STUDIES IN ROMANCE LANGUAGES: 8

THE SPANISH BALLAD IN ENGLISH

THE SPANISH BALLAD IN ENGLISH

BY

SHASTA M. BRYANT

THE UNIVERSITY PRESS OF KENTUCKY

LEXINGTON

Standard Book Number 0-8131-1280-X
Library of Congress Catalog Card Number 72-81314

A statewide cooperative scholarly publishing agency serving Berea College, Centre College of Kentucky, Eastern Kentucky University, Kentucky State College, Morehead State University, Murray State University, University of Kentucky, University of Louisville, and Western Kentucky University

Editorial and Sales Offices: Lexington, Kentucky 40506

PRINTED IN SPAIN

IMPRESO EN ESPAÑA

I.S.B.N. 84-399-1652-3

DEPÓSITO LEGAL: V. 3.902 - 1973

Artes Gráficas Soler, S. A. — Jávea, 28 — Valencia (8) — 1973

CONTENTS

PREFACE

A large number of Spanish romances, *or ballads, have been translated into English, but with minor exceptions, the only translations which are widely known are those of John Lockhart. In some ways this is unfortunate, since the popularity of Lockhart's work has tended to obscure the existence of equally good or better English versions of a great many traditional* romances. *James Young Gibson, especially, merits considerably more attention as a translator of Spanish ballads than he has received heretofore. Analysis of Gibson's efforts and those of the other translators studied in this work indicates that the English reader actually has a wide range of worthwhile and enjoyable materials which can provide him with a thorough introduction to a most important branch of Spanish literature. These materials are not always readily available, however, and the chief aim of this volume is to furnish a broader and perhaps more truly representative sampling from the English translations of* romances. *Besides the selections included herein, attention is directed to hundreds of others through the textual references and the appendixes.*

In addition to the fact that detailed study of a translation requires close comparison with the original, the inclusion of the Spanish texts with the English renditions implicitly recognizes that many persons familiar with the romances, *students of comparative literature and others, have more than a casual interest in and knowledge of the subject. The discussions are intended primarily for the nonspecialist, however, and the ability to read Spanish is not requisite to the understanding and appreciation of the ballads. I hope, rather, that the specimens reproduced here may encourage the general reader to extend what may be his first acquaintance with the* romances.

The Spanish texts are taken from various well-known anthologies, including the Cancionero de romances de Amberes, *first published around 1548 and re-issued by Menéndez Pidal in facsimile editions in 1914 and 1945; the* Romancero general *of Agustín Durán, which came out in Madrid in separate volumes between 1828 and 1832, and again in Volumes 10 and 16 of the* Biblioteca de Autores Españoles *in 1916 and 1921; and Wolf and Hofmann's* Primavera y flor de romances *(Berlin, 1856). Other than supplying accent marks and, in some cases, adjusting punctuation and capitalization, I have not attempted to modernize or standardize either the Spanish or the English texts. The Spanish text throughout this volume has, however, been unnaturally and arbitrarily divided to permit easier comparison of the translation.*

The translations were chosen as those most representative of either a particular theme or a given translation technique, or, in some instances, simply because the English version seemed an exceptionally good rendition of the romance *or was outstanding in some other way. Also, I considered it essential to an adequate presentation of the subject that the Spanish originals be included next to the English translations. There are several advantages to be derived from this method, not the least of which is that ballad sources for translations are frequently difficult to locate and identify. The translators found their texts in a variety of early collections, and many of these are not easily accessible. Other benefits from having the original* romance *placed side by side with the translation are more self-evident. A direct, point-by-point comparison is facilitated, accuracy and faithfulness of translation are quickly checked, and the overall merits or defects of the rendition are more obvious. The brief analyses and discussions accompanying many of the selections are intended not as complete studies, but rather to call attention to certain notable qualities and characteristics of the translator or his work.*

Grateful acknowledgement is made to the following for permission to reprint material covered by copyright: The Clarendon Press, Oxford, for "Oh tis May, the month of May," from European Balladry *by William J. Entwistle; the editors of the* Modern Language Quarterly, *for the translations by George W. Umphrey. Special thanks are also due Professor Harry Lee King of Wake Forest University and Professor Edward D. Terry of the University of Alabama. Both read the manuscript and offered helpful suggestions.*

S. M. B.

Wake Forest University
January 1973

INTRODUCTION

Spain has frequently and rightfully been called the "land of the *Romancero*." No other country possesses such a rich and varied treasure of ballad literature, nor is there any other country whose history, civilization, and life are concentrated so thoroughly in its popular poetry. Loved by the common man, studied and admired by the historian and literary scholar, and a continual source of inspiration to creative writers, the *romances* constitute one of the most important segments of Spanish literature and one of the most original and lasting tributes to the Spanish people.

The word *romance* comes from a Vulgar Latin term meaning "in the vernacular" and apparently was used at first to distinguish the Vulgar Latin speech (which was developing into Spanish) from Classic Latin. Archaic forms of the word appear frequently in the thirteenth and fourteenth centuries as synonyms for the Spanish language. By the fifteenth century, however, the word had come to mean the type of literary composition which we usually refer to as the ballad, although there are important differences in origin, form, and spirit between the Spanish ballads and the English ballads. Early collections of ballads were often called *romanceros,* and this word is still used to designate a group of ballads bound together in one volume. It is also used for a series of ballads dealing with one subject, but when used independently and capitalized, the term refers to the entire body of Spanish ballad literature and the ballad tradition.

In general, the *romances* may be described as short narrative poems, fragmentary in character, consisting of verses of sixteen syllables, divided into hemistichs or half-lines of eight syllables each, and employing assonance rather than rhyme. (Most printed versions, however, as will be evident from the texts reproduced in this study, are arranged on the page in the half-line or eight-syllable verses, and in fact this arrangement seems more in accord with the internal characteristics of the ballads.) The *romances* were originally composed to be sung to the accompaniment of music, usually that of the *vihuela,* a forerunner of the modern guitar, and while these poems are normally thought of as narrative compositions, many of them are quite lyrical. The typical ballad contains from twenty-five to fifty verses, though there are some with hundreds of verses.

In earlier ages, the tendency for the *romance* to be written in sixteen-syllable lines of monorhyming assonance was so widespread, and the association of this meter with the ballad so strong, that often other lyrical songs which seemed to have ballad subjects, but with different metrical forms, were converted to this type of verse.[1] However, many of the *romanceros* contain poems which do not fit the above description, and there are many compositions with a variety of meters and poetical combinations which are sometimes classified as *romances.* In the older *romanceros* it is not uncommon to find refrains, rounds, carols, and poetic glosses, as well as sonnets, *liras,* and other poems in the Italian manner. Because many of these compositions are highly lyrical in quality, often containing a delicate charm and grace, many of them were translated and placed among the true *romances,* without the translator's bothering to note that they are not ballads. The present study follows the practice of the collectors and translators and includes such poems in the lists of ballads which have been translated into English, being governed only by the requirements that the composition be referred to as a ballad by the translator and that it be included in the conventional *romanceros.*

The style of the *romances,* although chiefly responsible for their appeal to us, poses the greatest difficulty for the translator and is probably the reason why so few really superior translations have been made. Most critics emphasize the realistic austerity, the vividness of situation, the intensity of emotion, and the dignity and nobility which predominate. One might single out also the substitution of dialogue for narrative, the simplicity and directness, and a marked dramatic quality as basic characteristics. The poems are fragmentary in nature;

---

[1] Ramón Menéndez Pidal, *Flor nueva de romances viejos* (Madrid: Revista de Archivos, Bibliotecas y Museos, 1928), p. 23.

many of them begin abruptly without explanation or transition, often ending just as abruptly, a characteristic which can prove frustrating to the uninitiated, but which lends to the ballads an element of mystery and adds to their charm. An additional difficulty for the translator is the monorhyming assonance of the Spanish which very seldom has been carried over into English in a manner pleasing to the ear, so that the best of the English translations employ a rhyme completely foreign to the originals.

The question of when and how the *romance* originated has given rise to much discussion and no little disagreement. Earlier it was believed that some of the ballads were written near the time of the events described in them and were the product of collective, communal composition. According to this theory, these shorter poems were later used in the composition of the long epic poems of the twelfth and thirteenth centuries. These are the *romances viejos,* which do indeed bear a marked resemblance in subject matter and form to the historical epics. Later studies have tended to disprove this explanation, however, and the theories of the foremost authority on the *Romancero,* Ramón Menéndez Pidal, concerning the age and origin of the ballads, are now generally accepted. He believes that the oldest Spanish ballads which we know date back to no earlier than the fifteenth or late fourteenth centuries,[2] and that the *romances* began life as relatively short fragments of the longer epic compositions which had preceded them. According to this theory, as the long and somewhat monotonous epics began to decline in popularity, the most dramatic and popular parts were converted into ballads by the *juglares,* the professional poets and musicians who earned their livelihood by public recitations. Menéndez Pidal theorizes that this process began in the second half of the thirteenth century, with the period of greatest activity dating from the second half of the fourteenth to the first part of the sixteenth century.[3] (The oldest ballad text which has been preserved was set down in a mixture of Castilian and Catalan by a Majorcan student in Italy in 1421.)

Although many of the *romances viejos* closely parallel parts of the longer epic poems, most scholars agree that even the most historical

[2] Ibid., p. 8.

[3] Ramón Menéndez Pidal, *Romancero hispánico* (Madrid: Espasa Calpe, 1953), 1: 158.

of the old ballads cannot be thought to come completely from the epics, but were composed artificially and deliberately from the fifteenth century on, with an original epic or, perhaps more frequently, a prose reworking of an epic providing the inspiration. Menéndez Pidal and others also emphasize the important part played by successive performers in the evolution of the ballads to their present forms. Many individuals undoubtedly contributed to the creative process during the long history of oral transmission of the *romances,* so that the versions which finally reached us might be said to be, in a certain sense, the result of collective composition. The extremely large number of variants of a single ballad would seem to be one proof of the assertion that the *romances* were continually undergoing change.

If the earliest ballads were indeed fragments of longer historical epics, the ballad form and techniques were not long in being applied to novelesque or fictional themes, and some of the *romances novelescos* are probably as old as the historical ballads. At any rate, the scope of ballad themes was soon greatly enlarged, with the emphasis shifting in many cases from narrative to lyrical elements. The extent to which the ballad form was employed for other than historical subjects will be evident in the later discussion of the classification of the *romances.*

Although we are not sure when the ballad became popular with the lower classes, it came into favor in the courts around 1450, and according to Menéndez Pidal, ballads were sung at the courts of Alfonso V of Aragon, Enrique IV of Castile, and Ferdinand and Isabella.[4] There is much evidence that already by the end of the fifteenth century poets and critics were beginning to appreciate and study the ballad and that not only the man in the streets but also the aristocrats liked them and knew them by heart. Aurelio Espinosa has stated that all the traditional types had reached complete development by this time, adding that the richness of the later Golden Age literature is indebted to the retention of the forms and themes of the ballad in the oral tradition until the *romances* began to be printed and compiled in collections later in the sixteenth century.[5] The influence

[4] Menéndez Pidal, *Flor nueva,* p. 39.

[5] Aurelio Espinosa, *El romancero español: sus orígenes y su historia en la literatura universal* (Madrid: Biblioteca Española de Divulgaciones Científicas, 1931), p. 94.

of the ballad is indeed clearly visible in almost all the major genres of the Golden Age, especially the drama, novel, and lyric verse.

The first printed ballads to gain wide circulation were in the form of *pliegos sueltos* or loose copies, somewhat equivalent to the English "broadsides," [6] and the first important collection of *romances* was the *Cancionero de romances,* which was not dated but which is thought to have appeared around 1548. Many other collections were made during the latter half of the sixteenth century and the first half of the seventeenth, although the best and most extensive *romanceros* were compiled following the renewed interest in the ballad in the nineteenth century.

The charm and beauty of the ballads contained in the early collections and the appeal to national pride of the *romances históricos* resulted in their appearing in almost every branch of literature. In 1579 a Sevillan dramatist, Juan de la Cueva, used a ballad in the text of one of his plays, thus paving the way for the many other dramatists of the sixteenth and early seventeenth centuries who were to make wide use of this now-favorite literary form. Lope de Vega and Guillén de Castro, to name only two of the better known playwrights, were greatly attracted by the *romance,* and the point is frequently made that Castro's play *Las mocedades del Cid* is almost a storehouse of ballads. As a matter of fact, Castro used the ballads rather than the more famous epic poem on the Cid as source material for his drama. In similar fashion, the novelists drew on the ballads for inspiration, with *Las guerras civiles de Granada* of Ginés Pérez de Hita being perhaps the best known example, although Cervantes in *Don Quixote* also makes many references to the Spanish ballads and sometimes uses one of them as the basis for an adventure of the knight and his faithful squire, Sancho Panza.

Still another aspect of the interest which had been aroused by the old ballads is that the courtly poets soon began to copy the primitive poems and to use the ballad meter and techniques for their own compositions. As early as 1442 the poet Carvajal signed his name to *romances* printed in the *Cancionero de Stúñiga,* while Fray Iñigo de Mendoza, Juan del Encina, and Gil Vicente are other

---

[6] See the *Bulletin of Hispanic Studies* 42 (1965): 187, for a comparison of *pliegos sueltos* and English broadsides.

well-known early writers of ballads. Some of the collectors of ballads of the sixteenth century also were inspired to write their own *romances,* the most important of these being Lorenzo de Sepúlveda, Juan de Timoneda, and Pedro de Padilla. Some of the early English translators made use of their collections. In addition to their other works, Cervantes, Francisco Quevedo, Lope de Vega, and Luis de Góngora are known for their ballad compositions. Many lesser names are to be found among the list of known poets who contributed to the fund of ballad literature, and it is probably not overstating the case to affirm that in the century and a half during which ballads flourished most vigorously, almost every Spanish poet wrote at least a few or included some of the popular ones in his works. The tradition also spread to the other Romance languages and dialects spoken on the Iberian peninsula, all of which are represented by either original *romances* or variants of poems in Castilian.

By the middle of the seventeenth century, however, ballads were beginning to lose favor with the learned classes, although there is no indication that they ever suffered any loss of esteem among the common people. This is the period of the satirical ballads and the parodies and burlesque types which ridiculed the ancient favorites. Later, under the French classical influences and with the deemphasis of the national spirit which had been a factor in the general popularity of the ballads, these, like the plays of Lope de Vega and other national writers, fell into literary oblivion, from which they were rescued only by the Romantic movement of the nineteenth century.

There are no known English translations of the *romances* during the period of their first extended popularity, and the earliest translations which we have are a product of the interest aroused by the collections of the early part of the nineteenth century. Romanticists outside Spain are generally credited with reminding the Spaniards of this important part of their national heritage, and indeed the first two important collections of *romances* assembled during this period were published in other countries. These, the *Silva de romances viejos* of Jakob Grimm (Vienna, 1815) and the *Sammlung der besten alten spanischen Romanzen* of G. B. Depping (Leipzig, 1817), were followed by Agustín Durán's *Romancero general* in 1828-1832 and the *Primavera y flor de romances* of F. J. Wolf and C. Hofmann in 1856. Durán's anthology, originally published in five volumes and republished in two volumes in 1849-1851 in the *Biblioteca de Autores*

Españoles, contains more than 1,900 ballads and is still the most complete collection, while the Wolf and Hofmann selection offers 198 of the oldest and most popular *romances.* Several good anthologies have come out in this century, including reprints of some of the early *romanceros,* and one might cite in particular the *Flor nueva de romances viejos* of Menéndez Pidal, reprinted many times since 1928, and the *Romancero español* of Luis Santullano, first published in 1935. The fifth edition of the latter collection (Madrid, 1946) contains over 450 Castilian ballads of all kinds, plus several examples of Catalan and Spanish-Jewish *romances.*[7]

The interest, enthusiasm, and scientific investigation engendered by the rediscovery of the *Romancero* has continued down to the present, both in Spain and abroad. Among the famous literary figures in relatively recent times who have received inspiration from the ballads have been the Duque de Rivas, José Zorrilla, Eduardo Marquina, Antonio Machado, and García Lorca, while many important scholars have loved and studied the *romance* and have contributed to our knowledge concerning it. The efforts of Menéndez Pidal and others have indicated that the ballad tradition is still being maintained not only in the Iberian peninsula but also among the people of Spanish descent in other countries, and that traditional Spanish ballads are still preserved in the memory of many unlettered folk.

The richness and diversity of the *Romancero* is reflected in the terminology that has been developed to classify and identify the various kinds of poems which it embraces. Unfortunately, this terminology is not precise, although most of the classifications are intended to indicate something about the origin, age, subject matter, or style of the ballads included. Some familiarity with the terms most often used in the anthologies is helpful, however, in any discussion of the *romances* and their translation.

The oldest ballads are usually referred to as *romances viejos, romances primitivos,* or *romances tradicionales,* and a great number

---

[7] An excellent selection for the general reader, consisting of seventy ballads from the *Primavera y flor de romances,* carefully and generously annotated in English, is contained in C. Colin Smith's *Spanish Ballads* (Oxford: Pergamon Press, 1964). This edition also has a fine introduction which summarizes the latest research of Menéndez Pidal and others in the field of the traditional ballad.

of these deal with themes also found in the epic poems from which many of the ancient ballads seem to have derived. For most modern scholars, these terms denote those ballads that were transmitted by oral tradition, in contrast to the *romances nuevos,* those appearing after about 1550, whose characteristics were affected among other things by early publication. It should be noted, however, that some of the ballads written after 1550 were widely accepted by the common people and passed into the oral tradition, while a few of the *romances viejos* or *primitivos* were not discovered by the experts or published for the first time until well after the middle of the sixteenth century.[8] (See the index of *romances* for the ones included here which are known to have been in circulation prior to 1550.) Since the epics almost without exception were based on national history or tradition, most of the *romances viejos* are also *romances históricos.* The historical ballads were frequently imitated, however, in later periods, and it is best to define *romances históricos* as those ballads which treat the history, both true and legendary, of Spain during its formation as a nation, without drawing inferences as to age or origin. The truly primitive ones in this group are usually considered the best and the most original and have received by far the most attention of any of the Spanish ballads. Most critics would agree that, whether primitive or not, the historical ballads are the most important of any in the *Romancero.*

Perhaps the next most important category is comprised of ballads dealing with the Moors in Spain. These include the *romances fronterizos,* which depict events connected with the warfare along the *frontera* or border between the opposing Moorish and Christian forces, and the more idealized *romances moriscos.* Although sometimes used interchangeably, the two terms should not be considered synonymous since the border ballads are more closely akin to the historical ballads and are relatively old, while the *romances moriscos* describe the customs, manners, adventures, and loves of either real or pseudo-

[8] In addition to the references in his *Romancero hispánico,* Menéndez Pidal has interesting discussions of "traditional poetry" and the *romancero nuevo* in *Poesía popular y poesía tradicional en la literatura española,* Conferencia leída en All Souls College el lunes, día 26 de junio de 1922 (Oxford: Imprenta Clarendoniana, 1922), and in *De primitiva lírica española y antigua épica* (Buenos Aires: Espasa-Calpe Argentina, Colección Austral, 1951).

Moorish characters and are of a more recent date. There are numerous Moorish ballads, and while they sometimes are based on actual happenings, there is little historical accuracy in them, and most of them treat small incidents rather than the larger events which are the typical themes of the historical ballads. Although composed at a later date, many of the *romances moriscos,* and more especially the *romances fronterizos,* have inherited the ease, vigor, realism, and epic greatness of the earlier historical ballads and are more perfect in form, even though they may not always be as poetically inspired.

A third large and important category is the group of ballads concerned with the knights and ladies of the age of chivalry. These are the *romances caballerescos,* of which the largest subdivision is the collection of *romances carolingios* dealing with Roland, Charlemagne, Gaiferos, and other legendary figures of France. There are also various cycles covering Amadís, Lancelot and other knights of the Arthurian Round Table, Tristan and Isolde, as well as certain Italian heroes. Although some of these may have had their origin in epic poems, most of them are considered as *romances juglarescos,* that is, the work of a sophisticated *juglar* or courtly minstrel of the fifteenth century. They tend to be longer and more personal than the *romances viejos,* and more completely narrative in nature, with less of the economy and concentration characteristic of the older ballads.

Since some of the *romances caballerescos* recount the adventures of a knight not identified with any of the familiar chivalric cycles, such ballads have sometimes been called *romances novelescos,* but it seems more accurate to reserve this term for any isolated tale of adventure whose origin is thought to be fictional or whose hero remains unknown to history or tradition. There are a number of excellent ballads in this category, many of them developing themes from Spanish folklore. Marvelous or supernatural happenings, prophetic dreams, miracles, and other similar elements are frequently found in the *romances novelescos.* In contrast to the widespread occurrence of such motifs in the English ballads, the supernatural is not common in Spanish literature, and some critics have felt that the origin of these ballads could be traced to the influence of French and other European literature.[9]

---

[9] Chapters 7, 9, and 10 of Menéndez Pidal's *Romancero hispánico* discuss

One of the results of the widespread popularity of the ballad in the sixteenth century was the imitation of the traditional ballad by erudite poets. This most sincere form of flattery produced a large store of *romances eruditos,* which in some cases are reworkings of historic ballads, in others, original compositions copying the style of the ancient ballads. Most of the themes are from the printed chronicles, and often the poet seemed to be trying to fill gaps in the ballad versions of historical legends. These may have led in turn to the development of the *romances artísticos,* so called because of the evidence of conscious literary effort. The personal, artistic touch is more easily discernible, and the authors of many of these ballads are known. The lyrical element becomes much more pronounced in the artistic ballads (many are truly *romances líricos*), and every conceivable theme is introduced. They exhibit a more regular and polished form, but, with notable exceptions, suffer in comparison with the older, less studied compositions. Both types are now often called *romances artificiosos.*

Other kinds of ballads so numerous as to warrant separate classifications are the *romances amorosos, romances pastoriles, romances a lo divino* — the ballads treating religious themes — and at the other end of the scale, *romances vulgares,* which are the type composed and sung by beggars and other members of the lower classes, often relating crimes and descending to an extremely coarse level. The pastoral ballads are, of course, only a specialized type of love ballad, and both types can be, and often are, included in the category of artistic ballads. Other ballads essentially lyrical in nature, but not fitting exactly one of the classifications above, are usually placed among the *romances artísticos.*

Still another type of ballad includes those written during the time when the literary circles were beginning to tire of the rather extraordinary popularity enjoyed by the *romances.* The reaction eventually produced by an almost universal acceptance of the popular poetry was expressed in the form of satires and parodies of both ballad themes and forms, with the resulting compositions earning the name of *romances satíricos, jocosos,* or *burlescos.* Needless to say, few of these were of high literary value, and very few of them have been translated into English.

---

the rather complicated problems connected with the origins of the *romances caballerescos* and *novelescos.*

It is rather obvious that the classifications discussed above are extremely general, permitting a good deal of overlapping, so that one must necessarily be somewhat arbitrary in assigning ballads to a particular category. The editors of some of the *Romanceros* have sought to avoid this difficulty by attempting a more precise differentiation and by subdividing the larger categories into smaller units. The value of this procedure is debatable, however, and since most of the English translations fall rather conveniently into the more conventional groupings already mentioned, these will be used throughout this study.

Interest in the Spanish ballad in the English-speaking world began at a time when the *romances* were probably least appreciated in their native country. After several centuries of enormous popularity among all classes at every social level, the ballads had passed into relative obscurity in the eighteenth century as a result of changing literary tastes and the prevailing influence of Neoclassicism. Ignored and long forgotten by the majority of the native writers and intellectuals in Spain, the Spanish ballads were discovered in the early years of the nineteenth century by several romanticists in Germany, France, and England, who were quick to recognize the artistic merit of these compositions and to seek inspiration from them. In Weimar, for example, Friedrich Schlegel in 1802 presented a tragedy based on the Spanish ballad of Count Alarcos which immediately drew attention from all quarters to the aesthetic and literary values of the *Romancero.* Other German literary figures to be noted in connection with the fascination which the ballads exerted over them are Herder, Goethe, Hegel, and Jakob Grimm, who compiled the first of the important collections of this period. [10]

In France, interest in the *romances* soon reached high proportions also. Creuzé de Lesser, who in 1814 characterized the *Romancero* as an Iliad without a Homer, Victor Hugo, with similar terms in his praise of the ballads in 1829 and Louis Viardot, who in 1832 described the *romances* as "rhapsodies," furnish ample evidence of the high regard held for the Spanish ballads by the French during this period. [11] Other French writers who came under the influence of the

[10] See Espinosa, *El romancero español,* for a fuller account of German and French interest in the *romances.*

[11] Cited by Menéndez Pidal, *Flor nueva,* p. 44.

romance and who serve to emphasize the range of its popularity were Chateaubriand, Abel Hugo, Leconte de Lisle, and the Comte de Puymaigre, to name only a few of the many who became susceptible to the peculiar beauty of the ballad and who responded either with translations, public praise, or original compositions inspired by study of the ballads.

In England, the Spanish ballads seem to have been discovered even earlier than in France or Germany. In the middle of the eighteenth century, a Scotsman, Thomas Blackwell, in reviewing the life and works of Homer, had praised the Moorish ballads of Spain as samples of true popular poetry. A short time later Thomas Percy, author of the famous *Reliques of Ancient English Poetry,* became attracted to the Spanish *romances* through his study of the English ballads and in order to show certain similarities in the folksongs of the two countries included two translations in the first edition of the *Reliques,* published in London in 1765. Earlier, in a letter written in 1759, he had commented on the ballads to this effect: "To my hoard of these in my own language, I have added a small but curious collection of old Spanish ones." Although he published only two at that early date, he apparently was considerably interested in the *romances* and had planned to devote more attention to them at a later time. [12]

The forces set in motion by the Romantic movement are undoubtedly the principal reason for England's great interest in the literature of Spain during the early part of the nineteenth century, although other contributory causes may be noted. Chief among these are the events connected with the Napoleonic wars and the invasion of Spain by France. England had come into close contact with Spain in the common struggle against Napoleon, and English sympathies and admiration were greatly aroused by the heroic resistance of the Spanish against the French. Many of the intellectuals of the country not only lent their pens and voices to the cause of the Spanish but also worked actively to enlist funds and military support for their friends on the peninsula. Byron, Campbell, and Shelley wrote poetry expressing their sympathy for the Spanish, and Southey and Wordsworth are reported to have been particularly aroused by the events in Spain, with Words-

[12] Thomas Percy, *Ancient Songs (Chiefly on Moorish Subjects),* ed. David Nichol Smith (Oxford: Oxford University Press, 1932), pp. viii-ix.

worth aiding the cause by writing a tract concerning the relations between Great Britain, Spain, and Portugal.[13] Sir Walter Scott and his son-in-law, John Lockhart, also were interested in the events in Spain and followed closely the military action there, while Carlyle and Tennyson are included among other prominent literary figures known to have actively supported the Spanish cause.

It was only natural that the attention of these men, having first been attracted by political and military affairs in Spain, should turn to an examination and appraisal of that country's literature. The interest of Percy in the ballads has already been noted, and while he was apparently the first to recognize the value of this particular genre, appreciation of this and other types of Spanish literature spread quickly. As early as 1801, the Spanish language and literature were being praised as second only to English in beauty and variety,[14] while an example of the enthusiasm aroused by Spanish legend is seen in the fact that in the short period from 1811 to 1814 no less than three poems by different English authors appeared on the subject of Rodrigo, the last of the Gothic kings of Spain.

It is with the ballads, however, that we are concerned at present. Already in the first decade of the nineteenth century, considerable attention had been focused on them as is revealed by the number of translators and translations which had appeared by 1810. At least eight authors had published their versions of *romances* by then, to start the flow of English translations which would continue almost without interruption down to the present time. Some of the reasons for the interest in translations have already been indicated. Perhaps we should emphasize the obvious, however, and add that often quite different motives lay behind the work of the various translators. It has been suggested that there were three different states in the popularity of the *romances* and their translation in England.[15] In the first place, translations were made to serve as a parallel or comparison with the

[13] For a complete discussion of this period, see Erasmo Buceta, "El entusiasmo por España en algunos románticos ingleses," *Revista de filología española* 10 (1923): 1-25.

[14] See Erasmo Buceta, "Apuntes preliminares para un estudio de las traducciones inglesas de romances en el primer tercio del siglo XIX," in *Estudios eruditos* in memoriam *de Adolfo Bonilla y San Martín* (Madrid: Facultad de Filosofía y Letras de la Universidad Central, 1930), 2: 313.

[15] Ibid., p. 315.

English ballads. The renditions of Percy fall into this category. Second, there was interest in the ballads for their own sake; that is, their beauty and artistry were appreciated by the translator, and this appreciation led to translations of different types depending on the tastes of the individual. Finally, enthusiasm for certain themes led to collections of translations, in which the translator attempted to transcribe whole series of ballads in order to give his readers a more comprehensive picture of the subject under treatment. Thus, we have the collections of Moorish ballads, ballads on the Cid, ballads from the civil wars of Granada, and so forth.

In the United States, some of the same forces which were operative in England worked to produce translations of the *romances,* and to those mentioned earlier should be added the circulation and popularity of the early English translations, notably those of Lockhart. It is perhaps understandable that the American translations should begin much later than the English ones, and it seems appropriate that a famous American poet, William Cullen Bryant, should be the first of the translators with his publication in 1829 of several Moorish ballads. Although becoming acquainted with the Spanish ballads somewhat later than their English contemporaries, the Americans were equally enthusiastic in their praise of these poems, as illustrated by the remarks of Longfellow which accompanied his translations in 1833.[16] Likewise, the Americans were to continue their interest in translating the *romance* throughout the rest of that century and down to the present.

Although it would be presumptuous to attempt to treat and evaluate here the complete history of Spanish ballad translation in England and the United States, a rapid chronological survey may be useful as background information for the discussions accompanying some of the poems in this volume and as a supplement to the appendixes. In the following summary, brief mention will be made of all known English translations, regardless of merit and irrespective of the motives which produced them.

In view of the rather extraordinary popularity of the *romance* in Spain in earlier ages, it is surprising, perhaps, that no English trans-

[16] Henry Wadsworth Longfellow, *Outre-Mer,* rev. ed. (Boston: Houghton Mifflin Company, 1866), p. 218.

lations were made until the latter part of the eighteenth century. Such seems to be the case, however, since no translations have been discovered which are earlier than those of Thomas Percy. His *Reliques of Ancient English Poetry* (1765) contained two of the several ballads which he seems to have translated around 1760.[17] Percy had become interested in the Spanish ballad through his study of *Don Quixote* and Ginés Pérez de Hita's *Guerras civiles de Granada,* and he had intended to complete a volume of translations.[18] This plan was never carried out, however, and the net result of his efforts in this field is seven translations, mostly of *romances moriscos.* He tended toward literal translation and showed considerable skill, especially in his version of "Río-Verde, Río-Verde." This poem, which he called "Gentle River," was so highly regarded that it became a model for later translators.

Francis Carter, the next English translator, as far as is known, rendered only one ballad. In 1777, twelve years after Percy, he published a travel book, *A Journey from Gibraltar to Malaga,* which contained his version of "Ocho a ocho y diez a diez," a Moorish ballad. This ballad was published again in 1810 in a volume by Robert Harding Evans, to whom it sometimes is attributed.

Four years later, in 1781, John Pinkerton, in *Select Scottish Ballads,* published six translations important more for their historical value than for their poetic merit. In two dissertations preceding the ballads, he finds a resemblance of the *romances* to the Scottish ballads, and he explains why he includes the former in his book. He states: "Having in the first of the foregoing dissertations mentioned with applause the Spanish Ballads, or Romances, contained in the *Historia de las Guerras Civiles de Granada,* and that book being seldom to be met with, and written in a language of no wide study, the Editor has been induced to give a few translations from that work; the two which Dr. Percy has published having rather excited than gratified curiosity."[19]

---

[17] Complete bibliographical information on translators and their works will be found in Appendix B.

[18] Percy, *Ancient Songs,* p. v.

[19] John Pinkerton, *Select Scottish Ballads,* 2d ed. (London: J. Nichols, 1783), p. xlv.

Five of the six ballads are *romances moriscos,* and although the translator managed to capture some of the spirit and rhythm of the originals, Pinkerton's versions are unacceptable from the standpoint of faithfulness to their models.

In 1797 appeared the first of seven translations from Robert Southey, a poet from whom much might have been expected, but whose translations leave something to be desired. The *Letters Written during a Short Residence in Spain and Portugal* included his version of the ballad previously translated by Carter, "Ocho a ocho y diez a diez," and six others were published at a later date. Southey's translations are not entirely without merit, however, and undoubtedly would have been better if he had not tried to imitate the style of the originals by using assonance instead of rhyme. Very few of the later translators followed him in this respect, apparently convinced that too many of the more desirable qualities of a good translation are lost in the attempt to duplicate closely the peculiar poetic form of the *romance.* Southey demonstrated his originality in another way also, by being the first, and one of the few, to translate a satirical ballad.

The first author to publish English translations of Spanish ballads on a large scale was Thomas Rodd with his *Ancient Ballads from the Civil Wars of Granada and the Twelve Peers of France* (London, 1801). The title correctly points to Ginés Pérez de Hita's *Guerras civiles de Granada* as the source for most of Rodd's translations, and in 1803 he published an English translation of the first volume of this work. The *Ancient Ballads* contained sixty-four compositions, including an old English ballad, Percy's version of "Río-Verde," and several other miscellaneous pieces. Eleven years later, in 1812, Rodd published a second collection, repeating part of those found in the first group but also including the "Most Celebrated Ancient Spanish Ballads Relating to the Twelve Peers of France Mentioned in *Don Quixote.*" Some of the poems contained in these two books may be original compositions, rather than translations, since sources have been located for only sixty-one. Approximately one-third of these are Moorish ballads, one-third are *romances históricos,* and the remainder are from the Carolingian cycle of the ballads of chivalry. Rodd used the translations of Percy as models and, like Percy, was inclined toward a literal rendering. Although his renditions have been praised for their conscientious workmanship, they are deficient in the poetic qualities of the originals.

The next translator, John Hookham Frere, apparently translated only two ballads, but he has been hailed as a "poet of unsurpassed genius in the art of translation." [20] Frere, a minister to Spain, is best known in Spanish circles for his friendship with Angel de Saavedra, the Duque de Rivas, and their relationship furnishes another example of the influence of English Romanticism in Spain. Saavedra reportedly became familiar with the works of Byron, Scott, and other contemporary Romantics through Frere, and it was at the suggestion of the latter that he began his Romantic epic, *El moro expósito.* Frere translated many other pieces of Spanish literature, and it is to be regretted that he did not spend more time on the *romances.* His two translations, one a *romance artístico,* the other a historical ballad, are quite free, but both retain the spirit and emotion of the originals. They were published in 1804.

In 1808 appeared the next translation, a version of a well-known Carolingian ballad, by Matthew Gregory Lewis in an edition of his Gothic novel *The Monk: A Romance.* This book, which treated pseudo-Spanish themes, had caused quite a stir with its first appearance in 1796, and from it Lewis acquired the title "Monk" often associated with his name. Lewis later translated a total of six ballads, including five which had been treated by earlier writers, and his versions are generally regarded as being very good. In particular, they are noted for their highly rhythmic qualities and complicated rhymes.

Another famous writer whose work with ballad translations is somewhat disappointing is Sir Walter Scott. He published the first of only two ballads in a review of Southey's *Chronicle of the Cid* in the *Quarterly Review* in 1809, and the second in the *Ancient Spanish Ballads* of Lockhart, his son-in-law, in 1823. His two translations, "Ese buen Cid Campeador" and "Los fieros cuerpos revueltos," are both on Spanish historical themes and are of uneven merit. The latter is the better.

The first of several translators to concentrate on the historical ballads of the Cid was Henry Richard Fox, better known as Lord

[20] George W. Umphrey, "Spanish Ballads in English, Part I — Historical Survey," *Modern Language Quarterly* 6 (1945): 485.

Holland. Fox spent several years in Spain and was an admirer of Spanish culture. In 1806 he published *Some Account of the Life and Writings of Lope de Vega,* and in the second edition of this work in 1817 he included two *romances moriscos* and eight ballads dealing with the *mocedades* or youth of the Cid. The Moorish ballads are superior to the others.

In 1818 there appeared the widely read translations of Lord Byron in the fourth canto of *Childe Harold.* These, consisting of "En las torres de Alhambra," "Moro alcaide, moro alcaide," and "Paseábase el rey moro," although treating Spanish historical themes, deal mostly with Moorish subjects. Byron's translations are comparable in quality to his original work and are satisfying in most respects.

There are many indications of the attention which Spanish ballads were receiving in England in the early 1820s. The influential literary journal, *Blackwood's Magazine,* frequently included articles on the *Romancero* and translations by known or anonymous authors. Poems inspired by the *romances* may be found in this and other journals and in various poetry collections of the period.

The years 1820-1823 saw the translations of John Gibson Lockhart, the poet who more than any other single person familiarized the English-speaking world with the Spanish ballads. Lockhart had developed his enthusiasm for the *romances* during study in Germany, but published his first translations in the *Edinburgh Annual Register* and *Blackwood's Magazine.* His largest collection, *The Spanish Ballads,* came out in 1823, at the very height of the Romantic movement in England and was so successful that at least twelve subsequent editions have been published. The man and his book both deserve special attention, although limitations of space prevent more than a brief assessment of his unique contributions. These include, if one counts translations published in other sources, some sixty-seven versions which have been identified, representing thirty-six ballads on Spanish historical subjects and lesser numbers from the ballads of chivalry, the Moorish ballads, and the artistic ballads.

The success of *The Spanish Ballads,* called in most subsequent editions *Ancient Spanish Ballads,* was almost instantaneous, and the book has maintained its popularity through the years. The tenor of the praise that has been heaped upon it is indicated by the remarks of George Ticknor who called it "a work of genius beyond any of the sort known to me in any language."[21] The language of a later critic, George Umphrey, is more restrained, but his praise of Lockhart is still sufficiently lavish. Umphrey writes:

> He applied poetic gifts [to his translations] that barely failed to make him a good original poet. He had sure literary taste, a fine feeling for poetry, and notable mastery of verse technique.... Some ballad translators ... wrote better original poetry than Lockhart; others ... surpassed him in the finished technique of their verse; none of them entered so completely into the spirit of the ballads. The poetic inspiration of his best translations still gives to his *Ancient Spanish Ballads* first place in Spanish ballad translations; and the high praise given him by Ticknor may be considered a just tribute to his genius as a translator.[22]

With due regard to these opinions and to the unquestioned ability of Lockhart, it must be pointed out that some of his translations are far from being completely satisfactory. He tended to take excessive liberties with many of the ballads, and the more familiar one is with the originals, the less satisfied he is with Lockhart's versions. No one could deny that Lockhart was able to capture the ease and spirit of his material, but in doing so the result often resembles more an original composition than a translation. Another modern critic, Erasmo Buceta, states the case well when he says: "El mérito de los originales sobre que trabajó es muy vario y cuando los romances no son de la mejor calidad, puede decirse que se perfeccionan con su desembarazado tratamiento; pero cuando se trata, en cambio, de composiciones más delicadas, los amaneramientos de Lockhart les hacen perder miserablemente sus puntos más sutiles y sus contornos más finos y admirables."[23] One might add, without citing specific examples at this point, that some of Lockhart's translations are so farfetched as to raise doubts concerning whether he fully understood the verses he was translating.

As Buceta suggests, many of the ballads translated by Lockhart were not of the best quality, and the liberties which he took with them were undoubtedly intended to add to their poetic possibilities.

---

[21] George Ticknor, *History of Spanish Literature* (New York: Harper and Bros., 1849), 1: 127.

[22] Umphrey, "Spanish Ballads in English," p. 488.

[23] Erasmo Buceta, "Traducciones inglesas de romances en el primer tercio del siglo XIX," *Revue Hispanique* 62 (1924): 503.

In some cases the changes made were rather minor, while at other times he freely expanded or deleted whole lines or even more substantial portions. Frequently the sections omitted are not completely relevant to the main story, but in some poems the omissions do definitely affect adversely the overall portrayal of the models. At times he chose to compress somewhat the original materials, often achieving in this way a heightened effect or a more vivid expression, and this type of change is perhaps quite defensible. It seems somewhat more difficult to justify lengthy additions which introduce picturesque details and imaginative elements not found in the Spanish texts.

One must hasten to affirm, however, that most of his compositions do qualify as translations and therefore may be compared with others on the same subjects; in fact, they may even be used as criteria in judging the excellence of other translations. The only question that remains is whether Lockhart has been placed in proper perspective. To quote Buceta again:

> No puede negarse que la contribución de Lockhart fué de primera magnitud, y con mucho y sin hipérbole, la más importante en este ramo de producciones [Buceta was dealing with only the first third of the nineteenth century]; pero hay que confesar que su nombre siempre se cita como si fuese el único, o casi el único, que trabajase en este departamento literario. Concedo que fué su obra la de mayor mérito artístico, pero nunca tendremos un justo relieve de una provincia literaria si sólo prestamos atención a las cimas y desdeñamos los altibajos del terreno que tratamos de estudiar.[24]

Since I present here many of Lockhart's translations along with the originals, and with the versions of other translators, the reader may judge for himself the measure of success which the Scottish poet achieved.

Following Lockhart, and the first translator to become interested in the artistic and lyric ballads, was John Bowring, who published in 1824 *Ancient Poetry and Romances of Spain*. This work contained eighty-nine compositions which Bowring called ballads and 105 translations of other kinds of poetry from known Spanish poets. The book was planned as one of a series of translations of representative poetry from all nations. Of the eighty-nine ballads, sixty-four belong in the artistic category (including many that do not have the true ballad

---

[24] Buceta, "Apuntes preliminares," p. 313.

form), sixteen are ballads of chivalry, seven are on Moorish and Spanish historical subjects, and two are religious ballads. Some of these translations had been published earlier in the *London Magazine*.

Bowring's interpretations are quite literal but highly poetic, possessing to a considerable degree the simplicity and directness of the originals. One critic has said of this collection that "it conveys to a foreigner a more adequate idea of the beauties of Castilian lyric poetry than any native collection, so sure is the editor's taste in selection." [25] Other readers have been impressed by the excellence of these poems, but since the lyric ballads are not as representative of Spanish balladry as are other types, Bowring's work has received relatively little notice.

Bowring experimented with various types of rhyme in his translations and even attempted some in assonance. One Moorish ballad, published anonymously in the *Retrospective Review* in 1821, was translated primarily to show the effects of assonance in English, and the author commented on his rendition that "this must be read with indulgence. It is perhaps the first attempt to naturalize the asonantes of the peninsula; and Mr. Southey might teach us how perilous it is to embark on an almost untried ocean." [26] The rhymed translations remain Bowring's best, however, even though he achieved a certain degree of success in his experiments with assonance.

Whether stimulated by the appearance of the works of Lockhart and Bowring, or as a result of independent research, several authors were inspired to undertake ballad translation during this same period. In the years from 1823 to 1832 translations were brought out by Jeremiah Holmes Wiffen, George Moir, and George Borrow. Translations were also published anonymously during this time in *Fraser's Magazine*, the *Foreign Quarterly Review*, and the *Foreign Review and Continental Miscellany*. The average number of ballads from each of these sources is five, and a variety of types is represented, including several of the more popular *romances novelescos*. However, none of these translations is particularly outstanding.

It is about this time also that the *romance* was being discovered by American poets. In 1829 William Cullen Bryant translated three

---

[25] S. Griswold Morley, *Spanish Ballads* (New York: Henry Holt and Company, 1924), p. iv.

[26] "Poetical Literature of Spain," *Retrospective Review* 4 (1821): 358.

which may be considered as fair samples of the *Romancero,* followed in 1833 by Henry Wadsworth Longfellow with four.

Longfellow, who for many years was professor of Romance Languages at Harvard, left many indications of his love for Spanish, and his ballad translations attest to his ability in the language as well as to his skill as a poet. He had visited the peninsula for eight months in 1827, and thereafter his interest in Spanish never ceased, though the majority of his translations from this language were made during the next few years after his return. In addition to the ballads, some of the other works which he translated include parts of the *Siete partidas* of Alfonso el Sabio and the *Libro de buen amor* of Juan Ruiz, the "Coplas" of Jorge Manrique, sonnets from Quevedo and Lope de Vega, odes from Góngora, and selections from the *Quixote.*

Longfellow translated his ballads partly to refute the assertions of Robert Southey, who considered the *romances* inferior to English poetry and who had spoken somewhat disparagingly of them. They were published in *Outre-Mer* (1833), together with a lengthy section on Spain in which the American poet briefly describes the *Romancero* and praises it highly. The smoothness and seeming spontaneity of these compositions offer cause for regret that he translated only four.

Another American who published translations the same year as Longfellow was Caleb Cushing, who had been a Minister to Spain and who, at one time, was Attorney General for the United States. His *Reminiscences of Spain* (1833) contains fifteen historical ballads, including nine on the legendary Bernardo del Carpio and four from the cycle concerning the betrayal of the seven Infantes de Lara. His ballads could be described as being quite good, but not outstanding. They are usually praised more for their skillful technique than their poetic merit. It is interesting to note, however, that an anonymous reviewer of the *Reminiscences* stated that Cushing's translations were "very spirited and natural, and, we should think, would convey a better impression of the originals, than Mr. Lockhart's."[27]

In 1845 translations appeared in the *United States Magazine and Democratic Review* from the pens of two other Americans. One of

[27] "Cushing's Reminiscences of Spain," *New England Magazine* 4 (1833): 428.

these, Wallace S. Cone, combined several ballads into one long and very loose translation which tells the story of the seduction in the eighth century of the beautiful La Cava by Rodrigo, the last king of the Goths. The other translator, Edward Maturin, was also excessively free in his interpretations, but he did succeed in rendering extremely spirited versions of twenty-one historical and legendary ballads.

An interesting group of ballads translated by John Oxenford appeared in 1846 in the *New Monthly Magazine.* Oxenford, an English dramatist and critic, had prepared a series of articles on the legends and romances of several European countries, and his translations of the *romances* were arranged so as to relate some of the stories from the legendary history of Spain. He has sixteen translations, five each on Bernardo del Carpio and the Infantes de Lara, and three each on the kings Alfonso and Rodrigo. His translations are literal and read well, although they are not poetically inspired.

In 1849 George Ticknor, Longfellow's successor in Romance Languages at Harvard, translated eleven of the Spanish ballads to serve as examples for the chapters on the *Romancero* in his *History of Spanish Literature.* He has five ballads on Spanish historical themes, three artistic ballads, one Carolingian ballad of chivalry, one Moorish, and one satirical ballad. His translations have been called "good, but not distinguished," and "accurate and stylistically correct," although lacking the "divine spark." [28]

Four translations by Sir Edmund Head in 1868 show considerable skill, and one of them, which had also been included in Ticknor's *History,* is a good example of a Carolingian ballad. The same praise cannot be given, unfortunately, to the *Ballads of the Cid,* published by Gerrard Lewis some years later in 1883. This book does deserve some comment, however, if only to emphasize the extent to which a translator can fall short of his mark. Lewis's idea — to complete a group of translations that would tell in verse the story of the Cid — was admirable, but he did not possess the ability to do justice to his materials. The thirty-four compositions which make up this work are completely lacking in the poetic qualities so characteristic of the originals. Furthermore, the author made no effort to observe the letter

[28] Umphrey, "Spanish Ballads in English," p. 492.

of his models; on the contrary, he apparently felt free to combine variants and embellish the narrative at will to make a more complete account. Possibly the only thing that could be said in favor of Lewis's translations is that taken together these poems present a fairly complete history of the highlights of the Cid's career.

In marked contrast to the work of Gerrard Lewis, the Cid ballads of James Young Gibson have earned him a place comparable to that of Lockhart among the translators of Spanish ballads. Gibson, also a Scotsman, studied extensively in England and Germany and, although licensed as a Presbyterian clergyman, devoted himself almost exclusively to literature. He visited Spain in 1871-1872 and became so enthusiastic over the language and literature of that country that at one time he thought of attempting a comprehensive collection of songs, ballads, and poetry which would reflect and illustrate Spanish history. The vast quantity of material involved caused him to give up this idea, but in 1887, after his death, his ballad translations were published in a two-volume edition called *The Cid Ballads and Other Poems and Translations from Spanish and German.* Gibson translated more ballads than any other poet (130), and more different types are represented. In addition to his Cid ballads, he has thirteen historical ballads, seven Moorish ballads, thirteen ballads of chivalry, thirteen artistic ballads, and one satirical ballad.

In spite of the decline in interest in this type of literature by the time Gibson's book appeared (the editors cautiously limited the edition to 500 copies), it met with favorable comment in literary circles. A reviewer for the *Academy,* after first discussing the poems from the German and a few original compositions which were also included, continued:

> If we turn to these translations, and especially to those from the *Romancero del Cid,* we think the reader has here almost as perfect a representation of the originals as can well be conveyed in a foreign tongue. Those in the shorter ballad metre are perhaps generally better than those in longer verse; but one has only to compare this translation with its predecessors to show its superiority. It is needless to say that there is no misconception of the Spanish as in some of Lockhart's ballads . . . or in Byron's.[29]

---

[29] Review of *The Cid Ballads,* by James Young Gibson, *Academy* 32 (1887): 100.

The critic for the *Saturday Review* also liked the book, commenting on it in the following terms:

> Of the translations included in these two volumes, *The Cid Ballads* [*sic*] deserve to have the first place. They are, on the whole, admirably well done, with scrupulous adhesion to the spirit of the letter which is the essence of a good translation. Compared with Lockhart's or any other preceding versions, they must be allowed to have the palm, at least as regards fidelity. . . . The exquisite little poems . . . "Rosa fresca, Rosa fresca," "Fonte frida, Fonte frida," — the despair of translators, are among the happiest of Mr. Gibson's successes. Aided by his native Scotch he has been able to make them almost as pretty as the originals.[30]

This initial recognition of Gibson's ballad work has been repeated from time to time in the years since his death whenever any scholar has taken the trouble to examine it. Thus in 1911 S. Griswold Morley commented that "Gibson's work is always careful and never in bad taste, and his selection is superior to Lockhart's."[31] In 1945 George Umphrey voiced the opinion that "Gibson's translations, especially of the Cid ballads, are in some ways superior to those of Lockhart. They are just as spirited and spontaneous, and have the added advantage of much greater faithfulness to the originals."[32]

The ballads presented in the following pages will demonstrate the validity of the judgments cited above, since the majority of the translations included are Gibson's. There are at least two reasons why it seems desirable to concentrate on his work, somewhat to the exclusion, perhaps, of that of other translators. First, in spite of their acknowledged excellence, his ballads are little known outside the small circle of specialists in the ballad field. Second, the study of his translations offers, in effect, a résumé of the work of almost all the other translators. He transcribed a greater number of ballads and of more different types than any other translator, and he made use of most of the known techniques and patterns. These factors, combined with a high level of artistry and craftsmanship, make of his translations worthy examples in English of Spanish balladry.

---

30 Review of *The Cid Ballads,* by James Young Gibson, *Saturday Review* 64 (1888): 234.

31 Morley, *Spanish Ballads,* p. xxxiv.

32 Umphrey, "Spanish Ballads in English," p. 492.

In 1901 appeared another large collection of ballads which again inspires a slight feeling of regret for the misused opportunity of the translator. As part of a volume on Moorish literature, Epiphanius Wilson translated seventy-five *romances moriscos* intended to illustrate the vivid descriptions and dramatic qualities of this class of ballads. Wilson obviously aimed for as literal a rendition as possible, and some of his translations come close to duplicating the characteristics he was seeking to demonstrate. There are too many failures, however, and the overall impression is unfavorable.

No other large collections of ballad translations were published in the first half of the twentieth century, but for the sake of completeness I will mention briefly numerous small groups and isolated samples which were made public. In 1913 Sophie Jewett translated three *romances* for a book on the folk music of southern Europe. A short time later James Elroy Flecker published one of the many versions in English of the popular ballad of "Conde Arnaldos," and in 1919 the literary historian J. D. M. Ford transcribed for a book on Spanish literature two *romances históricos* illustrative of the series celebrating the legends of Fernán González and Bernardo del Carpio. The following year Ida Farnell translated "Conde Arnaldos," also for a book on literature. In 1921, and again in 1941, Georgiana King published ballad translations, as did the poet Yvor Winter in the 1927 volume of *Poetry* magazine.

A Master's thesis by Luella Thurston Little in 1937 presents an interesting comparison of the contrasting versions by different translators of four separate *romances,* and the author, in addition to reviewing some of the scholarly opinion concerning the criteria for translation, offers an original interpretation of a Carolingian ballad.

The following year the Hispanic Society of America included eight ballads from six authors in *Translations from Hispanic Poets.* The selections emphasized lyrical elements with four artistic ballads, two Moorish ballads, one historical ballad, and one ballad of chivalry. It may be worthwhile to note in passing that the latter, "Conde Niños," with its theme of intertwining plants growing from the graves of ill-fated lovers, resembles the old English ballad "Barbara Allen" and is one of the relatively few Spanish ballads containing supernatural elements. Another book on European folk songs in 1939 accounts for nine ballad translations by W. J. Entwistle representing all the major categories of *romances,* and in the 1940s there were quite competent ballad translations by Nicholson B. Adams, Edwin Honig, John Masefield, and George W. Umphrey. Umphrey's versions were made primarily to demonstrate that assonance could be carried over successfuly into English, and although the effect is not as pleasing as in the Spanish originals, the point is well made.

With one exception the only new translations to appear in the second half of this century have been isolated examples such as those by Paul T. Manchester (1951) and Eleanor L. Turnbull (1955). However, the 1961 edition of *Spanish Ballads* by W. S. Merwin offers an extensive selection comprising almost every kind of *romance,* including Catalan and Spanish-Jewish ballads. These compositions are somewhat unusual in that the translator chose to forgo both rhyme and assonance in an effort to preserve the rhythm and literal sense of the originals. Consequently, the more than seventy poems of this collection are readable and faithful translations, but lack the lyrical and poetical qualities of the models.

Interest in the *romances* probably reached a peak in the first third of the nineteenth century, with more English translations made at that time than in any comparable period since. It is equally evident, however, that enthusiasm for the ballads did not cease with the passing of the Romantics, so that a more or less steady stream of translations has continued into the present. Over seven hundred versions in English of more than four hundred and fifty different *romances* attest to the vitality of this genre and the attraction it has held for the English-speaking student of Spanish literature.

Although practically all categories of ballads in the *Romancero* are represented by translations, the translators have shown a marked preference for the historical ballads and for those dealing with Moorish subjects. Not surprisingly, perhaps, the most famous of all Spanish heroes, the Cid Campeador, accounts for the largest number of ballads on a single subject, with approximately one hundred and fifty-five translations. The *romances caballerescos* and *novelescos* and the artistic ballads have not been neglected, however, and there are many fine specimens in English to illustrate these classifications.

Quite a large number of *romances* have been translated by more than one author, and for some there are as many as ten different versions in English. The following ballads, identified by the first lines, since the majority of the *romances* do not have titles, may be studied in five or more translations: "Abenámar, Abenámar — moro de la morería"; "Fonte-frida, fonte-frida — fonte-frida y con amor"; "Moro alcaide, moro alcaide — el de la vellida barba"; "Ocho a ocho y diez a diez — Sarracinos y Aliatares"; "Paseábase el rey moro — por la ciudad de Granada"; "Por el mes era de mayo — cuando hace la calor"; "Quién hubiese tal ventura — sobre las aguas del mar"; "Rosa fresca, rosa fresca — tan garrida y con amor"; "Sale la estrella de Venus — al tiempo que el sol se pone."

It is difficult to single out any one Spanish ballad translator as the most outstanding among the many who have labored in this field. Included in the work of some of the best are compositions whose failure to reflect to any significant extent the qualities of the originals emphasizes again the difficulty of the sometimes underestimated art of poetry translation. Nevertheless, among those whose ballads most consistently reveal an understanding of the spirit of the *romances* and the ability to transcribe understanding and appreciation into acceptable English verse are Lockhart, Gibson, Bowring, Longfellow, Monk Lewis, and John Hookham Frere. Cushing, Oxenford, Percy, and Lord Byron also certainly deserve favorable mention in any discussion of the Spanish ballad in English. Lockhart remains the best-known and for that reason, possibly, the most popular of the English translators, but there is much reason to believe, as I hope the translations in this volume will show, that first place should go to Gibson.

Chapter I

THE CID BALLADS

THE POPULARITY OF SPAIN'S GREATEST FOLK HERO, El Cid Campeador, dates from a few years after his death in 1099. He was born Rodrigo, or Ruy, Díaz de Vivar, near the city of Burgos in northern Spain around the middle of the eleventh century. His deeds, both legendary and real, were first celebrated in the twelfth-century epic *El poema de mío Cid* and later in the much more romantic and extravagant *Mocedades de Rodrigo* (The Youth of Rodrigo) of the late fourteenth or early fifteenth century. The most complete account of the Cid's life and adventures is to be found in the hundreds of ballads in which he appears either as the principal or secondary figure. Not only does he seem to have been the favorite topic for the unknown authors to whom we are indebted for the *romances,* but a substantial number of these poems have been put into English. Some of the ballads of the Cid may be fragments or reworkings of portions of the old epic, but the majority are relatively late compositions which reflect the tendencies and tone of the *Mocedades,* rather than the austere realism of the *Poema.* They are usually arranged so as to trace the chronology of the Cid's life from boyhood to his death. Accordingly, the first translation in James Young Gibson's collection is the ballad relating how Rodrigo was tested by his father, Diego Laínez, to determine if the youth had the qualities necessary to avenge an insult which the old man had suffered from the arrogant Count Lozano. The opening lines are as follows:

Cuidando Diego Laínez	Diego Lainez brooding sat,
Por las menguas de su casa,	His house was on decline,
Fidalga, rica y antigua,	More ancient, rich and noble
Antes de Iñigo y Abarca;	Than old Abarca's line.
Y viendo que le fallecen	He saw the Count Lozano,
Fuerzas para la venganza	Each day that flitted by,
Y que por sus luengos años	Ride past his door with mocking lip
Por sí no puede tomalla,	And insult in his eye.
Y que el de Orgaz se pasea	He had no hope of vengeance,
Libre y exento en la plaza,	He had no strength to fight,
Sin que nadie se lo impida,	His drooping arm with weight of years
Lozano en el nombre y gala	Had lost its power to smite.
No puede dormir de noche	By night he could not slumber,
Ni gustar de las viandas,	By day he could not eat,
Ni alzar del suelo los ojos	Nor lift his eyes from off the ground,
Ni osa salir de la sala;	Nor walk along the street.
Nin fablar con sus amigos,	He dare not meet his comrades,
Antes les niega la fabla,	Nor talk of bygone fame,
Temiendo que les ofenda	Lest they should shrink with horror back
El aliento de su infamia.	Before his breath of shame.
Estando, pues, combatiendo	But while he writhed in anguish,
Con estas honrosas bascas,	And mourned his honor true,
Para usar desta esperiencia	The wisdom that had come with years
Que no le salió contraria	Now taught him what to do.

The verse pattern used here is the quatrain of four- and three-stress lines, eight and six syllables, iambic, with frequent omission of the fourth stress in the first line. This type of meter was a favorite with all translators and is used by Gibson more than any other pattern. Some transposition of verses is noticeable in the first three stanzas, but there is little addition to or omission of ideas. For the most part, Gibson prefers to stay even closer to a line-for-line translation, as illustrated by his handling of the remaining stanzas of this ballad:

Mandó llamar sus tres fijos	He bade his sons be summoned
Y sin fablalles palabra,	Of words he uttered none,
Les apretara uno a uno	But took their noble tender hands,
Los fidalgos tiernas palmas.	And grasped them one by one.

Non para mirar en ellos
Las chirománticas rayas,
Que aquel fechicero abuso
No había nacido en España.

Y poniendo al honor fuerza
A pesar del tiempo y canas,
A la fría sangre y venas,
Nervios y arterias heladas,

Les apretó de manera
Que dijeron: —¡Señor, basta!
¿Qué intentas o qué pretendes?
¡Déxanos ya, que nos matas! —

Mas cuando llegó a Rodrigo,
Casi muerta la esperanza
Del fruto que pretendía,
Que a do no piensan se halla,

Encarnizados los ojos
Cual furiosa tigre hircana,
Con mucha furia y denuedo
Le dice aquestas palabras:

—Soltedes, padre, en malhora
Soltedes, en hora mala,
Que a no ser padre, no hiciera
Satisfacción de palabras,

Antes con la mano mesma
Vos sacara las entrañas,
Faciendo lugar el dedo
En vez de puñal o daga.—

Llorando de gozo el viejo
Dijo: —Fijo de mi alma,
Tu enojo me desenoja,
Y tu indignación me agrada,

Esos bríos, mi Rodrigo,
Muéstralos en la demanda
De mi honor que está perdido,
Si en ti no se cobra y gana.—

'Twas not to trace the mystic lines
  Foreboding joy or pain;
For such device of witchery
  Was then unknown in Spain.

His honour lent him vigor
  In spite of age and pain,
Of pithless nerves and languid blood,
  That ran in frozen veins.

So fierce his grip and cruel,
  "Enough, Señor," they cry;
"What dost thou mean, what dost thou wish?
  Unhand us, or we die!"

But when he reached Rodrigo,
  And hope was almost gone,
He reaped the fruit he longed to find
  Where he expected none.

For, like Hyrcanian tiger,
  With burning bloodshot eyes,
And fury mounting in his cheeks,
  The youth with daring cries:

"Unhand me, wretched father,
  Unhand me now in haste!
For wert thou not my father, I
  Not many words would waste;

I'd pluck thy quivering entrails out,
  I'd do it with my hand;
And make my finger serve the place,
  Of dagger or of brand!"

For joy the old man wept and cried,
  "Enough, my darling boy!
Thine anger drives my anger back,
  Thy fury gives me joy!

These arms of thine, Rodrigo mine,
  Make ready for the fight,
To give me vengeance on my foe,
  And make my honour bright."

Contóle su agravio, y dióle
Su bendición, y la espada
Con que dió al conde la muerte
Y principio a sus fazañas.

He told him all his grief, and gave
His blessing and the sword,
With which Rodrigo slew the count,
And grew a famous lord.

Gibson seems to have transcribed from two versions of this *romance,* and the one from which the second portion is taken is slightly different from the one first cited. The translation is accurate and literal, yet the vigor and spirit of the original are preserved. The rather naive note on witchery is carefully carried over, and the angry reaction of Rodrigo is reproduced exactly.

Gibson's next ballad continues the above situation as the Cid readies himself for combat against the offending count. The four- and three-stress iambic pattern is well illustrated by the opening stanzas.

Pensativo estaba el Cid,
Viéndose de pocos años,
Para vengar a su padre
Matando al Conde Lozano.

The Cid he was of tender age,
And deep in thought he stood
How best to right his father's wrongs
In Count Lozano's blood.

Miraba el bando temido
Del poderoso contrario,
Que tenía en las montañas
Mil amigos asturianos:

He looked upon his powerful foe,
Surrounded by his train,
Who from the wild Asturian hills
Could bring a thousand men:

Miraba como en las cortes
Del rey de León Fernando
Era su voto el primero,
Y en guerras mejor su brazo.

Who in the court of Ferdinand
Shone out the foremost star,
His voice in council ever first,
His arm the best in war.

Todo le parece poco
Respecto de aquel agravio,
El primero que se ha fecho
A la sangre de Laín Calvo.

Full little recked he of the man,
But much of the disgrace,
The first that e'er had cast a stain
On Layn Calvo's race.

Al cielo pide justicia,
A la tierra pide campo,
Al viejo padre licencia,
Y a la honra esfuerzo y brazo.

From Heaven he begged for justice,
From Earth a field of fight;
Permission from his aged Sire,
From Honour manly might.

Non cuida de su niñez,
Que en naciendo, es costumbrado
A morir por casos de honra
El valiente fijodalgo.

He minded not his tender age,
For from his very youth
A Cavalier is trained to die
For honour and for truth.

Descolgó una espada vieja
De Mudarra el castellano,
Que estaba vieja y mohosa
Por la muerte de su amo:

He took him down an ancient sword,
Mudarra's of Castile;
It seemed to mourn his master's death,
That old and rusty steel.

Y pensando que en ella sola
Bastaba para el descargo,
Antes que se la ciñese
Así le dice turbado:

And knowing well that it alone
Would for the deed suffice,
Before he girt it round his waist,
The youth with daring cries:

—Faz cuenta, valiente espada,
Que es de Mudarra mi brazo,
Y que con su brazo riñes,
Porque suyo es el agravio.

"O valiant sword, bethink thee,
Mine is Mudarra's arm;
A cause like his thou hast to right,
A quarrel and a harm.

Bien sé que te correrás
De verte así en la mi mano,
Mas no te podrás correr
De volver atrás un paso.

I know full well thou blushest now
Thy master's hand to lack;
But never wilt thou have to blush
To see me turn my back.

Tan fuerte como tu acero
Me verás en campo armado;
Tan bueno como el primero
Segundo dueño has cobrado,

As true as is thy tempered steel
Thou'lt find me on the field;
Thy second master, like thy first,
Was never born to yield.

Y cuando alguno te venza,
Del torpe fecho enojado,
Fasta la cruz en mi pecho
Te esconderé muy airado.

But should the foeman master thee;
Not long the shame shall rest;
Up to the hilt I'll drive thee straight,
And sheathe thee in my breast.

Vamos al campo, que es hora
De dar al Conde Lozano
El castigo que merece
Tan infame lengua y mano.—

To meet the Count Lozano
The hour is now at hand;
And woe betide that braggart knight,
His shameless tongue and hand."

Determinado va el Cid,
Y va tan determinado,
Que en espacio de una hora
Quedó del Conde vengado.

So dauntlessly the Cid goes forth,
So high his spirits mount,
That in the space of one short hour
He met and slew the Count.

Following his successful encounter with the count, the young Cid returns to his grieving father with the dramatic evidence that the stain on the family honor has been erased. The version is, again, that of Gibson.

Llorando Diego Laynez
Yace sentado a la mesa,
Vertiendo lágrimas tristes
Y tratando de su afrenta,

Y trasportándose el viejo,
La mente siempre inquieta,
De temores muy honrados
Va levantando quimeras,

Cuando Rodrigo venía
Con la cortada cabeza
Del conde, vertiendo sangre,
Y asida por la melena.

Tiró a su padre del brazo
Y del sueño lo recuerda,
Y con el gozo que trae
Le dice de esta manera:
— Veis aquí la yerba mala;
Para que vos comáis buena;

Abrid, mi padre, los ojos,
Y alzad la faz, que ya es cierta
Vuesa honra, y ya con vida
Os resucita de muerta.

De su mancha está lavada,
A pesar de su soberbia,
Que hay manos que no son manos,
Y esta lengua ya no es lengua.

Yo os he vengado, señor,
Que está la venganza cierta
Cuando la razón ayuda
A aquel que se arma con ella. —

Piensa que lo sueña el viejo,
Mas no es así, que no sueña,
Sino que el llorar prolijo
Mil caracteres le muestra;
Mas al fin alzó los ojos
Que fidalgas sombras ciegan,
Y conoció a su enemigo,
Aunque en la mortal librea.

Diego Lainez sat at meat,
And woebegone was he;
His head was drooping on his breast,
And tears were falling free.

He groaned aloud, and could not rest,
But brooded o'er his pain;
And phantoms, conjured by his fears,
Kept flitting through his brain.

'Twas then Rodrigo, fresh from fight
Before his father stood;
He held the Count's head by the hair,
All dripping down with blood.

He touched his father on the arm,
And roused him up to eat;
"See, father, here the bitter herb
Will make thy banquet sweet!

Thou now may'st open wide thine eyes,
And raise aloft thy head;
Thine honour's safe, and new-born life
I bring thee from the dead.

Thine every stain is washed away,
And though the fight was sore,
These hands they are no longer hands,
This tongue a tongue no more.

I have avenged thee, good my Lord,
For vengeance must alight
When good and righteous is the cause
And arms defend the right."

The old man thought it but a dream;
At length he raised his eyes,
And recognized his former foe,
Although in deadly guise.

—Rodrigo, fijo del alma,
Encubre aquesa cabeza,
No sea otra Medusa
Que me trueque en dura piedra

"Veil, veil that head, Rodrigo mine,
And come to me alone,
Lest like a fierce Medusa
It turn me into stone!

Y sea tal mi desventura
Que antes que te lo agradezca
Se me abra el corazón
Con alegría tan cierta.

And let me clasp thee to my breast,
And thank my gallant boy,
Lest this poor heart ere that be done
Should burst with sudden joy!

¡Oh conde Lozano infame!
El cielo de ti me venga,
Y mi razón, contra ti,
Ha dado a Rodrigo fuerzas.

O shameless Count Lozano,
Heaven's vengeance comes at length,
And this my righteous feud with thee
Hath given Rodrigo strength!

Siéntate a yantar, mi fijo,
Do estoy, a mi cabecera,
Que quien tal cabeza trae,
Será en mi casa cabeza.

Now take, my son, the seat I fill,
And eat in peace thy bread;
Who brings me such a head as this
Shall of my house be Head!"

Gibson's customary meter is evident in the above translation, as is his usual concern with accuracy. In one instance he has combined and shortened eight verses of the original into four of the English ("Piensa que lo sueña el viejo," etc.), but the essential idea is retained and, in fact, the change may be an improvement. The verse pattern is quite regular, perhaps more than is normally the case in Gibson's ballads, but not excessively so. The words are in good taste and well chosen to avoid a sense of the grotesque, yet convey the full impact of a rather shocking scene.

Lord Holland, who also translated several ballads from the boyhood of the Cid, may have had the above *romance* in mind when he remarked that "while I have endeavoured to preserve the sparks of spirit which occasionally enliven these popular songs, the whole object of my translation would have been defeated had I softened any vulgarity, or disguised any absurdity of the rude originals." [1] His version of the above poem, like Gibson's, is certainly not softened, and it would appear to be only a matter of choice as to which of the two translations is the better.

---

[1] Henry Richard Fox, Lord Holland, *Some Account of the Lives and Writings of Lope Félix de Vega Carpio and Guillén de Castro* (London, 1817), 2: 13.

The next ballad in Gibson's collection introduces the theme of the Cid's quarrel with the king and presents the hero in a somewhat unfavorable light. Gibson rendered it in the characteristic quatrains of four- and three-stress lines, maintaining a close agreement with the Spanish lines throughout. It was also translated by Lockhart, whose version may be studied here; the original is apparently very old.[2]

Cabalga Diego Laínez
Al buen rey besar la mano;
Consigo se los llevaba
Los trescientos hijosdalgo.
Entre ellos iba Rodrigo
El soberbio castellano;
Todos cabalgan a mula,
Solo Rodrigo a caballo;
Todos visten oro y seda,
Rodrigo va bien armado;
Todos espadas ceñidas,
Rodrigo estoque dorado;
Todos con sendas varicas,
Rodrigo lanza en la mano;
Todos guantes olorosos,
Rodrigo guante mallado;
Todos sombreros muy ricos,
Rodrigo casco afilado,
Y encima del casco lleva
Un bonete colorado.
Andando por su camino,
Unos con otros hablando,
Allegados son a Burgos;
Con el rey se han encontrado.
Los que vienen con el rey
Entre sí van razonando:
Unos lo dicen de quedo,
Otros, lo van preguntando:
—Aquí viene entre esta gente
Quien mató al conde Lozano.—
Como lo oyera Rodrigo,
A hito los ha mirado:
Con alta y soberbia voz
De esta manera ha hablado:
—Si hay alguno entre vosotros
Su pariente o adeudado,
Que le pese de su muerte,
Salga luego a demandallo,
Yo se lo defenderé
Quiera a pie, quiera a caballo.
Todos responden a una:
—Demándelo su pecado.—
Todos se apearon juntos
Para el rey besar la mano,
Rodrigo se quedó solo
Encima de su caballo.
Entonces habló su padre,
Bien oiréis lo que ha hablado:
—Apeáos vos, mi hijo,
Besaréis al rey la mano,
Porque él es vuestro señor,
Vos, hijo, sois su vasallo.—
Desque Rodrigo esto oyó,
Sintióse más agraviado:
Las palabras que responde
Son de hombre muy enojado.
—Si otro me lo dijera
Ya me lo hubiera pagado;
Mas por mandarlo vos, padre,
Yo lo haré de buen grado.—
Ya se apeaba Rodrigo
Para al rey besar la mano;
Al hincar de la rodilla
El estoque se ha arrancado.
Espantóse de esto el rey
Y dijo como turbado:
—Quítate, Rodrigo, allá,
Quítate me allá, diablo,

[2] See Ramón Menéndez Pidal, *Flor nueva de romances viejos*, 8th ed. (Buenos Aires: Espasa-Calpe, Colección Austral, 1950), p. 198, n. 4.

Que tienes el gesto de hombre,
Y los hechos de león bravo.—
Como Rodrigo esto oyó
Apriesa pide el caballo:
Con una voz alterada,
Contra el rey así ha hablado:
—Por besar mano de rey
No me tengo por honrado;
Porque la besó mi padre
Me tengo por afrentado.—
En diciendo estas palabras
Salido se ha del palacio:
Consigo se los tornaba
Los trescientos hijosdalgo:
Si bien vinieron vestidos,
Volvieron mejor armados,
Y si vinieron en mulas
Todos vuelven en caballos.

Lockhart's translation offers a different verse pattern, and one which is just as characteristic of his work as the four- and three-stress lines are of Gibson's. This is the seven-stress, fourteen-syllable line with caesura, which he arranges in quatrains. The first stanza is a typical variation of six-stress lines.

Now rides Diego Laynez to kiss the good king's hand;
Three hundred men of gentry go with him from his land;
Among them young Rodrigo, the proud knight of Bivar;
The rest on mules are mounted, he on his horse of war.

They ride in glittering gowns of soye, — he harnessed like a lord;
There is no gold about the boy, but the crosslet of his sword.
The rest have gloves of sweet perfume, — he gauntlets strong of mail;
They broidered cap and flaunting plume, — he crest untaught to quail.

All talking with each other thus, along their way they passed,
But now they've come to Burgos, and met the king at last;
When they came near his nobles, a whisper through them ran, —
"He rides amidst the gentry that slew the Count Lozan." —

With very haughty gesture Rodrigo reined his horse,
Right scornfully he shouted, when he heard them so discourse; —
"If any of his kinsman or vassals dare appear,
The man to give them answer, on horse or foot, is here."

"The devil ask the question," thus muttered all the band; —
With that they all alighted to kiss the good king's hand,
All but the proud Rodrigo, he in his saddle stayed, —
Then turned him to his father (you may hear the words he said).

"Now light, my son, I pray thee, and kiss the good king's hand,
He is our Lord, Rodrigo, we hold him of our land."
But when Rodrigo heard him, he looked in sulky sort, —
I wot the words he answered, they were both cold and short.

"Had any other said it, his pains had well been paid,
But thou, sir, art my father, thy word must be obeyed." —
With that he sprung down lightly, before the king to kneel,
But as the knee was bending, out leapt his blade of steel.

The king drew back in terror, when he saw the sword was bare;
"Stand back, stand back, Rodrigo! in the devil's name beware!
Your looks bespeak a creature of father Adam's mould,
But in your wild behavior you're like some lion bold."

When Rodrigo heard him say so, he leapt into his seat,
And thence he made his answer, with visage nothing sweet, —
"I'd think it little honor to kiss a kingly palm,
And if my father kissed it, thereof ashamed I am."

When he these words had uttered, he turned him from the gate,
His true three hundred gentles behind him followed straight;
If with good gowns they came that day, with better arms they went,
And if their mules behind did stay, with horses they're content.

Lockhart's translation is quite satisfactory and has perhaps less monotony than Gibson's version of this ballad, although there is an occasional jarring note in such rhymes as "stayed—said" and "palm—am." One is also impelled to question the choice of "father Adam's mould" for "gesto de hombre," and the last line of the translation seems a somewhat weak ending. In general, however, Lockhart has preserved both the spirit and the idea quite well, and possibly the only major defect for the modern reader is the nineteenth-century phraseology. Unfortunately, translations, even good ones, seem to become dated more quickly than original compositions, which is one reason why new versions continue to be made.

Following the scene above, Ximena Gómez, daughter of the slain count, comes to the king to demand vengeance for the death of her father in a ballad which has been translated by Gibson, Lockhart, and Lord Holland. Gibson's version accompanies the Spanish.

Grande rumor se levanta	At Burgos in the palace
De gritos, armas y voces	Was heard the din of arms,
En el palacio del Rey	And there arose a mighty clamour
Donde son los ricos-homes:	With shouting and alarms.
Baja el Rey de su aposento	The King he left his chamber,
Y con él toda la corte,	With all his men of state,

Y a las puertas de palacio
Hallan a Ximena Gómez

And saw Ximena Gomez stand
Before the palace gate.

Desmelenado el cabello,
Llorando a su padre el conde,
Y a Rodrigo de Vivar
Ensangrentado el estoque.

She tore her hair; with streaming eyes
Her father's death deplored,
And cursed Rodrigo of Bivar
And eke his bloody sword.

Vieron al soberbio mozo
El rostro airado que pone
De Doña Ximena oyendo
Lo que dicen sus clamores:

The haughty stripling stood aloof
With anger in his eyes,
While loud Ximena Gomez gave
Her clamours to the skies:

—Justicia, buen Rey, te pido,
Y venganza de traidores,
Así lo logren tus fijos
Y de sus fazañas goces,

"I ask for justice, noble king,
And vengeance on the bad;
Thy sons shall reap the fruit thereof,
And thou thyself be glad.

Que aquel que no la mantiene
Del rey no merece el nombre,
Nin comer pan en manteles,
Nin que le sirvan los nobles.

The king who does not justice grant
Deserveth not to reign,
Nor eat his bread at tables spread
Nor have a noble train.

Mira, buen Rey, que deciendo
De aquellos claros varones
Que a Pelayo defendieron
Con castellanos pendones;

Good king, my sires were barons bold,
Of high renown and skill,
Who gathered to Pelayo's host,
With banners of Castile.

Y cuando no fuera así,
Tu brazo ha de ser conforme,
Dando venganza a los chicos
Con rigor de los mayores.

But were I as low as I am high,
Thine arm should equal fate,
In giving vengeance to the small
With rigour of the great.

Y tú, matador rabioso,
Tu espada sangrienta corre
Por esta humilde garganta
Sujecta a su duro golpe.

And thou, wild swordsman, take thy [sword,
And deal a deadly blow,
And pierce this tender throat of mine,
Till all the blood shall flow.

Mátame, traidor, a mí,
No por muger me perdones,
Mira que pide justicia
Contra ti Ximena Gómez.

Slay me, o traitor to my peace,
Nor heed a woman's cry;
It is Ximena Gomez calls
For vengeance from on high.

Pues mataste un caballero
El mejor de los mejores,
La defensa de la fe,
Terror de los Almanzores,

Thou giv'st to death a gallant knight,
The flower of the noblesse
A brave defender of the faith,
The scourge of heathenness.

No es mucho, rapaz villano,
Que te afrente y te deshonre.
La muerte, traidor, te pido,
No me la niegues ni estorbes. —

En esto viendo Ximena
Que Rodrigo no responde,
Y que tomando las riendas
En su caballo se pone,

El rostro volviendo a todos,
Por obligallos da voces,
Y viendo que no le siguen,
Dice: "Venganza, señores."

It is not much, thou base-born youth,
To heap on thee disgrace;
Come, traitor, pierce me to the heart
Nor turn away thy face."

Her burning glance was on the youth,
Rodrigo gave no heed;
But took the reins into his hands,
And leapt upon his steed.

She turned her to the nobles round,
And uttered taunting words;
But none would move, though loud she [cried:
"Avenge me, good my lords!"

Lockhart exhibits in his translation of this poem another popular long-line ballad meter, with six stresses and either twelve or thirteen syllables with caesura. This is his favorite alternative to the seven-stress line. The first lines will give an idea of the technique employed:

Within the court at Burgos a clamor doth arise,
Of arms on armor clashing, of screams, and shouts, and cries;
The good men of the King, that sit his hall around,
All suddenly upspring, astonished at the sound.

In this and the other stanzas, Lockhart maintains the spirit of the poem quite well, but his version is somewhat deficient in literalness and smoothness when compared to either Gibson's or the original.

The next ballad, "Día era de los reyes," continues Ximena Gómez's complaint to the king and introduces her unusual solution to her grievance. Some of its variants are very old.

Día era de los Reyes,
Día era señalado,
Cuando dueñas y doncellas
Al Rey piden aguinaldo,

Si no es Ximena Gómez,
Hija del Conde Lozano,
Que puesta delante el Rey
Desta manera ha hablado:

— Con mancilla vivo, Rey,
Con ella vive mi madre;

It was the feast-day of the Kings,
A high and holy day,
When all the dames and damosels
The King for hansel pray.

All save Ximena Gomez,
The Count Lozano's child,
And she has knelt low at his feet,
And cries with dolour wild:

"My mother died of sorrow, King,
In sorrow still live I;

Cada día que amanece
Veo quien mató a mi padre,

I see the man who slew my Sire,
Each day that passes by.

Caballero en un caballo
Y en su mano un gavilane;
Otras veces un halcón
Que trae para cazare,

A horseman on a hunting horse,
With hawk in hand rides he;
And in my dove-cot feeds his bird,
To show his spite at me.

Y por me hacer más enojo
Cébalo en mi palomare:
Con sangre de mis palomas
Ensangrentó mi briale.

My little doves, both young and old
He cruelly strikes down;
The trickling blood from out their breasts
Has stained my silken gown.

Enviéselo a decir,
Envióme amenazare
Que me cortará mis haldas
Por vergonzoso lugare,

I sent to tell him of my grief,
He sent to threaten me,
That he would cut my skirts away,
Most shameful for to see!

Me forzará mis doncellas
Casadas y por casare;
Matarme un pagecico
So haldas de mi briale.

That he would put my maids to scorn,
The wedded and to wed,
And underneath my silken gown
My little page strike dead!

Rey que no hace justicia
No debía de reinare,
Ni cabalgar en caballo,
Ni espuela de oro calzare,

The King deserveth not to reign
Who justice doth withhold,
Nor ride upon a horse of war,
Nor wear a spur of gold;

Ni comer pan en manteles,
Ni con la Reina holgare,
Ni oír misa en sagrado,
Porque no merece mase.—

Nor eat his bread at tables spread,
Nor dally with the Queen,
Nor hear the mass in holy kirk,
Nor bear the sword, I ween."

El Rey de que aquesto oyera
Comenzara de hablare:
—¡Oh válame Dios del cielo!
Quiérame Dios consejare:

The King was grave, and thought aloud,
When he the matter knew:
"O God of heaven, be now my aid,
And teach me what to do!

Si yo prendo o mato al Cid,
Mis Cortes se volverane;
Y si no hago justicia
Mi alma lo pagarae.

If I should seize or slay the Cid,
My Cortes will rebel;
But if I fail to right her wrongs,
God's wrath will fall as well!"

—Ten tú las tus Cortes, Rey,
No te las revuelva nadie,
Y al que a mi padre mató
Dámelo tú por iguale,

"Fear not thy Cortes, noble King,
But list to my desire,
And deign to give me as my mate
The man who slew my sire.

Que quien tanto mal me hizo
Sé que algún bien me harae. —
Entonces dijera el Rey,
Bien oiréis lo que dirae:

For he who did me so much ill
I trow, will bring me cheer."
The King was in a mindful mood,
And what he said ye'll hear:

— Siempre lo oí decir,
Y agora veo que es verdade,
Que el seso de las mugeres
Que non era naturale:

"It often hath been told to me,
And now I know it true,
That women's wits are wondrous strange
And passing nature too!

Hasta aquí pidió justicia,
Ya quiere con él casare:
Yo lo haré de muy buen grado,
De muy buena voluntade,

For till this hour she justice seeks,
And now with him will wed;
With pleasure and a right goodwill
I'll do the thing she said.

Mandarle quiero una carta,
Mandarle quiero llamare. —
Las palabras no son dichas,
La carta camino vae,

I'll send a letter to the Cid,
My summons to obey."
The words are neither mild nor sweet,
The letter goes its way.

Mensagero que la lleva
Dado la había a su padre.

Off rides the messenger with speed,
And gives it to the Sire.
The Cid regards him with a frown,
And mutters in his ire:

— Malas mañas habéis, Conde,
No os las puedo yo quitare,
Que cartas que el Rey os manda
No me las queráis mostrare.

"Thou hast but sorry manners, Count,
Much better would I see;
Thou hast a letter from the King,
And keep'st it back from me."

— No era nada, mi fijo,
Sino que vades alláe,
Quedaos vos aquí, mío hijo,
Yo iré en vuestro lugare.

"It is a trifle, good my son,
Thyself at court to show;
But rest thee here in peace, my son,
And in thy place I'll go."

— Nunca Dios tal cosa quiera
Ni Santa María lo mande,
Sino que adonde vos fuéredes
Que allá vaya yo delante.

"Now God forbid, and Mary blessed,
That such a thing should be;
Wherever thou art bound to ride,
I'll ride in front of thee!"

In addition to Gibson's version, accompanying the Spanish above, there is an anonymous translation of this ballad in the *Foreign Review and Continental Miscellany*, Vol. 4, 1829.

Although the translation above is quite literal, two differences between it and the original are noted. In both cases Gibson has taken the reading of a variant of this ballad, the one which begins "En Burgos está el buen rey." While the two versions are identical in many respects, the second one has Ximena say: "Con manzilla vivo, rey; con ella murió mi madre," not "con ella vive mi madre," as in the verses above. It also includes the two lines preceding Rodrigo's words to his father. By bringing in these two minor points, Gibson has strengthened his poem and made the last portion more self-explanatory.

The next ballad deals with one of the youthful exploits of the Cid as he begins to build a reputation for himself. Gibson gives it his usual straightforward treatment.

Reyes moros en Castilla Entran con grande alarido; De moros son cinco reyes, Lo demás mucho gentío.	The Moorish kings have reached Castile, With shoutings and alarms. Five valiant kings of Moorish blood, With all their men of arms.
Pasaron por junto a Burgos, A Montes-Doca han corrido, Y corriendo a Belforado, También a Santo Domingo,	And they have skirted Burgos' walls, At Montesdoca tarried; And they have Belforado ta'en, And St. Domingo harried.
A Nájera y a Logroño, Todo lo habían destruido. Llevan presa de ganados, Muchos cristianos cautivos,	Nacera's and Logroño's walls, They've levelled with the ground; Have captured many flocks and herds, And many a Christian bound.
Hombres muchos y mujeres, Y también niñas y niños. Ya se vuelven a sus tierras Bien andantes y muy ricos,	Both men and women, boys and girls, Are fast within their toils; Right merrily they homeward march, And laden with their spoils.
Porque el rey, ni otro ninguno, A quitárselo han salido. Rodrigo cuando lo supo En Vivar el su castillo,	Shame on the king and nobles all Who see it from afar! The tidings reach Rodrigo's ears In his castle of Bivar.
(Mozo es de pocos días, Los veinte años no ha cumplido) Cabalga sobre Babieca, Y con él los sus amigos,	He's still a youth of tender age, Not twenty years hath he; On Bavieca forth he rides, With goodly company.
Apellidara a la tierra, Mucha gente le ha venido. Gran salto diera en los moros: En Montes-Doca el castillo	He sends a message through the land, Draws round an armed host; At Montesdoca battle gives, Where Moors must pay the cost.

Venciera todos los moros
Y prendió los reyes cinco.
Quitárales la gran presa
Y gentes que iban cautivos,

He takes the five kings every one.
  The Moors in terror flee;
He gathers back the wealthy spoils,
  And sets the captives free.

Repartiera las ganancias
Con los que le habían seguido,
Los reyes trajera presos
A Vivar el su castillo,

He makes division of the prey
  Amongst his men of war;
The captive kings he sends in chains
  To his castle of Bivar.

Entrególos a su madre,
Ella los ha recibido,
Soltólos de la prisión,
Vasallage han conocido,

He sends them to his mother's charge
  She gives them kindly care;
From chains and prison they are freed,
  And vassalage they swear.

Y a Rodrigo de Vivar
Todos lo han bendecido.
Loaban su valentía,

With many a tearful word they bless
  Rodrigo of Bivar,
And sound aloud with praises high,
  His valiant deeds of war.

Sus parias le han prometido,
Fuéronse para sus tierras
Cumpliendo lo que habían dicho.

And they have sworn with many an oath,
  To give him tribute due;
And when the band reached Moorish
  They kept their promise true. [land,

Gibson has injected one sentiment into the translation which, although implied in the Spanish, is not openly stated. This is the reproach to the king and other nobles ("Shame on the king and nobles all"). Only one other addition to ideas can be noted ("The Moors in terror flee"), and nothing has been deleted. Barring this exception, the translation seems to be almost perfect. Monotony is avoided by the use of eye rhymes, e.g., "host—cost," "war—Bivar," which seem to have been used intentionally for this purpose. The interior rhyme in the next to last line gives the impression of a small flourish as the author signs off. It is a peculiarity often noted in Gibson's poems.

Lockhart also did a very good job of translating this ballad, although, as usual, his version is not quite as literal as Gibson's.

The foregoing ballads have suggested the future relationship between the young Cid and Ximena Gómez, and the one which follows relates how the unfortunate situation arising from her father's death is to be resolved. It has been translated by Gibson, Lockhart, and Lord Holland. Gibson's version accompanies the Spanish.

De Rodrigo de Vivar
Muy grande fama corría;
Cinco Reyes ha vencido
Moros de la Morería.

It is Rodrigo de Bivar
His fame it groweth grand,
For he has conquered five great Kings,
Five Kings of Moorish land.

Soltólos de la prisión
Do metidos los tenía,
Quedaron por sus vasallos,
Sus parias le prometían.

From prison he has led them out,
Where fast in chains they lay;
And they have homage sworn to do,
And fitting tribute pay.

En Burgos estaba el Rey
Que Fernando se decía;
Aquesa Ximena Gómez
Ante el buen Rey parecía:
Humilládose había ant'el
Y su razón proponía:

The King in Burgos holds his court,
The good King Ferdinand;
In haste Ximena Gomez comes,
To kiss her liege's hand.

— Fija soy yo de Don Gómez
Que en Gormaz condado había,
Don Rodrigo de Vivar
Le mató con valentía,

"I am Don Gomez' daughter true,
In Gormaz Count was he;
Of all the daughters that he had,
I'm youngest of the three.

La menor soy yo de tres
Hijas que el Conde tenía,
Y vengo a os pedir merced
Que me hagáis en este día,

Rodrigo, with his arm of might,
My honoured Sire did slay;
I come to ask a boon, my lord,
A boon from thee this day:

Y es que aquese Don Rodrigo
Por marido yo os pedía.
Ternéme por bien casada,
Honrada me contaría,

That Don Rodrigo thou wilt give
To be my lord and head:
I'll hold me honoured by the gift,
And think myself well wed.

Que soy cierta que su hacienda
Ha de ir en mejoría,
Y él mayor en el estado
Que en la vuestra tierra había.

For sure I am that wealth and fame
Are now at his command;
And of his peers he yet shall rank
The highest in the land.

Hareisme así gran merced,
Hacer a vos bien vernía,
Porqu'es servicio de Dios,
Y yo le perdonaría
La muerte que dió a mi padre
Si el aquesto concedía. —

To grant my boon will bring thee luck,
For it is Heaven's desire;
And I will pardon to my spouse
The death he gave my sire."

El Rey hobo por muy bien
Lo que Ximena pedía,

Ximena's wishes pleased the King;
He sent a message straight,

Escrebiérale sus cartas,
Que viniese, le decía,
A Plasencia donde estaba,
Qu'es cosa que le cumplía.

And to Placencia called the Cid,
On matters of the state.

Rodrigo, que vió las cartas
Que el Rey Fernando le envía,
Cabalgó sobre Babieca,
Muchos en su compañía:
Todos eran hijosdalgo
Los que Rodrigo traía,

Soon as Rodrigo read the words
Writ by the royal hand,
On Bavieca forth he rode,
And with a goodly band;

Armas nuevas traían todos,
De una color se vestían.
Amigos son y parientes,
Todos a él lo seguían.
Trescientos eran aquellos
Que con Rodrigo venían.

Three hundred gallant gentlemen,
Kinsmen and friends of yore;
Alike they dressed in rich attire,
New shining arms they bore.

El Rey salió a recibirlo,
Que muy mucho lo quería,
Díjole el Rey: —Don Rodrigo,
Agradézcoos la venída,

The king went forth to meet the band,
For well he loved the youth;
And with a gracious smile he said,
"Thou'rt welcomed here in sooth.

Que aquesa Ximena Gómez
Por marido a vos pedía,
Y la muerte del su padre
Perdonada os la tenía:

The fair Ximena Gomez here
Desires to be thy wife;
And to the man will pardon give
Who took her father's life.

Yo vos ruego que lo hagáis,
Dello gran placer habría,
Hacervos he gran merced,
Muchas tierras os daría.

To see thee wed so fair a dame
My heart with joy will swell;
And I will give thee honours great,
And many lands as well."

— Pláceme, Rey, mi señor,
(Don Rodrigo respondía)
En esto y en todo aquello
Que tu voluntad sería. —

"To do thy will in this and all,
My lord, I'm nothing loath."
With this Rodrigo took her hand,
And plighted there his troth.

There are several lines in the Spanish following Rodrigo's agreement to the marriage which destroy the unity present up to that point and which Gibson left off. He had another reason for doing so, since he planned to translate several other ballads which developed in greater detail the events mentioned in this part. His translation shows no unusual features, but is consistently accurate and satisfactory.

The next ballad is one of the relatively few in Spanish which deal with the miraculous or the supernatural. It relates the story of the Cid's encounter with a leper who turns out to be St. Lazarus.

Celebradas ya las bodas,
A do la corte yacía
De Rodrigo con Jimena,
A quien tanto el Rey quería,
El Cid pide al Rey licencia
Para ir en romería
Al apóstol Santiago,
Porque así lo prometía.

The marriage festival was o'er,
The feasting and the games;
The Cid would go to pay his vow
At the shrine of great St. James.

El Rey túvolo por bien
Muchos dones le daría;
Rogóle volviese presto
Que es cosa que le cumplía.

The King he gave his glad consent,
Nor was in kindness slack,
But loaded him with presents rich,
And bade him soon be back.

Despidióse de Jimena,
A su madre la daría,
Diciendo que la regale,
Que en ello merced le haría,

Rodrigo sent Ximena home
Beneath his mother's care,
To treat her as beseemed a bride
So noble and so fair.

Llevaba veinte fidalgos,
Que van en su compañía:
Dando va muchas limosnas,
Por Dios y Santa María,

And with him twenty gentlemen
Rode forth in close array;
Much alms for God and Mary's sake
They scattered on the way.

Y allá en medio del camino,
Un gafo le aparecía
Metido en un tremedal,
Que salir dél no podía.

When they had gone but half the road
A leper came in sight,
Who struggled in a slimy pool,
And cried in woeful plight:

Grandes voces está dando;
Por amor de Dios pedía
Que le sacasen de allí
Pues d'ello se serviría.

"Good gentlemen, for love of God,
Assist me in my need!
Release me from this fearful place,
And Heaven send you speed!"

Cuando lo oyera Rodrigo
Del caballo descendía;
Ayudólo a levantar
Y consigo lo subía.

Rodrigo lighted from his horse,
While thus the leper cried,
And drew him from the miry pool,
And placed him by his side.

Lleváralo a su posada,
Consigo cenado había;
Ficiérales una cama,
En la cual ambos dormían.

He took him to the strangers' inn,
And gave him meat and bread;
He led him to his chamber fine,
And shared with him his bed.

Hacia allá a la media noche,
Ya que Rodrigo dormía,
Un soplo por las espaldas
El Gafo dado le había,

At midnight while Rodrigo slept,
And all around was still,
Lo! from the leper came a breath
That made his shoulders thrill;

Tan recio, que por los pechos
A Don Rodrigo salía.
Despertó muy espantado,
Al Gafo buscado había;

A shock so sudden and so sharp
That through his breast it ran;
Alarmed Rodrigo started up
And sought the leper man.

No le hallaba en la cama,
A voces lumbre pedía:
Traídole habían lumbre,
Y el Gafo no parecía.

He could not find him in the bed
For light aloud he cried;
But when the lighted lamp was brought,
No leper man they spied.

Tornádose había a la cama;
Gran cuidado en sí tenía
De lo que le aconteciera,
Mas un hombre a él venía
Vestido de blancos paños,
Deste manera decía.

He turned again unto his bed,
In great alarm and fright;
When lo! a man stood by his side
All dressed in garments white.

—¿Duermes, o velas, Rodrigo?
—No duermo, le respondía;
Pero ¿dime tú quien eres,
Que tanto resplandecías?

"Rodrigo, dost thou sleep or wake?"
"I do not sleep," he said;
"But tell me, stranger, who thou art,
With glory round thy head?"

—San Lázaro soy, Rodrigo,
Que yo a fablarte venía.
Yo soy el gafo a que tú
Por Dios tanto bien facías.

"I am St. Lazarus, my son,
And come to speak with thee;
That leper man, whom thou didst treat
With Heaven's own charity.

Rodrigo, Dios bien te quiere,
Y otorgado te tenía,
Que lo que tu comenzares
En lides o en otra vía,

Rodrigo, God doth love thee well,
Thy fame shall aye increase;
And all that thou beginn'st to do
In battle or in peace,

Lo cumplirás a tu honra
Y crecerás cada día:
De todos serás temido,
De cristianos y morisma,

That shalt thou end with honour great,
No foe shall strike thee down;
And Moorish men and Christians too
Shall tremble at thy frown.

Y que los tus enemigos Empecer no te podrían. Morirás tu muerte honrada, Tu persona no vencida: Tu serás el vencedor, Dios su bendición te envía. —	And thou shalt die an honoured death Unconquered in the strife; Thou shalt be victor to the last, And Heaven crown thy life."
En diciendo estas palabras, Luego desaparecía. Levantóse Don Rodrigo, Y de hinojos se ponía:	The gracious words are hardly said, When lo! the vision flees; Rodrigo raised him from his bed, And fell upon his knees.
Dió gracias a Dios del cielo, También a Santa María Y ansí estuvo en oración Hasta que fuera de día.	He praised aloud the God of Heaven, And blessed Mary's name; And thus he knelt alone in prayer Until the morning came.
Partióse para Santiago, Su romería cumplía; De allí se fue a Calahorra. A donde el buen Rey yacía.	To Santiago he set forth, His pilgrimage he made; To Calahorra he returned, Where then the good King stayed.
Recibiéralo muy bien, Holgóse de su venida; Lidió con Martín González, En el campo le vencía.	The King he bade him welcome back, Nor was his joy concealed; He fought Gonsalez in the lists, And left him on the field.

Some condensation is noted in the transcription of the first eight lines, and the translator has given the leper's words in the first person for greater dramatic effect. Otherwise, the original is followed quite closely, and the manner and spirit are carefully reproduced. The first line of the translation seems an especially good opening, and with the exception of "leper man" for "gafo," the choice of expression throughout is apt.

There is another version of this ballad which begins "Ya se parte Don Rodrigo / que de Vivar se apellida" and which was translated by Lockhart with the title "The Cid and the Leper." Although it is quite similar to the one above, the basic differences reduce its usefulness for comparison with Gibson's translation.

The next two ballads, while concerning the Cid only indirectly, represent an interesting exchange between Ximena and the king. The age-old complaint of the lonely wife to her husband's employer is brought over convincingly in the first translation with complete justice to the original. Gibson manages to voice Ximena's sentiments in such a way as to reflect the particular age and circumstances, but with a universality which would be understood and appreciated by any English reader at any time.

En los solares de Burgos
A su Rodrigo aguardando
Tan en cinta está Ximena,
Que muy cedo aguarda el parto.

Ximena sat in her mansion house
In Burgos, pale with care;
For though her time had fully come
Rodrigo was not there.

Cuando además dolorida,
Una mañana en di-santo,
Bañada en lágrimas tiernas
Tomó la pluma en la mano,

It was upon a Sunday morn,
Her heart was far from light;
And while her tender tears ran down
She took her pen to write.

Y después de haberle escrito
Mil quejas a su velado,
Bastantes a domeñar,
Unas entrañas de mármol,

And first she wrote some wailing lines
Unto her husband dear,
And told a thousand griefs might melt
A heart of stone to hear.

De nuevo tomó la pluma
Y de nuevo tornó al llanto,
Y desta guisa le escribe
Al noble Rey Don Fernando.

Again she let the tears fall down
Again to write began
Unto the good King Ferdinand:
And thus the letter ran:

"A vos, mi señor el Rey,
El bueno, el aventurado,
El magno, el conqueridor,
El agradecido, el sabio,

"To you, my honoured lord and King,
The good, the fortunate,
In war the strong, in peace the wise,
The generous, and the great,

La vuesa sierva Ximena,
Fija del Conde Lozano,
A quien vos marido disteis
Bien así como burlando,

Ximena, Count Lozano's child,
Your servant most distressed,
To whom you gave a loving spouse,
Though surely 'twas in jest,

Desde Burgos os saluda
Donde vive lacerando:
Las vuesas andanzas buenas
Llévevoslas Dios al cabo.

Doth greet you well from Burgos here,
Although in doeful need,
And prays that God would bless your [hopes,
And crown them with good speed.

Perdonadme, mi señor,
Si no os fablo muy en salvo,
Que si mal talante os tengo
Non puedo disimulallo.

My lord, I pray you pardon me,
If proper words I lack;
For right or wrong, whate'er I think,
I cannot well keep back.

¿Qué ley de Dios vos enseña
Que podáis por tiempo tanto,
Cuando afincáis en las lides,
Descasar a los casados?

What law of God permitteth you
While on the field you tarry,
For such a grievous length of time,
The married to unmarry?

¿Qué buena razón consiente
Que a un garzón bien domeñado,
Falagüeño y homildoso
Le mostréis a ser león bravo?

What reason urgeth you to change
A youth of manners mild,
So winning and so grave withal,
Into a lion wild?

¿Y que de noche y de día
Le traigáis atraillado
Sin soltalle para mí
Sino una vez en el año?

You hold him fast by night and day,
And weary out his life;
And give him leave but once a year
To see his wedded wife.

Y esa que me le soltáis
Fasta los pies del caballo
Tan teñido en sangre viene
Que pone pavor mirallo;

And when he comes, as well he may,
He comes in such a plight,
Blood-stained down to his horse's feet,
I cannot look for fright.

Y cuando mis brazos toca,
Luego se duerme en mis brazos;
En sueños gime y forceja,
Que cuida que está lidiando.

And when he holds me in his arms,
He sinks to sound repose;
Or groans and struggles in his dreams,
As if he charged his foes.

Apenas el alba rompe
Cuando lo están acuciando
Los esculcas y adalides
Para que se vuelva al campo.

And scarcely has the morning dawned,
He calls for sword and shield;
For all the scouts and guides come round
To urge him to the field.

Llorando vos lo pedí,
Y en mi soledad cuidando
De cobrar padre y marido,
Ni uno tengo, ni otro alcanzo;

I sought Rodrigo at your hands,
To fill my father's place;
But sire and husband both are gone,
And woeful is my case.

Que como otro bien no tengo
Y me lo habedes quitado,
En guisa le lloro vivo
Cual si estuviera finado.

You gave me once a husband dear,
You've taken what you gave;
And here I mourn a living spouse,
As if he filled a grave.

Si lo facéis por honralle.
Mi Rodrigo es tan honrado
Que no tiene barba y tiene
Cinco Reyes por vasallos.

You think to give Rodrigo fame,
Enough he has in truth;
He holds five Kings as vassals true,
Though still a beardless youth.

Yo finco, señor, en cinta
Que en nueve meses he entrado,

My husband's child lies 'neath my breast,
Nine months are well nigh run;

Y me podrán empecer
Las lágrimas que derramo.

Such harmful tears as those I shed
I fain, good King, would shun.

Non permitáis se malogren
Prendas del mejor vasallo
Que tiene cruces bermejas
Ni a Rey ha besado mano.
Respondedme en poridad
Con letras de vuesa mano,
Aunque al vueso mandadero
Le pague yo su aguinaldo.

Return an answer, writ by you,
And well the matter guard;
And if the bearer bring it safe,
He'll earn a good reward.

Dad este escrito a las llamas
Non se faga de palacio,
Que a malos barruntadores
Non me será bien contado."

Consign this letter to the flames,
Nor let the palace know;
For talking tongues may tell the tale,
And I should feel the blow."

Now comes the king's answer:

Pidiendo a las diez del día
Papel a su secretario,
A la carta de Ximena
Responde el Rey por su mano.

One morning at ten, with paper and pen,
The King sat in his chair;
And he would send Ximena back
An answer then and there.

Después de facer la cruz
Con cuatro puntos y un rasgo,
Aquestas palabras finca
A guisa de cortesano:

And first of all he made the Cross,
With four points and a dash;
And like a gallant man he wrote
With hurried pen and rash:

"A vos, Ximena la noble,
La del marido envidiado,
La homildosa, la discreta,
La que cedo espera el parto,

"To you, Ximena, noble dame,
Whose spouse may envied be,
The modest maid, the prudent wife,
The mother soon to be,

El Rey que nunca vos tuvo
Talante desmesurado
Vos envía sus saludos
En fe de quereros tanto.

The King, who never thinks you bold,
Whatever tale you tell,
Doth send his loving greetings back,
Because he likes you well.

Decísme que soy mal Rey
Y que descaso casados,
Y que por les mis provechos
Non curo de vuesos daños:

Bad King you call me 'cause, forsooth,
The married I unmarry,
And rob you of your dearest rights,
While in the field I tarry.

Que estáis de mí querellosa
Decís en vuesos despachos,

You tax me with a grievous wrong,
And sad it is to hear

Que non vos suelto el marido
Sino una vez en el año,

Y que cuando vos le suelto
En lugar de falagaros
En vuesos brazos se duerme
Como viene tan cansado.

Si supiérades, señora,
Que vos quitaba el velado
Por mis enamoramientos,
Fuera con razón quejaros;

Mas si solo vos lo quito
Para lidiar en el campo
Con los moros convecinos,
Non vos fago mucho agravio.

A non vos tener en cinta,
Señora, el vueso velado,
Creyera de su dormir
Lo que me habedes contado;

Pero si os tiene, señora,
Con el brial levantado....
No se ha dormido en el lecho
Si espera en vos mayorazgo:

Y si en el parto primero
Un marido os ha faltado,
No importa, que sobra un Rey
Que os fará cien mil regalos.

Non le escribades que venga,
Porque aunque esté a vueso lado
En oyendo el atambor
Será forzoso dejaros.

Si non hubiera yo puesto
Las mis huestes a su cargo,
Ni vos fuerais más que dueña,
Ni el fuera más que un fidalgo.

Decís que vueso Rodrigo
Tiene Reyes por vasallos:
¡Ojalá como son cinco
Fueran cinco veces cuatro!

That I will let your husband go
But only once a year.

And when he comes to see his wife,
Instead of love's delight,
He falls asleep within your arms,
And sleeps the livelong night.

Fair lady, your complaints are just,
Your anger I deserve,
If I keep back your husband dear
My selfish ends to serve.

But when I hold him in the camp,
To combat with the strong,
And put to rout the neighbouring Moors,
In faith I do no wrong.

Rodrigo's sleep, that wondrous tale,
Might well my pity move,
Did you not bear beneath your breast
The sweetest pledge of love.

He did not sleep so sound, I wis,
If wider gowns you wear;
Nor was his love so very cold,
Since he expects an heir.

If when your first-born sees the light
Your spouse be far away,
The King with hundred thousand gifts
Will make his coming gay.

Write not, I pray, to bid him come,
For were he at your side,
Soon as he hears the sounding drum
He would be bound to ride.

Had I not given him men of war,
To aid him with their might,
You would be still a simple dame,
And he a nameless knight.

You tell me that five Moorish Kings
To be his vassals swore;
I would that they, instead of five,
Were rather five times four;

Porque teniéndolos él
Sujetos a su mandado
Mis castillos y los vuesos
No hubieran tantos contrarios.

That they were now beneath his feet,
And captive to his spear;
Then all my castles and your own
Would have no foes to fear.

Decís que entregue a las llamas
La carta que me habéis dado:
A contener heregías
Fuera digna de tal pago;

You bid me take your letter,
And thrust it in the grate;
And if it heresies contain,
It well deserves the fate.

Mas si contiene razones
Dignas de los siete sabios,
Mejor es para mi archivo
Que non para el fuego ingrato.

But if the Seven Sages all
Its wisdom would admire;
'Tis better in my royal desk
Than in the cruel fire.

Y porque guardéis la mía
Y non la fagáis pedazos,
Por ella a lo que parierdes
Prometo buen aguinaldo.

And if my own be kept as well,
And not in pieces torn,
Then I'll bestow a handsome gift
Upon the babe unborn.

Si fijo, prometo dalle
Una espada y un caballo,
Y dos mil maravedís
Para ayuda de su gasto.

If 'tis a boy, I'll give to him
A sword and eke a horse;
And good two thousand maravédis,
That he may run his course.

Si fija, para su dote
Prometo poner en cambio
Desde el día que naciere,
De plata cuarenta marcos.

But if a daughter, I'll lay out,
The day that she is born,
Full forty marks of silver fine,
Due on her wedding morn.

Con esto ceso, señora,
Y no de estar suplicando
A la Virgen vos alumbre
En los peligros del parto."

With this I close, O lady fair;
Receive it as its worth;
And may the Virgin guard you well
In perils of the birth.

Both translations are admirably done and could hardly be improved. The personalities of both Ximena and the king are clearly revealed, and the king's gentle teasing of Ximena in the second poem, so clearly and humorously expressed in the English, is a faithful reproduction of the Spanish. Gibson shows remarkable ability in both translations in assimilating and recreating the spirit of his originals without doing violence to the ideas. In only one place has he left anything out, this being the four lines near the end of the first translation referring to the "mejor vasallo que tiene cruces bermejas." The reason for this omission is unclear.

The ballad which follows is one of the several accounts of how the Cid received his Moorish title. Gibson's is the only version.

En Zamora está Rodrigo
En cortes del Rey Fernando,
Padre del rey sin ventura,
A quien llamaron don Sancho,
Cuando llegan mensajeros
De los reyes tributarios
A Rodrigo de Bibar,
Al cual dicen humillados:

Rodrigo in Zamora dwelt,
At the court of Ferdinand;
When from the Moorish vassal Kings
Came messengers to hand:

— Buen Cid, a ti nos envían
Cinco reyes tus vasallos,
A te pagar el tributo
Que quedaron obligados,

"Good Cid," they said on bended knees,
"Five Kings, thy vassals true,
Have sent us here with homage meet
To give thee tribute due.

Y por señal de amistad
Te envían más cien caballos,
Veinte blancos como armiños,
Y veinte rucios rodados.

A hundred horses they have sent,
Their friendly court to pay;
The twenty are like ermine white,
The twenty dapple-grey;

Treinta te envían morcillos
Y otros tantos alazanos,
Con todos sus guarnimientos
De diferentes brocados,

The thirty sorrel, thirty black,
All in state arrayed,
With costly gay caparisons
Of gold and fine brocade.

Y más a Doña Ximena
Muchas joyas y tocados,
Y a vuestras dos fijas bellas,
Dos jacintos muy preciados,

And to thy wife Ximena
Rich veils and jewels fair;
And to thy lovely daughters
Two jacinths wondrous rare.

Dos cofres de muchas sedas
Para vestir tus fidalgos. —
El Cid les dijera: — Amigos,
El mensaje habéis errado,

And coffers two of divers silks
To make thine esquires gay."
"Good friends," replied Rodrigo,
"Your message goes astray;

Porque yo no soy señor
Adonde está el Rey Fernando;
Todo es suyo, nada es mío,
Yo soy su menor vasallo. —

For I am here no lord of yours,
Where sits King Ferdinand;
The whole is his, there's nothing mine,
His vassal here I stand."

El Rey agradeció mucho
La humildad del Cid honrado,
Y dixo a los mensajeros:
— Decidles a vuestros amos

The King was much content to hear
Rodrigo's humble words;
And to the messengers he said:
"Go tell your noble lords

Que aunque no es rey su señor Con un rey está sentado, Y que cuanto yo poseo El Cid lo ha conquistado,	That if Rodrigo be not King, Next to the King he stands; And to his strength and prowess I owe my wealth and lands.
Y que estoy muy contento En tener tan buen vasallo.— El Cid despidió a los moros Con dones que les ha dado,	To have a vassal such as he A king may well be proud." The Moors were sent with gifts away, And sang his praises loud.
Siendo desde allí adelante El Cid Ruy Díaz llamado, Apellido entre los moros De homes de valor y estado.	They call him in their tongue Good Cid, To speak his rank and fame: And in all tongues Cid Ruy Diaz Thereafter is his name.

The translator has deleted two lines referring to the unfortunate king Don Sancho, since this ballad does not concern him in any way and since his story is to be told in later ballads. The statement of the gift of the horses is handled very skillfully with only a minor change in the word order of the Spanish and with a slight addition to the description of the trappings. The dialogue of the English version seems so natural and idiomatic that one is tempted to doubt the accuracy of the translation until it is checked. However, "Your message goes astray" and similar passages are found to be almost exact renderings of the original, and even those words which are not word-for-word translations are found to be almost perfect English equivalents. Only the last stanza is a little disappointing, since what is said explicitly in the Spanish about the significance of the name is only implied in the translation. The term is actually a derivation of the Arabic word *sayyid*, "lord."

The next two ballads, numbers twenty and twenty-one in Gibson's collection, although appearing separately in the *romanceros*, constitute a single unit. They introduce the background for the Cid's adventures in Zamora. Cervantes has Sancho make reference to the second one in the fifth chapter of the second part of the *Quixote*. Both are very old.

Doliente estaba, doliente, Ese buen rey don Fernando; Los pies tiene cara oriente Y la candela en la mano.	The King was dying, slowly dying, The good king Ferdinand; His feet were pointed to the East, A taper in his hand.
A su cabecera tiene Arzobispos y perlados;	Beside his bed, and at the head, His four sons took their place;

A su mano derecha tiene
Los sus hijos todos cuatro:
Los tres eran de la reina
Y el uno era bastardo.

The three were children of the Queen,
The fourth of bastard race.

Ese que bastardo era
Quedaba mejor librado:
Arzobispo es de Toledo
Y en las Españas perlado.

The bastard had the better luck,
Had rank and noble gains;
Archbishop of Toledo he,
And Primate of the Spains.

— Si yo no muriera, hijo,
vos fuérades Padre Santo,
Mas con la renta que os queda,
Bien podréis, hijo, alcanzarlo.

"Thou might'st be Holy Father, boy,
Were I not doomed to die;
But with thy boundless wealth, my son,
Thou still may'st soar as high."

While thus they stood Urraca came,
The fair Infanta she,
And while she looked upon her sire,
She said right bitterly:

The second ballad begins at this point:

— Morir vos queredes, padre,
¡San Miguel vos haya el alma!
Mandastes las vuestras tierras
A quien se vos antojara:

"Saint Michael, keep thy soul! my sire,
If now thou yield the ghost;
Thy good broad lands thou hast be- [queathed
To those who urged thee most;

Diste a don Sancho a Castilla,
Castilla la bien nombrada,
A don Alfonso a León
Con Asturias y Sanabría,
A don García a Galicia
Con Portugal la preciada,

To good Don Sancho comes Castile,
Castile the fair and gay-
To Don Alonso proud Leon,
Don Garcia has Biscay.

Y a mí, porque soy mujer,
¡Dejáisme desheredada!
Irme he yo de tierra en tierra
Como una mujer errada;

But as for me, a woman weak,
No heritage have I;
And I may wander through these lands
A lonely maid, or die.

Mi lindo cuerpo daría
A quien bien se me antojara,

But 'tis not justice, noble sire,
And honour may be lost;
Myself I'll give and all I have
To him who urges most;

A los moros por dinero Y a los cristianos de gracia; De lo que ganar pudiere, Haré bien por vuestra alma. —	To Christians for the favour's sake, To Moors for bread and dole; And all the wealth I gain will go In masses for thy soul."
Allí preguntara el rey: — ¿Quién es ésa que así habla? Respondiera el arzobispo: — Vuestra hija doña Urraca. — Calledes, hija, calledes, No digades tal palabra, Que mujer que tal decía Merecía ser quemada.	"Peace, peace, my daughter," cried the [King, "Thy sex such language shames; The woman who can use such words Doth well deserve the flames.
Allá en tierra leonesa Un rincón se me olvidaba, Zamora tiene por nombre, Zamora la bien cercada,	In old Castile there stands a town, Thou may'st hereafter claim; A town well-peopled and well-walled, Zamora is its name.
De un lado la cerca el Duero, Del otro peña tajada.	On this side runs the Douro round, On that bold rocks do frown; The Moorish land is all about — In truth a noble town!
¡Quien vos la quitare, hija, La mi maldición le caiga! — Todos dicen: Amén, amén, Sino don Sancho que calla.	Who dares to take it from thy hands, My curse be on his head!" They all replied, "Amen, Amen!" Don Sancho nothing said.

The last stanza of Gibson's first translation above, which serves as an introduction to the second ballad, is not his own invention, but is rather the reading of the last four lines of a variant of this *romance,* the one which begins "Doliente se siente el rey." Gibson apparently chose the one above as his model because it is more succinct, but he needed the last four lines from the other to bring in effectively the second ballad.

His rendering of both ballads is spirited and vivid, and the language bold and vigorous. The opening stanza of the first translation sets the scene, and in the remaining verses the relationship between the king and his children and between the children themselves is deftly portrayed. The outline of the family situation in both the original and the translation merits praise, since as usual Gibson's translation is quite literal. In one or two places he has amplified the original slightly, e.g., "Had rank and noble gains," "A lonely maid, or die," "and a town well-peopled," but such additions represent only a minor extension of the original idea. The pregnant final stanza of the last ballad, very effectively stated in the English, is an almost exact word-for-word translation of the original.

The following ballad, one of the *romances viejos,* continues the chain of events initiated in the preceding poem as the eldest son of Ferdinand, King Sancho, lays bare his desire to reunite the kingdoms divided at his father's death. The Cid is only a secondary figure in most of the ballads dealing with Sancho, but each one adds to his reputation for wisdom and courage. Gibson's translation is accurate in letter and spirit, being a close parallel of the Spanish throughout. It portrays the Cid as recognizing that what the king is doing is wrong and so advising him, but nevertheless voicing his willingness to prove his loyalty in whatever manner the king requires. The opening stanza presents a device observed on other occasions in Gibson's work — the beginning of a translation predominantly in the four- and three-stress pattern with a quatrain of three-stress lines.

Rey don Sancho, rey don Sancho, Ya que te apuntan las barbas, Quien te las vido nacer, No te las verá logradas.	Don Sancho, King Don Sancho, Thy beard is early shown! But he who sees it budding Will never see it grown!
Aquestos tiempos andando Unas Cortes ordenara, Y por todas las sus tierras Enviaba las sus cartas:	It happened on a certain day A Council he would hold; And he has sent his letters round To all his Barons bold.
Las unas iban de ruego, Las otras iban con saña, A unos ruega que vengan, A otros amenazaba. Ya que todos son llegados, De esta suerte les hablara:	And some he called with furious threat, And some he did beseech; And when they all had gathered round He thus took up the speech;
— Ya sabéis, los mis vasallos, Cuando mi padre finara, Como repartió sus tierras A quien bien se le antojara:	"My vassals, when my father's time Had come to yield the ghost, Ye know how he bequeathed his lands To those who urged him most;
Las unas dió a doña Elvira, Las otras a doña Urraca,	To Dame Elvira some he gave, To fair Urraca others;

Las otras a mis hermanos;

And others still, though all were mine,
He shared amongst my brothers.

Todas éstas eran mías,
Porque yo las heredaba.
Ya que yo se las quitase
Ningún agravio aquí usaba,
Porque quitar lo que es mío
A nadie en esto dañaba. —

I am the rightful heir of all,
I claim them every one;
And if I seize what is my own
I do offence to none."

Todos miraban al Cid
Por ver si se levantaba,
Para que responda al rey
Lo que en esto le agradaba.

All eyes were fixed upon the Cid,
To see if he would rise,
And give an answer to the King,
An answer he would prize.

El Cid, que vee que le miran,
De esta suerte al rey habla:
— Ya sabéis, rey mi señor,
Como, cuando el rey finara,

Their dumb request the Cid obeyed,
And to the King he said;
"Thou know'st O King, that when thy
Lay dying on his bed, [sire

Hizo hacer juramento
A cuantos allí se hallaban:
Que ninguno de nosotros
Fuese contra lo que él manda,

He took a firm and solemn oath
Of all who were at hand,
That none of us would ever act
Against his last command;

Y que ninguno quitase
A quien él sus tierras daba.
Todos dijimos amén,
Ninguno lo rehusara.

That none of us would ever seize
From any one his share;
'Amen!' we all of us replied,
No man refused to swear;

Pues ir contra el juramento
No hallo ley que lo manda;
Mas si vos queréis, señor,
Hacer lo que os agradaba,

To act against a solemn oath
No law doth give consent;
But if it is thy will, O King,
If thou on this art bent,

Nos no podemos dejar
De obedecer vuestra manda;
Mas nunca se logran hijos
Que al padre quiebran palabra.

As vassals true, we're bound to do
Whate'er thou dost require;
But never son has prospered yet
When faithless to his sire;

Ni tampoco tuvo dicha
En cosa que se ocupaba,
Nunca Dios le hizo merced,
Ni es razón que se la haga.

Nor ever did he gain success
In aught that he might try;
God's blessing never went with him,
Nor is there reason why!"

King Sancho does not heed the good advice of the Cid, however, and his men begin their preparations for battle. Gibson describes the effect this has on Ximena in a translation that is quite different in style and spirit from the ones previously studied. The refrain, so common in English ballads, is not frequently found in the *romances,* and the references to Mars and Apollo, London cloth and Milan — in fact, the entire tone and mood of the poem — seem out of place in a ballad on Spanish historical subjects. The translator, however, took no undue liberties. Even though it is too sentimental for modern tastes, the translation is an excellent rendition of both spirit and ideas. The lines "Mas nosotros trocaremos / las almas y corazones" have been altered slightly, but the change is minor and not inappropriate. The translation of the refrain is exact, although perhaps slightly more emphatic and less plaintive than the Spanish. Although the stanza arrangement is different, the verse pattern is quite similar to Gibson's preceding translations.

Al arma, al arma sonaban
Los pífaros y atambores;
Guerra, fuego, sangre dicen
Sus espantosos clamores.

To arms! to arms! The pipes and drums
Are sounding near and far;
Their horrid discords tell the tale
Of blood and flames and war.

El Cid apresta su gente,
Todos se ponen en orden,
Cuando llorosa y humilde
Le dice Ximena Gómez:
— *Rey de mi alma, y desta tierra* [*Conde,*
¿Por qué me dejas? ¿Dónde vas, [*adónde?*

The Cid has summoned all his men,
In battle-rank they stand;
When lo! Ximena weeping comes
And takes him by the hand:
"King of my soul! Lord of the country [round!
Why dost thou leave me? Whither art [thou bound?

Que si eres Marte en la guerra,
Eres Apolo en la corte,
Donde matas bellas damas
Como allá moros feroces.
Ante tus ojos se postran
Y de rodillas se ponen
Los Reyes moros, las hijas
De Reyes cristianos nobles:
— *Rey de mi alma, y desta tierra* [*Conde,*
¿Por qué me dejas? ¿Dónde vas, [*adónde?*

Mars in the tent thou art, but still
Apollo in the hall;
Here lovely maidens die for thee,
As there the Moormen fall.
Both Moorish Kings and daughters fair
Of royal Christian race
Do bend their knees and droop their [eyes
At one glance of thy face;
"King of my soul! Lord of the country [round!
Why dost thou leave me? Whither art [thou bound?"

<table>
<tr><td>Ya truecan todos las galas
Por lucidos morriones,
Por arneses de Milán
Los blandos paños de Londres:
Las calzas por duras grevas,
Por mallas guantes de flores;
Mas nosotros trocaremos
Las almas y corazones.
—Rey de mi alma, y desta tierra [Conde,
¿Por qué me dejas? ¿Dónde vas, [adónde?</td><td>For morrions strong his gala-dress
Now changes every man;
The soft broad-cloth of London
For harness of Milan;
For greaves of steel his silken hose,
For mail his scented gloves;
But we must change our wedded joys
For widowed hearts and loves.
"King of my soul! Lord of the country [round!
Why dost thou leave me? Whither art [thou bound?"</td></tr>
<tr><td>Viendo las duras querellas
De su querida consorte,
No puede sufrir el Cid
Que no la consuele y llore.
—Enjugad, señora, dice,
Los ojos hasta que torne.—
Ella mirando los suyos
Su pena publica a voces:
—Rey de mi alma, y desta tierra [Conde,
¿Por qué me dejas? ¿Dónde vas, [adónde?</td><td>The Cid could hardly hide his tears
While she her grief expressed:
With many a tender word and look
He drew her to his breast:
"Señora, till thy spouse return,
These eyes of thine be dried!"
She fondly looked into his own,
But still aloud she cried:
"King of my soul! Lord of the country [round!
Why dost thou leave me? Whither art [thou bound?"</td></tr>
</table>

Gibson continues with his customary stanza division in the next translation which voices King Sancho's strong desire and intention to have Zamora. Several stanzas will be observed to have only three stresses in the first line—an effective variation frequently noted in his use of this meter.

<table>
<tr><td>Llegado es el Rey Don Sancho
Sobre Zamora esa villa:
Muchas gentes trae consigo,
Que haberla mucho quería.</td><td>The King, Don Sancho, and his host
Have reached Zamora's town;
His heart was aching to possess
A place of such renown.</td></tr>
<tr><td>Caballero en un caballo
Y el Cid en su compañía,
Andábala al rededor,
Y el Rey así al Cid decía:</td><td>The King went forth to spy the walls,
The Cid was by his side;
And much he thought and much he said
As round it they did ride:</td></tr>
<tr><td>—Armada está sobre Peña
Tajada toda esta villa,
Los muros tiene muy fuertes,
Torres ha en gran demasía,</td><td>"How firmly on its massive rock
This armed town doth stand!
Its circling walls how thick and strong
Its many towers how grand!</td></tr>
</table>

Duero la cercaba al pie,
Fuerte es a maravilla,
No bastan a la tomar
Cuantos en el mundo había:

Around its feet the Douro foams,
  It is of matchless form;
A world in arms would scarce suffice
  To take this town by storm!

Si me la diese mi hermana
Más que a España la querría.
Cid, a vos crió mi padre,
Mucho bien fecho os había;

My sister, should she give it me,
  I'd love it more than Spain;
O Cid, my father brought thee up,
  Nor was his love in vain;

Fízoos mayor de su casa
Y caballero en Coímbra
Cuando la ganara a moros.
Cuando en Cabezón moría,

He dubbed thee Knight in Coimbra's town,
  That from the Moors he won;
Thou wert the Captain of his house
  When he died in Cabezón.

A mí y a los mis hermanos
Encomendado os había;
Jurámosle allí en sus manos
Facervos merced cumplida.

Thee to my brother's care and mine
  He dying did commend;
Upon his hands we took an oath
  To treat thee as a friend;

Fíceos mayor de mi casa,
Gran tierra dado os tenía
Que vale más que un condado
El mayor que hay en Castilla.

I made thee Captain of my house,
  I gave thee 'neath my seal
More lands than any Baronie,
  The best in all Castile.

Yo vos ruego, Don Rodrigo,
Como amigo de valía,
Que vayades a Zamora
Con la mi mensagería,

I ask thee, Don Rodrigo,
  I ask thee as a friend,
That thou will to Zamora bear
  The message I shall send;

Y a Doña Urraca mi hermana
Decid que me dé esa villa
Por gran haber o gran cambio,
Como a ella mejor sería.

And beg my sister she will not
  The town to me refuse,
For solid gold or good exchange,
  Whichever she may choose.

A Medina de Rioseco
Yo por ella la daría
Con todo el Infantazgo,
Y también le prometía

Medina on the Seco
  I'll give her with goodwill,
With all its wealthy appanage,
  And more I'll promise still.

A Villalpando y su tierra,
O Valladolid la rica,
O a Tiedra, que es buen castillo,

I'll give her Villapando,
  And all the country there;
Or else Valladolid the rich,
  Or Tiedra's castle fair.

Y juramento le haría
Con doce de mis vasallos
De cumplir lo que decía;
Y si no lo quiere hacer,
Por fuerza la tomaría. —

To keep my troth, with twelve good men
I'll take a solemn vow;
But if she give it not with grace,
By force I'll take it now."

El Cid le besó la mano,
Del buen Rey se despedía,
Llegado había a Zamora
Con quince en su compañía.

The Cid he kissed the royal hand,
And gave his steed the rein;
And he has reached Zamora's town,
With fifteen in his train.

The princess Urraca's reaction to her brother's threat is related in Gibson's next translation.

Entrado ha el Cid en Zamora,
En Zamora, aquesa villa,
Llegado ha ante Doña Urraca
Que muy bien lo recibía,

The Cid has entered Zamora's town
And eke its palace-halls;
The Infanta kindly welcomes him,
And at her feet he falls.

Dicho le había el mensaje
Que para ella traía,
Doña Urraca que lo oyó
Muchas lágrimas vertía,

He has told the message of the King,
He has told it to her face;
The Infanta's heart is very sore,
Her tears flow down apace.

Diciendo: —¡Triste cuitada!
Don Sancho ¿qué me quería?
No cumpliera el juramento,
Que a mi padre fecho había:

"O luckless I! O faithless King!
I could not love him more;
And is it thus he keeps the oath
He to my father swore?

Que aun apenas fuera muerto,
A mi hermano Don García
Le tomó toda su tierra
Y en prisiones lo ponía,
Y cual si fuese ladrón
Agora en ellas yacía.

My brother Don Garcia's lands
He took against his vow;
And put him like a thief in chains,
And there he is lying now.

También a Alfonso mi hermano
Su reino se lo tenía;
Huyóse para Toledo,
Con los moros está hoy día.

My brother Don Alfonso's realm
He took away as well;
And he has to Toledo fled,
Amongst the Moors to dwell.

A Toro tomó a mi hermana,
A mi hermana Doña Elvira;
Tomarme quiere a Zamora,
¡Gran pesar yo recibía!

He has taken Toro from Elvira,
Elvira my sister fair;
And now he claims Zamora too,
To drive me to despair.

Muy bien sabe el rey Don Sancho
Que soy mujer femenina,
Y non lidiaré con él,
Mas a furto o paladina
Yo haré que le den la muerte,
Que muy bien lo merecía. —

He thinks I am a woman weak;
But to Don Sancho tell
That, fair or foul, I'll give to him
The death he merits well!"

Levantóse Arias Gonzalo
Y respondido la había:
— Non lloredes vos, señora,
Yo por merced os pedía

Up rose Arias Gonzalo,
And gravely he did say:
"My lady, do not sorrow thus,
For pity's sake, I pray.

Que a la hora de la cuita
Consejo mejor sería
Que non acuitarvos tanto,
Que gran daño a vos vendría.

In such a trying hour as this
'Twill better counsel be
To face the danger with good heart,
Or harm may come to thee.

Hablad con vuesos vasallos,
Decid lo que el Rey pedía,
Y si ellos lo han por bien
Dadle al Rey luego la villa;

Speak to thy noble vassals round,
And hear what they will say;
And if they judge the King has right,
Give up the town this day.

Y si non les pareciere
Facer lo que el Rey pedía,
Muramos todos en ella,
Como manda la hidalguía. —

But if they think it is not good
To obey the King's commands,
Then let us die within its walls,
As Chivalry demands!"

La Infanta tuvo por bien
Facer lo que le decía;
Sus vasallos la juraron
Que antes todos morirían
Cercados dentro en Zamora
Que no dar al Rey la villa.

The Infanta called her nobles round;
They scorned so base a thing,
And swore that they would rather die,
Than yield it to the King.

Con esta respuesta el Cid
Al buen Rey vuelto se había:
El Rey cuando aquesto oyó
Al buen Cid le respondía:
— Vos aconsejasteis, Cid,
No darme lo que quería,

The Cid brought back this answer;
The King's eyes flashed with fire:
"It is thou, O Cid, hast counselled them
To hinder my desire!

Porque vos criasteis dentro
De Zamora aquesa villa,
Y a no ser por la crianza
Que en vos mi padre facía,

Because within Zamora's walls
Thy youthful days were spent;
Did not my father's love to thee
And last commands prevent,

Luego os mandara enforcar;
Mas de hoy en noveno día
Os mando vais de mis tierras
Y del reino de Castilla.

I'd place thee in a dungeon deep;
But now obey my will,
That nine days hence thou leave my [lands
And kingdom of Castile!"

Gibson has inserted one or two lines that are not in the original such as the Cid's falling at Urraca's feet and her statement of her love for her brother. On the whole, however, the transcription is quite literal. Urraca's sentiments are well expressed and reflect perfectly her indignation at her brother's action and her determination to keep her kingdom. The last three stanzas of the translation, which should be read as one unit, are seen to correspond perfectly to the last fourteen lines of the original which also admit of little separation.

The effect produced by an extra syllable in some of the lines above may be contrasted with that brought about by the omission of a syllable as illustrated by a few of the verses below. The subject matter is a continuation of the situation above, and the translation straightforward and accurate, with the exception of the substitution of "fifteen" for "five hundred" in the next-to-the-last stanza.

El Cid fué para su tierra:
Con sus vasallos partía
Para Toledo, do estaba
Alfonso cuando fuía.

The Cid, with all his vassals,
Has left his native land;
And he has to Toledo gone,
To join Alfonso's band.

Los condes y ricos-homes
Al rey Don Sancho decían,
No perdiese tal vasallo,
Y de tanta valentía

The nobles and the grandees
Were troubled at the sight:
"Good King, we pray thee do not lose
A vassal of such might.

Como es Ruy Díaz el Cid.
Qu'es muy grande su valía.
El Rey vido qu'es muy bien
Facer lo que le decían,

As Ruy Diaz, the noble Cid,
Whose power o'ermasters all;
Much wilt thou lose in losing him,
And worse may yet befall."

Y fablando a Diego Ordóñez
Mandóle que al Cid le diga
Que se venga luego a él
Que como bueno lo haría,

The King was pleased to hear their [words
And cried right hastily:
"Ride forth, Ordoñez, to the Cid,
Wherever he may he,

And tell him that the King desires
To see him back again;

Y que le haría el mayor De los que en su casa había.	Will make him chief of all his house, And captain of his train."
Ordoño fué tras del Cid, Su mensaje le decía: El Cid se había aconsejado Con los suyos que tenía, Si haría lo que el Rey manda:	Ordoñez rode to reach the Cid, His message to present; The Cid took counsel of his men What answer should be sent.
Su parecer les pedía. Que se vuelva al Rey dijeron, Pues su disculpa le envía; El Cid con ellos se vuelve, El Rey cuando lo sabía	They all advised him to return, Since now they did entreat him; The Cid turned back with all his men, The King rode forth to meet him.
Dos leguas salió a él Quinientos van en su guía. El Cid cuando vido al Rey De Babieca descendía,	Two leagues he rode upon the way, With fifteen of his force; But when the Cid had spied the King He lighted from his horse.
Besóle luego las manos, Para el real se volvía Y todos los castellanos Gran placer con él habían.	He kissed with grace the royal hand, He rode to camp that night; And all the nobles of Castile Received him with delight.

The next series of ballads, some of which are *romances viejos,* returns us to Zamora and the conflict between Sancho and Urraca. Two knights from the Zamoran camp begin the action.

Riberas del Duero arriba Cabalgan dos zamoranos: Las divisas llevan verdes, Los caballos alazanos,	Along the Douro's bank there ride Two gallant Zamorese On sorrel steeds; their banners green Are fluttering in the breeze.
Ricas espadas ceñidas, Sus cuerpos muy bien armados, Adargas ante sus pechos, Gruesas lanzas en sus manos,	Their armour is of finest steel, And rich their burnished brands; They bear their shields before their [breasts; Stout lances in their hands.
Espuelas llevan ginetas Y los frenos plateados. Como son tan bien dispuestos Parecen muy bien armados,	They ride their steeds with pointed spurs, And bits of silver fine; More gallant men were never seen, So bright their arms do shine.

Y por un repecho arriba
Salen más recios que galgos,
Y súbenlos a mirar
Del real del rey Don Sancho.

More swift than greyhounds on the course
They gallop up the height;
The camp of King Don Sancho
Turns out to see the sight.

Desque a otra parte fueron
Dieron vuelta a los caballos,
Y al cabo de una gran pieza
Soberbios ansí han fablado:

With might they curb their prancing steeds
Upon the further side;
And from a lofty rugged knoll
They shout with mickle pride:

—¿Tendredes dos para dos,
Caballeros castellanos,
Que puedan armas facer
Con otros dos zamoranos,
Para daros a entender

"If there be two Castilian knights,
Who wish to strike a blow
With other two Zamorans,
We give them here to know,

No face el Rey como hidalgo
En quitar a Doña Urraca
Lo que su padre le ha dado?

Their King hath not demeaned himself
As seems a gallant Knight,
To seize Urraca's town and lands,
Her own by gift and right.

Non queremos ser tenidos,
Ni queremos ser honrados,
Ni rey de nos faga cuenta,
Ni conde nos ponga al lado,
Si a los primeros encuentros
No los hemos derribado,

No more from King and Barons bold
Shall we deserve renown
If at the first encounter
We do not strike them down.

Y siquiera salgan tres,
Y siquiera salgan cuatro,
Y siquiera salgan cinco,
Salga siquiera el diablo,
Con tal que no salga el Cid,
Ni ese noble rey Don Sancho,

Let three come forth, or four or five,
The Devil if he choose;
But with Don Sancho or the Cid
We must the fight refuse.

Que lo habemos por señor,
Y el Cid nos ha por hermanos:
De los otros caballeros
Salgan los más esforzados.

The King he is our royal liege,
The Cid esteems us brothers;
But of the noble knights around
We'll fight with any others."

Oídolo habían dos condes
Lo cuales eran cuñados:
—Atended, los caballeros,
Mientras estamos armados.—

Two Counts, true foster-brothers they,
Come forth at the alarm;
"Wait here, Sir Knights, we pray of you,
While we retire to arm!"

Piden apriesa las armas,
Suben en buenos caballos,
Caminan para las tiendas
Donde yace el rey Don Sancho:

They seek their arms with frantic haste,
On noble steeds they spring,
And gallop to the royal tent,
Where sits their lord the King:

Piden que los dé licencia
Que ellos puedan hacer campo
Contra aquellos caballeros,
Que con soberbia han hablado.

"O grant us license, noble King,
Forth to the field to ride
Against these boastful Cavaliers,
Whose words are full of pride!"

Allí fablara el buen Cid,
Que es de los buenos dechado.
— Los dos contrarios guerreros
Non los tengo yo por malos,

Then up and spake the gallant Cid,
None braver e'er was seen:
"The two opposing warriors
Are not so bad, I ween;

Porque en muchas lides de armas
Su valor habían mostrado,
Que en el cerco de Zamora
Tuvieron con siete campo:

For they in many a strife of arms
Have proofs of valour given;
And round about Zamora's walls
Have battle done with seven;

El mozo mató a los dos,
El viejo mató a los cuatro;
Por uno que se les fuera
Las barbas se van pelando. —

The youth he fought and killed his two,
The old man slew his four;
And for the one who turned and fled,
Their beards they plucked and tore."

Enojados van los condes
De lo que el Cid ha fablado:
El Rey cuando ir los viera
Que vuelvan está mandando;

The Counts have heard his taunting [words,
Their cheeks with fury burn;
The King who sees them thus depart,
Commands them to return.

Otorgó cuanto pedían,
Más por fuerza que de grado.
Mientras los condes se arman,
El padre al fijo está hablando:

More by constraint than right goodwill
He yields to their request;
And while they buckle on their arms,
The Sire his son addressed:

— Volved, fijo, hacia Zamora,
A Zamora y sus andamios,
Mirad dueñas y doncellas,
Como nos están mirando:

"Turn to Zamora now, my son,
Zamora and its towers;
See how the dames and damsels look,
Their faces fixed on ours.

Fijo, no miran a mí,
Porque ya soy viejo y cano;
Mas miran a vos, mi fijo,
Que sois mozo y esforzado.

They do not look at me, my son,
For I am grey and old;
Their eyes are turned to thee, my son,
For thou art young and bold.

Si vos facéis como bueno
Seréis d'ellas muy honrado;
Si los facéis de cobarde,
Abatido y ultrajado.

If thou shouldst do thy duty well,
Of them thou shall have fame;
But if thou act the coward's part,
They'll cover thee with shame.

Afirmaos en los estribos,
Terciad la lanza en las manos,
Esa adarga ante los pechos,

Sit well upon thy stirrups,
And firmly grasp thy lance;
And place thy shield before thy breast,
All ready to advance.

Y apercibid el caballo,
Que al que primero acomete
Tienen por más esforzado. —

Stir up thy steed to furious charge,
And urge him to the fight;
For he who first attacks his man
Is held the boldest knight!"

Apenas esto hubo dicho,
Ya los condes han llegado;
El uno viene de negro,
Y el otro de colorado:

The Counts arrive; one clad in black,
And one in crimson bright;
The opposing ranks each other meet,
And furious is the fight.

Vanse unos para otros,
Fuertes encuentros se han dado,
Mas el que al mozo le cupo
Derribólo del caballo,
Y el viejo al otro de encuentro
Pasóle de claro en claro.

The youth has quick unhorsed his man,
With sturdy stroke and true;
The Sire has pierced the other's mail,
And sent his lance right through.

El Conde, de que esto viera,
Huyendo sale del campo,
Y los dos van a Zamora
Con vitoria muy honrados.

The horseless knight, pale at the sight,
Ran hurrying from the fray;
Back to Zamora ride the twain,
With glory crowned that day!

Gibson has done a fine job of translating a ballad which itself is also very good. His translation is highly colorful and poetic and at the same time faithful in all respects to the model. His skill in using various standard poetic devices is well displayed here. He begins with alliteration in the first two stanzas ("sorrel steeds"; "burnished brands"), uses repetition and alliteration effectively in "let them come forth, or four, or five," brings in a mosaic rhyme in "They do not look at me, my son . . . Their eyes are turned to thee, my son," and adds a final finishing touch with the interior rhyme of the "horseless knight, pale as the night." The challenging spirit of the two Zamorans is reproduced in an excellent fashion, as is the fatherly advice given to the youth by Arias Gonzalo. In short, it must be adjudged a satisfying translation on all counts.

During the ensuing siege, the impetuous King Sancho is killed by a traitor from the Zamoran camp whom he had unwisely trusted, and the ever-faithful Cid proposes that one of his knights challenge the Zamorans to avenge the treachery. Another translation by Gibson provides the details.

Muerto yace el rey Don Sancho,
Bellido muerto le había;
Pasado está de un venablo
Y gran lástima ponía.

Cold, cold in death Don Sancho lay,
And round about his bier
There stood the flower of all Castile;
They shed full many a tear.

Llorando estaba sobre él
Toda la flor de Castilla;
Don Rodrigo de Vivar
Es el que más lo sentía:
Con lágrimas de sus ojos
D'esta manera decía:

Pale stood Rodrigo of Bivar,
And lowly bent his head;
And while the tears came coursing down
He thus with sorrow said:

— ¡Rey, Don Sancho, señor mío,
Muy aciago fué aquel día
Que tú cercaste a Zamora
Contra la voluntad mía!

"O King Don Sancho, master mine,
That day was full of ire,
When thou didst compass Zamora's walls
Against my strong desire.

Quien te lo aconsejó, Rey,
A Dios ni al mundo temía,
Pues te fizo quebrantar
La ley de caballería. —

Whoever counselled thee, O King,
Nor God nor man feared he;
Because he urged on thee to break
The law of Chivalry.

Y viendo el hecho en tal punto
A grandes voces decía:
— Que se nombre un caballero,
Antes que se pase el día,
Para retar a Zamora
Por tan grande alevosía. —

But since this fatal deed is done,
To name a knight 'tis time,
To challenge Zamora and its men
For such a bloody crime."

Todos dicen que es muy bien;
Mas nadie al campo salía:
Témense de Arias Gonzalo
Y cuatro hijos que tenía.
Mancebos de gran valor,
De gran esfuerzo y estima.

" 'Tis well, 'tis well," they all reply,
But each the duty shuns;
They stand in awe of Arias
And his four mighty sons.

Mirando estaban al Cid,
Por ver si lo aceptaría,

The Cid looks round with steady eye
To see if none will go;

Y el de Vivar, que lo entiende,
D'esta manera decía:

He understands the matter well,
And forth his words do flow:

—Caballeros fijosdalgo,
Ya sabéis que non podía
Armarme contra Zamora,
Que jurado lo tenía:

"Ye know full well, my noble knights,
That I have sworn an oath,
Against Zamora ne'er to arm—
I cannot break my troth;

Mas yo daré un caballero
Que combata por Castilla,
Tal, que estando él en el campo
No sintáis la falta mía.—

But I will give a Champion bold
To combat for Castile,
And while for me he takes the field,
My want ye shall not feel."

Levantóse Diego Ordóñez,
Que a los pies del Rey yacía:
La flor es de los de Lara
Y lo mejor de Castilla:

Up rose Don Diego Ordoñez,
At the King's feet he did rest;
The flower of Lara's house was he,
Of all Castile the best.

Con voz enojosa y ronca
D'esta manera decía:
—Pues el Cid había jurado
Lo que jurar no debía,

With hoarse and angry voice he cries,
And eke with mickle scorn:
"Since that the Cid has sworn an oath
He never should have sworn,

No es menester que señale
Quien la batalla prosiga:
Caballeros hay en ella
De tanto esfuerzo y valía

He has no right to choose a knight
His champion to be;
But there be many knights around
As good and brave as he.

Como el Cid, aunque es muy [bueno,
Y yo por tal lo tenía;
Mas si queréis, caballeros,
Yo lidiaré la conquista

No doubt the Cid is good and brave,
And I do hold him so;
But if ye will, my noble knights,
'Tis I will strike the blow.

Aventurando mi cuerpo,
Poniendo a riesgo mi vida,
Pues que la del buen vasallo
Es por su Rey ofrecida.

My body and my life I'll risk,
And down the gauntlet fling;
A vassal's life is best bestowed
When ventured for his King!"

The translation omits the opening lines about the traitorous Bellido and the "venablo," but otherwise it is accurate and complete. The qualities of the sons of Arias Gonzalo, "mancebos de gran valor, de gran esfuerzo y estima," are summed up with no loss of force in the short but expressive phrase "four mighty sons." The situation in the Cid's camp is skillfully outlined as he puts the matter plainly to his knights and waits for someone to volunteer for what everyone knows will be a difficult job. Finally Diego Ordóñez, somewhat resentful at being forced into the affair, accepts the Cid's proposal and rides forth to hurl his own challenge to the opposing forces. Gibson draws from several *romance* variants for the following translation.

Ya cabalga Diego Ordóñez,
Del real se había salido
De nobles piezas armado
En un caballo morcillo:

Don Diego Ordoñez rides away
From the royal camp with speed,
Armed head to foot with double mail,
And on a coal-black steed.

Va a reptar los zamoranos
Por la muerte de su primo,
Que mató Bellido D'Olfos,
Hijo de D'Olfos Bellido.

He rides to challenge Zamora's men,
His breast with fury filled;
To avenge the King Don Sancho,
Whom the traitor Dolfos killed.

—Yo os repto, los zamoranos,
Por traidores fementidos,
Repto a todos los muertos,
Y con ellos a los vivos:

He reached in haste Zamora's gate,
And loud his trumpet blew;
And from his mouth like sparks of fire
His words in fury flew:

"Zamorans, I do challenge ye,
Ye traitors born and bred;
I challenge ye all, both great and small,
The living and the dead;

Repto hombres y mujeres,
Los por nascer y nascidos;
Repto a todos los grandes,
A los grandes y a los chicos,
A las carnes y pescados,
Y a las aguas de los ríos.—

I challenge the men and women,
The unborn and the born;
I challenge the wine and waters,
The cattle and the corn.

Within your town that traitor lives
Our King who basely slew;—
Who harbour traitors in their midst
Themselves are traitors too.

I'm here in arms against ye all
The combat to maintain;
Or else with five and one by one,
As is the use in Spain!"

Allí habló Arias Gonzalo,
Bien oiréis lo que hubo dicho:

Out spake Arias Gonzalo:
"I had better ne'er been born
Than brand myself as such a knave,
And worthy of such scorn.

— ¿Qué culpa tienen los viejos?
¿Qué culpa tienen los niños?

Your words are very bitter, Count,
And bitter is your tongue;
What harm have done the old men?
What harm have done the young?

¿Qué merecen las mujeres,
Y los que no son nascidos?
¿Por qué reptas a los muertos,
Los ganados y los ríos?

What curse rests on our women,
Or on the babes unborn?
Or why defy the very dead,
The cattle and the corn?

Bien sabéis vos, Diego Ordóñez,
Muy bien lo tenéis sabido.
Que aquel que repta concejo
Debe de lidiar con cinco. —
Ordóñez le respondió:
— Traidores heis todos sido. —

If you challenge all the Council,
You must fight with five or fall!"
Ordoñez gruffly answered:
"Ye are traitors, one and all!"

The following lines are taken from a second *romance* on this subject:

....
Arias Gonzalo, ese viejo,
....
Después que hubo entendido
Lo que Ordoño ha razonado.
....
D'esta manera ha fablado:

Old Arias grows pale with wrath,
And hastens from the walls;
He gathers all the people round,
And in their midst he calls:

— Varones de grande estima
Los pequeños y de estado,
Si hay alguno entre vosotros
Que en aquesto se haya hallado
Dígalo muy prontamente;
De decillo no haya empacho:

"Ye barons bold, and townsmen all,
Confess while yet 'tis time,
If any one of ye perchance
Have part in such a crime.

Mas quiero irme d'esta tierra
En Africa desterrado,
Que no en campo ser vencido
Por alevoso y malvado. —

I'd rather go to Afric's land,
And fill an exile's grave,
Than vanquished be in such a cause,
And held a traitor knave!"

Todos dicen a una voz.
Sin alguno estar callado:
— Mal fuego nos mate, Conde
Si en tal muerte hemos estado;
No hay en Zamora ninguno,
Que tal hubiese mandado.

They all replied with one accord,
No man was silent there:
"May evil fire consume us, Count,
If such a crime we share.

El traidor Bellido D'Olfos
Por si solo lo ha acordado;
Muy bien podéis ir seguro;
Id con Dios, Arias Gonzalo.

Vellido Dolfos, he alone,
  Designed the bloody deed;
Go forth in comfort, Arias,
  And Heaven send thee speed!"

This challenge by Diego Ordóñez is one of the most famous in Spanish literature, and there are many versions of it contained in the old ballads. The one given above is that of the *Cancionero de romances* [3] which Gibson indicates he used as the basic source. He obviously had access to several other versions, however, since the elements contained in the translation which appear to be additions to the original are all found in other *romances* on the subject. The last part of the translation, starting with Arias's speech to his townspeople, is from the one beginning "Después que Bellido D'Olfos, ese traidor afamado." What at first glance appears to be a very loose translation is found, then, to be a fairly literal rendering of several fragments of *romances* rearranged into a unified composition which is superior to any single one of the sources. The spirit of the originals is carefully retained in spite of the rearrangement of ideas, and the harsh bitterness of the challenge comes through with all its native vigor. Compression of action and elimination of unnecessary details constitute much of the charm of the *romances,* but in this series on Zamora, almost too much was pruned out. Gibson has corrected this in his translation, yet not added enough to dilute the strength of the original.

In the next translation, however, a long poem describing the outcome of the challenge to the Zamorans, Gibson returns to his usual practice of staying close to his source.

Ya se salen por la puerta,
Por la que salía al campo,
Arias Gonzalo, y sus hijos
Todos juntos a su lado.
Él quiere ser el primero

Forth from the gate rides Arias
  And his four sons to the fight;
For he had claimed to be the first
  To prove his honour bright.

Porque en la muerte no ha estado
De Don Sancho, mas la Infanta
La batalla le ha quitado,
Llorando de los sus ojos
Y el cabello destrenzado:

The Infanta heard him with dismay,
  And would not grant his prayer;
She came to him with weeping eyes
  And with dishevelled hair:

[3] *Cancionero de romances* (Antwerp: En Casa de Martín Nucio [n.d.]). This is frequently referred to as the *Cancionero sin año.* It appeared around 1548 and is the first of the *romanceros.*

— ¡Ay! ruégovos por Dios, dice,
El buen conde Arias Gonzalo,
Que dejéis esta batalla
Porque sois viejo y cansado:

"For God's sake, I entreat thee, Count
My noble friend and bold,
That thou wilt leave this battle-field,
For thou art worn and old.

Dejáisme desamparada
Y todo mi haber cercado;
Ya sabéis como mi padre
A vos dejó encomendado
Que no me desamparéis,
Ende más, en tal estado. —

My father with his dying breath
Consigned me to thy care;
And now thou leavest me alone
When I am in despair!"

En oyendo aquesto el Conde
Mostróse muy enojado:
— Dejédesme ir, mi señora,
Que yo estoy desafiado,
Y tengo de hacer batalla
Porque fui traidor llamado. —

"My lady, suffer me to go,"
With angry voice he cried,
"They've called me traitor to my face,
And I have been defied!"

Con la Infanta, caballeros
Junto al Conde han rogado
Que les deje la batalla,
Que la tomaran de grado.

The knights around took up the word,
And urged the Infanta's prayer:
"Count, leave the field to us, and trust
The battle to our care!"

Desque el Conde vido aquesto
Recibió pesar doblado;
Llamara sus cuatro hijos,
Y al uno d'ellos ha dado

Now doubly pained was Arias
That he the fight must shun;
He called his gallant four around,
And to his favourite son

Las sus armas y su escudo,
El su estoque y su caballo.
Al primero le bendice
Porque era dél muy amado:

He gave his armour and his shield,
His sword and battle-steed,
And blessed the youth he loved so well,
And bade him then God speed.

Pedrarias había por nombre,
Pedrarias el castellano.
Por la puerta de Zamora
Se sale fuera y armado;

His name was Pedro Arias,
Of true Castilian race;
He rode full-armoured through the gate
And proudly took his place:

Topárase con Don Diego
Su enemigo y su contrario:
— Sálveos Dios, Don Diego Or-
[dóñez,
Y él os haga prosperado,
En las armas muy dichoso,
De traiciones libertado:

"God save thee, Don Diego,
May Heaven smile on thee,
And make thee fortunate in arms,
And from all traitors free.

Ya sabéis que soy venido
Para lo que está aplazado,
A libertar a Zamora
De lo que le han levantado.—

Thou knowest well that I am here,
And have this combat sought,
To free Zamora from the charge
Which thou hast foully brought."

Don Diego le respondiera
Con soberbia que ha tomado:
—Todos juntos sois traidores,
Por tales seréis quedados.—

Ordoñez turned to him and said
With dark and haughty brow:
"Ye all of ye are traitors,
And I will prove it now!"

Vuelven los dos las espaldas
Por tomar lugar del campo,
Hiriéronse juntamente
En los pechos muy de grado;

On this they wheeled their prancing [steeds,
And round the field they pressed;
They couched their lances, charged at [once,
And struck full on the breast.

Saltan astas de las lanzas
Con el golpe que se han dado;
No se hacen mal alguno
Porque van muy bien armados.

Their lances quivered with the shock,
And wide the splinters flew;
But little harm was done, I ween,
Their armour was so true.

Don Diego dió en la cabeza
A Pedrarias desdichado,
Contárale todo el yelmo
Con un pedazo del casco;

Again they charged; Diego's lance
Struck Pedro on the head;
It pierced his helmet and his brow
With ghastly wound and red.

Desque se vido herido
Pedrarias y lastimado,
Abrazárase a las clines,
Y al pescuezo del caballo:

The luckless Pedro felt the wound,
And staggered 'neath the blow;
And grasping wild his charger's mane,
Upon its neck fell low.

Sacó esfuerzo de flaqueza
Aunque estaba mal llagado,
Quiso ferir a Don Diego,
Mas acertó en el caballo,

Though deep his wound and weak his [arm,
He gathered up his force
For one last blow against his foe,
But only touched his horse.

Que la sangre que corría
La vista le había quitado:
Cayó muerto prestamente
Pedrarias el castellano.

The blood that trickled down his face
His eyes and vision sealed;
So fell Don Pedro Arias,
And died upon the field.

Don Diego que vido aquesto
Toma la vara en la mano,
Dijo a voces: —¡Ah Zamora!

When Don Diego saw him fall
He waved his baton high,
And turning to Zamora's walls,
He thus aloud did cry:

¿Dónde estás, Arias Gonzalo?
Envía el hijo segundo,
Que el primero ya es finado. —

"Where art thou, Arias Gonzalo?
Send forth thy second son;
The first is lying on the field,
His race on earth is run!"

Envió el hijo segundo,
Que Diego Arias es llamado.
Tornara a salir Don Diego
Con armas y otro caballo,
Y diérale fin a aqueste
Como al primero le ha dado.

The second came, Diego hight,
And though he fought right well,
Ordoñez fought with better luck,
And like the first, he fell.

El Conde viendo a sus hijos,
Que los dos le han ya faltado,
Quiso enviar al tercero
Aunque con temor doblado.

Sad was the Count to see the sight,
That both his sons were slain;
The third he summoned to his side,
Although with double pain.

Llorando de los sus ojos
Dijo: — Ve, mi hijo amado,
Haz como buen caballero
Lo que tú eres obligado:

With brimming eyes aloud he cries:
"Go forth, my darling son,
Go forth like gallant knight to do
The deed that must be done!

Pues sustentas la verdad,
De Dios serás ayudado:
Venga las muertes sin culpa,
Que han pasado tus hermanos. —

It is the truth thou dost maintain,
And God will be thy stay,
And give thee vigour to avenge
Thy brothers slain this day."

Hernán D'Arias, el tercero,
Al palenque había llegado;
Mucho mal quiere a Don Diego,
Mucho mal y mucho daño.

Hernando Arias, the third,
Forth to the lists he bore,
And cursed Diego as he rode,
And speedy vengeance swore.

Alzó la mano con saña
Un gran golpe le había dado;
Mal herido le ha en el hombro,
En el hombro y en el brazo.

With furious hand he dealt a blow
To do him deadly harm;
Diego's shoulder felt the smart,
His shoulder and his arm.

Don Diego con el su estoque
Le hiriera muy de su grado,
Hiriéralo en la cabeza,
En el casco le ha tocado.

On this Diego drew his blade,
And struck with might and main;
So swift the blow it cleft the casque,
And lighted on the brain.

Recudó el hijo tercero
Con un gran golpe al caballo,
Que hizo ir a Don Diego
Huyendo por todo el campo.

The wild youth hit Diego's horse,
And cut its bridle rein;
The maddened charger cleared the lists,
And galloped round the plain.

Así quedó esta batalla
Sin quedar averiguado
Cuáles son los vencedores,
Los de Zamora o del campo.

And thus the combat ended,
Nor was it e'er revealed
If 'twere Zamora or the Camp
That day had won the field.

Quisiera volver Don Diego
A la batalla de grado,
Mas no quisieron los fieles,
Licencia no le han dado.

Diego fain would fight again,
So fierce was his intent;
The umpires judged the matter well,
But would not give consent.

The spirit of the original has been maintained well, although there is the usual transposition of a few lines to fit the rhyme scheme. The reference to Don Sancho is left out, but the lines "For he had claimed to be the first / To prove his honour bright" perhaps convey the idea better. There is no discussion of the second son's performance in the original, and the translator treats him briefly also, although he does imagine him to have "fought right well." This translation does not read as well as some of Gibson's other poems and lacks some of the ease of composition of the original, but otherwise it is satisfactory.

The next translation, number forty-one in the first edition of Gibson's *The Cid Ballads,* was left out of the second edition, possibly because the subject matter is also covered in the translation of "En Santa Gadea de Burgos," which comes a few pages later. It offers one explanation for the ill feeling between the Cid and King Alfonso, who had come to power in Castile with the death of his brother, Don Sancho. The ultimate exile of the Cid by Alfonso is the incident which begins the *Poema de mío Cid.*

En Toledo estaba Alfonso,
Que non cuidaba reinar;
Desterrárale Don Sancho
Por su reino le quitar:

Alfonso in Toledo dwelt,
No thought had he to reign;
Don Sancho drove him from the land,
His crown and realm to gain.

Doña Urraca a Don Alfonso
Mensajero fué a enviar;
Las nuevas que le traían
A él gran placer le dan.

To him the Lady Urraca sends
Her messengers with speed;
The letters they have brought to him
Right pleasant are to read:

—Rey Alfonso, rey Alfonso,
Que te envían a llamar;
Castellanos y leoneses
Por rey alzado te han,

"Alfonso, King Alfonso,
As monarch thee we own;
Castilians both and Leonese
Have raised thee to the throne.

Por la muerte de Don Sancho, Que Bellido fué a matar: Solo entre todos Rodrigo, Que no te quiere acetar,	Alone Rodrigo still declines To give thee homage due, Because of King Don Sancho's death, Whom base Vellido slew.
Porque amaba mucho al Rey Quiere que hayas de jurar Que en la su muerte, señor, No tuviste que culpar.	For much he loved the King, Señor, And he would have thee swear, That in the matter of his death Thou hadst no thought nor share."
— Bien vengáis, los mensajeros, Secretos queráis estar, Que si el rey moro lo sabe Él aquí nos detendrá. —	"Right welcome are ye, messengers, Let none the matter know; For were the Moorish King aware, He would not let us go."
El conde Don Peranzures Un consejo le fué a dar, Que caballos bien herrados Al revés habían de herrar.	The Count Don Peranzures Has counselled them that night To have their horses' shoes reversed, And take to instant flight.
Descuélganse por el muro, Sálense de la ciudad, Fueron a dar a Castilla Do esperándolos están.	By night they leap the Castle walls, And from the city steal; The people all are filled with joy When they have reached Castile.
Al Rey le besan la mano, El Cid no quiere besar, Sus parientes castellanos Todos juntado se han.	They stoop to kiss the royal hand, The Cid he has no heart; And all his kinsmen of Castile Are there to take his part:
—Heredero sois, Alfonso, Nadie os lo quiere negar; Pero si os place, señor, Non vos debe de pesar Que nos fagáis juramento	"Alfonso, none will dare deny That thou art rightful heir; But do not take offence, Señor, That we would have thee swear,
Cual vos lo quieren tomar, Vos y doce de los vuesos, Los que vos queráis nombrar, De que en la muerte del Rey Non tenedes que culpar.	Thyself, and twelve men of thy court, Whom thou wilt choose to name, That in Don Sancho's bloody death Ye had no part nor blame!"
— Pláceme, los castellanos, Todo os lo quiero otorgar. — En Santa Gadea de Burgos Allí el Rey se va a jurar;	"Men of Castile, it pleaseth me This day to grant your prayer; To Santa Gadea of Burgos Let us go forth to swear!"

Rodrigo tomó la jura
Sin un punto más tardar,
Y en un cerrojo bendito
Le comienza a conjurar:

To swear the King and his chosen twelve
Rodrigo is not loath;
Upon the sacred iron bolt
He puts them to the oath:

— Don Alfonso, y los leoneses,
Veníos vos a salvar
Que en la muerte de Don Sancho
Non tuvisteis que culpar,
Ni tampoco d'ella os plugo,
Ni a ella disteis lugar:

"Alfonso, and ye Leonese,
I charge ye here to swear
That in Don Sancho's death ye had
By word or deed no share!

Mala muerte hayáis, Alfonso,
Si non dijerdes verdad,
Villanos sean en ella
Non fidalgos de solar,

Alfonso, if thou tell not truth,
Be thine a death of shame;
May villain peasants strike thee down,
Not gentlemen of name;

Que non sean castellanos,
Por más deshonra vos dar,
Sino de Asturias de Oviedo
Que non vos tengan piedad.

Not nobles of Castilian blood,
But, to thy foul disgrace,
Asturian men of Oviedo,
That fierce and cruel race!"

— Amén, amén, dijo el Rey,
Que non fuí en tal maldad. —

"Amen, Amen," Alfonso cried,
"I scorn so foul a thing!"
"Amen, Amen," the twelve replied,
"We answer for the King!"

Tres veces tomó la jura.
Tantas le va a preguntar.
El Rey viéndose afincado,
Contra el Cid se fué a airar:

Three times the Cid has given the oath,
Three times the King has sworn;
With every oath his anger burned,
And thus he cried with scorn:

— Mucho me afincáis, Rodrigo,
En lo que no hay que dudar,
Cras besarme heis la mano,
Si agora me hacéis jurar:

"Thou swearest me, where doubt is none,
Rodrigo, to thy sorrow;
The hand that takes the oath to-day
Thou hast to kiss to-morrow!"

— Si, señor, dijera el Cid,
Si el sueldo me habéis de dar
Que en la tierra de otros reyes
A fijosdalgos les dan.

"Agreed, Señor," replied the Cid,
"If thou wilt give me pay,
As other Kings in other lands
Do give their knights this day;

Cuyo vasallo yo fuere
También me lo ha de pagar;
Si vos dármelo quisiéredes,
A mi placer me vendrá. —

Whose vassal I consent to be
Must pay like the rest;
If thou agree to do so now,
I yield to thy request!"

El Rey por tales razones	The King grew pale to hear his words,
Contra el Cid se fué a enojar;	And turned him from the Cid;
Siempre desde allí adelante	And from that hour for many a day
Gran tiempo le quiso mal.	His wrath could not be hid.

This *romance* is also one of the very old ones, and Gibson has been faithful in his transcription. Nothing is left out and little added. A sense of logic has caused him to give Alfonso's twelve witnesses a part in the oath, but in other respects he has given a literal rendering. He conveys very well the king's resentment at the severity of the oath and the feeling that the Cid is emphasizing his own importance and the king's dependence on him. The king's reminder to the Cid and the implied threat that the positions are soon to be reversed is made slightly more explicit in the translation by the lines "Thou swearest me where doubt is none / Rodrigo, to thy sorrow." The translator is careful throughout to express the feelings of the two men in words as close to the spirit of the original as possible, yet in a manner that will thoroughly explain the situation to the English readers.

There are several of the old ballads which suggest the reasons for the king's displeasure with the Cid, but the one which follows is one of the most interesting and perhaps the most unusual. Wolf and Hofmann put it among the *romances primitivos.*

En las almenas de Toro,	Upon the walls of Toro
Allí estaba una doncella,	There stood a maid of grace;
Vestida de negros paños,	Her dress was of the inky black,
Reluciente como estrella:	And like a star her face.
Pasara el rey Don Alfonso,	By chance the King Alfonso
Namorado se había d'ella,	That day came riding by;
	And as he looked he loved her,
	And thus aloud did cry:
Dice: — Si es hija de rey	"An gif she be a King's daughter,
Que se casaría con ella,	Then she shall wive with me;
Y si es hija de duque	An gif she be a Duke's daughter,
Serviría por manceba. —	My leman she shall be!"
Allí hablara el buen Cid,	Out spake the Cid and answered
Estas palabras dijera:	Unto the good King there;
— Vuestra hermana es, señor,	"Señor, she is thy sister,
Vuestra hermana es aquella.	She is thy sister fair!"

— Si mi hermana es, dijo el Rey,
Fuego malo encienda en ella:
Llámenme mis ballesteros;
Tírenle sendas saetas,

"May evil fire consume her,
  If she my sister be;
Now ho! my gallant bowmen,
  Send each a shot for me!

Y a aquel que la errare
Que la corten la cabeza. —
Allí hablara el Cid,
D'esta suerte respondiera.
— Mas aquel que la tirare
Pase por la misma pena.

The man who misses," cried the King,
  "His blood shall dye the sward!"
"The man who hits her," quoth the Cid,
  "Shall have the same reward!"

— Ios de mis tiendas, Cid,
No quiero que estéis en ellas.

Now wroth was King Alfonso,
  And a loud oath he swore:
"Go forth from out these tents of mine,
  And enter them no more!"

— Pláceme, respondió el Cid,
Que son viejas, y no nuevas:
Irme he yo para las mías,
Que son de brocado y seda,

"It pleaseth me," replied the Cid,
  "For very old they be;
Mine own of silk and gold brocade
  Are better far for me!

Que no las gané holgando,
Ni bebiendo en la taberna;
Ganélas en las batallas
Con mi lanza y mi bandera.

I gained them not in ladies' bower,
  Nor birling at the wine;
I gained them on the battlefield
  With this good lance of mine!"

There is a strong lyrical quality in the original which stands out immediately in the translation and which is seen to have been achieved with no sacrifice of ideas or spirit. The repetition of certain phrases, which is an important adjunct to the lyric effect, is used effectively in the translation, and the choice of expression is excellent. In several of the shorter *romances* Gibson has tended toward the use of the three-stress lines as a solution to the problem of conveying the rapid action and extreme concentration of the originals. This is evident here. He shows great skill in matching the simplicity and conciseness of his model — which is an excellent illustration of the technique — and the thirty-six lines of the translation compare favorably with the thirty-four of the original. The bit of dialect in the third stanza is unusual, but in other respects the translation is extremely satisfactory.

The next translation, a different description of the oath imposed upon King Alfonso by the Cid, is found in Spanish in two ancient versions, both of which contain many lines that are identical, but which vary enough in spirit and in certain small details to be considered separate compositions. The first, which begins "En Santa Agueda de Burgos," portrays the Cid as slightly more respectful to the king than the one included here. Gibson has again made use of both versions, but the spirit of the translation is definitely that of the second version which it accompanies.

En Santa Gadea de Burgos
Do juran los fijosdalgo,
Allí le toma la jura
El Cid, al rey castellano.

Las juras eran tan fuertes,
Que a todos ponen espanto;
Sobre un cerrojo de hierro
Y una ballesta de palo:

— Villanos mátente, Alfonso,
Villanos, que non fidalgos
De las Asturias de Oviedo,
Que no sean castellanos.

Mátente con aguijadas,
No con lanzas ni con dardos;
Con cuchillos cachicuernos,
No con puñales dorados;

Abarcas traigan calzadas,
Que non zapatos con lazos;
Capas traigan aguaderas,
Non de contray, ni frisado;

Con camisones de estopa,
Non de holanda, ni labrados;
Vayan cabalgando en burras,
Non en mulas ni caballos;

Frenos traigan de cordel,
Non de cueros fogueados;
Mátente por las aradas,
Non por villas ni poblados,

Y sáquente el corazón
Por el siniestro costado,
Si non dijeres verdad
De lo que te es preguntado,

In Santa Gadea of Burgos,
Where the knights were wont to swear,
Alfonso has come before the Cid,
To take a strong oath there.

He has placed his hand on the iron bolt,
And eke on the wooden bow;
So strong are the oaths that sudden fear
Strikes all the crowds below.

"Alfonso, may villains slay thee,
Not noble men and leal;
Asturian boors of Oviedo,
Not gentry of Castile!

May they slay thee with cattle-goads,
And not with lance in fight;
With their horny-hefted crooked knives,
And not with daggers bright!

On their feet be sandals of hide,
Not shoes of leather gay;
On their shoulders be mantles of straw,
Not broad-cloth of Contray.

Their skirts of the flaxen tow;
Not holland fine and wide;
On asses, and not on mules or steeds,
May they go forth to ride!

Their bridles be of the hempen cord,
And not of the leather brown;
And may they slay thee in the fields,
And not in a peopled town!

Out by the sinister side
May they pluck thy heart away,
If when the oath is put to thee,
Thou tell not truth this day!

Si fuiste, ni consentiste En la muerte de tu hermano.—	Alfonso, hadst thou art or part In that foul deed and blow, That sent thy brother to his death, Make answer, Yes or No!"
Jurado tiene el buen Rey, Que en tal caso no es hallado;	So strong the oath and fearful, The king declined to swear, When up and spake a noble knight, His favourite standing there:
	"Take thou the oath and fear not, It is the better plan; For never King was perjured yet, Nor Pope beneath the ban!"
Pero con voz alterada Dijo muy mal enojado:	"No!" cries the King, "upon my oath!" And three times he hath sworn; Then from the altar to the Cid He turns with mickle scorn:
—Cid, hoy me tomas la jura, Después besarme has la mano.—	"Right badly hast thou sworn me, Cid, Right badly, to thy sorrow; The hand upraised in oath this day Thou hast to kiss to-morrow!"
Respondiérale Rodrigo; D'esta manera ha fablado: —Por besar mano de rey No me tengo por honrado; Porque la besó mi padre Me tengo por afrentado.	"To kiss a kingly hand and all Doth not beseem my race; And if my father kissed it once, I hold it as disgrace!"
—Vete de mis tierras, Cid, Mal caballero probado, Y no me estés más en ellas Desde este día en un año.—	"Cid, quit these realms of mine in haste, Thou knight of evil fame; And see that for a year from this Thou enter not the same!"
—Pláceme, dijo el buen Cid, Pláceme, dijo, de grado, Por ser la primera cosa, Que mandas en tu reinado: Tú me destierras por uno, Yo me destierro por cuatro.—	"Señor, to obey thy first command Doth please me to the core; Thou send'st me away for a single [year— I banish myself for four!"
Ya se despide el buen Cid, Sin al Rey besar la mano,	With this the Cid has left the King, Nor deigned to kiss his hand;

Con trescientos caballeros,	And with him thrice a hundred knights,
Esforzados fijosdalgo;	All gentry of the land.
Todos son hombres mancebos,	They all were youths of mettle and [might,
Ninguno hay viejo ni cano;	No grey-beard to be seen;
Todos llevan lanza en puño	They all bore lances in their hands
Con el hierro acicalado,	Of tempered steel and keen;
Y llevan sendas adargas	They all had buckles on their arms,
Con borlas de colorado.	With bosses crimson-bright;
	The Cid I trow had a gallant band
	Within his camp that night.

The translation closely parallels the above model down to the point at which the king hesitates to answer. Here Gibson has gone to the other version for the incident of the knight who urges the king to swear, returning to the above with the lines "Por besar mano de rey / No me tengo por honrado." It is interesting to note that these two lines and the two which follow are found in a ballad treated earlier, "Cabalga Diego Laínez." Gibson uses the translation he made for them the first time, changing slightly the third line of his stanza which read in the earlier translation, "If my sire hath kissed it now." The rather cavalier attitude of the Cid which comes out strongly in the original is handled well in the translation, which deserves praise for its fidelity to both letter and spirit.

Gibson's next translation, number forty-five in his first edition, is practically a line-for-line rendition of King Alfonso's sentencing of the Cid to exile. It is an excellent example of the care he took to parallel not only the general spirit of the originals but every nuance. A few phrases have been reworded slightly, but no objection can be found with reference to ideas, spirit, or ease of composition.

—Si atendéis que de los brazos	"Dost thou expect that arms of ours
Vos alce, atended primero,	To raise thee shall be given?
Si no es bien que con los míos	As well expect that with thy hands
Cuide subirvos al cielo:	I'll bear thee up to heaven!
¡Bien estáis afinojado,	Tis well to see thee on thy knees,
Que es pavor veros enhiesto!	Thou man of fearful face!
¡Que asiento es, asaz debido,	To men of proud and haughty mien
El suelo, de los soberbios!	The ground's the fitting place.

¡Descubierto estáis mejor,
Después que se han descubierto
De vuesas altanerías
Los mal guisados excesos!

Tis better that thy head be bared,
To all the world revealed,
Since now thy scheming plans are bared,
However well concealed.

¿En qué os habéis empachado,
Que dende el pasado invierno
Non vos han visto en las Cortes,
Puesto que Cortes se han fecho?

What hindered thee this winter past
To take at Court thy place!
Though many a Council has been held,
We have not seen thy face!

¿Por qué siendo cortesano
Traéis la barba y cabello
Descompuesto, y desviada
Como los padres del yermo?

A courtier thou, and man of rank,
What makes thee bold to wear,
Like any unkempt Eremite,
Dishevelled beard and hair?

¡Pues aunque vos lo pregunto,
Asaz que bien os entiendo!
¡Bien conozco vuesas manas
Y el semblante falagueño!

Although I ask thee questions now,
No answer I entreat;
For well I know thy manners free,
And eke thy bold deceit!

Querréis decir que cuidando
En mis tierras y pertrechos
Non cuidades de aliñarvos
La barba y cabello luengo.

Thou'lt tell me that my lands and gear
Were put beneath thy care,
And left no time to set to rights
Thy beard and tangled hair!

Al de Alcalá contrallasteis
Mis treguas, paz y concierto,
Bien como si el querer mío
Tuviérades por muy vueso:

At Alcala, when peace I sought,
Thou thwartedst my design,
As if, forsooth! my wish and plans
Must all give way to thine!

A los fronterizos moros
Diz que tenéis por tan vuesos
Que os adoran como a Dios;
¡Grandes algos habréis d'ellos!

Thou'lt tell me that the border Moors
Before thy feet do bow,
And give thee honour like a god —
They pay thee well, I trow!

Cuando en mi jura os hallasteis,
Después del triste suceso
Del Rey Don Sancho mi herma- [no,
Por Bellido traidor muerto,

When at my brother Sancho's death,
Slain by Vellido's hand,
I came to take my rightful throne,
Alone didst thou withstand!

Todos besaron mi mano,
Y por rey me obedecieron:
Solo vos me contrallasteis
Tomándome juramento:

The nobles all did kiss my hand,
And pledged their knightly troth;
Thou single-handed didst presume
To put me to the oath!

En Santa Gadea lo fice
Sobre los cuatro Evangelios,

In Santa Gadea's holy church
I took the shameful test,

Y en el ballestón dorado
Teniendo el cuadrillo al pecho.

On the Gospels four, on the gilt cross-bow,
With a dagger to my breast!

Matárades a Bellido
Si ficierais como bueno,
Que no ha faltado quien dijo
Que tuvisteis asaz tiempo:

Thou mightst have struck Vellido down,
Hadst thou been valiant there;
For men aver that thou hadst time
Sufficient and to spare.

Fasta el muro lo seguisteis,
Y al entrar la puerta dentro
¡Bien cerca estaba quien dijo,
Que non osasteis de miedo!

Thou didst pursue him to the wall,
The gate was wide and clear;
But standers-by were heard to say
That thou didst stop through fear!

Y nunca fueron los míos
Tan astutos y mañeros,
Que cuidasen que Don Sancho
Muriese por mis consejos:

No friends of mine were so astute,
So shrewd as to divine
That King Don Sancho met his death
By any plot of mine.

Murió porque a Dios le plugo
En su juicio secreto,
Quizá porque de mi padre
Quebrantó sus mandamientos.

He died because God willed it so,
Perchance in righteous ire,
Because he broke the strict commands
And wishes of my sire.

Por estos desaguisados,
Desavenencias y tuertos,
Con título de enemigo
De mis reinos vos destierro.

For this and all that thou hast done,
With malice and design,
I brand thee foe, and bid thee go
From out these realms of mine!

Yo tendré vuesos condados
Fasta saber por entero,
Con acuerdo de los míos,
Si confiscárvoslos puedo.

Thy good broad lands I will retain,
The sentence to await,
Whereby my Courts, if right it seem,
Shall judge them confiscate.

¡Non repliquedes palabra,
Que vos juro por San Pedro,
Y por San Millán bendito,
Que vos enforcaré luego! —

Reply not with a single word,
Nor evil manners show,
Or by Saint Peter and Saint Millan,
To prison thou shalt go!"

Estas palabras le dijo
El rey Don Alfonso el Sexto,
Inducido de traidores,
Al Cid, honor de sus reinos.

These shameful words the king addressed,
Alfonso Sixth of Spain,
To Don Rodrigo of Bivar,
The glory of his reign.

Gibson has a curious note following the translation given above. He states, "I have been obliged to supply the last verse [stanza?] of this and of the following ballad."[4] The last four lines of the following ballad, "Téngovos de replicar," in which the Cid responds to the king's charges, and the last stanza of the translation are as follows:

Estas palabras decía
El noble Cid, respondiendo
A las querellas injustas
Del rey Don Alfonso el Sexto.

In tones like these the noble Cid
  A worthy answer made
To all the bitter words his King
  The sixth Alfonso made.

Since it is obvious that Gibson's lines are translations of the accompanying Spanish and not his own invention, the reason for the note is puzzling. The best explanation is that when he first made his translations, he was using versions of the two *romances* which included only the lines in quotes and was, therefore, forced to write his own stanzas explaining who the speakers were. Later he must have found the versions quoted above, rewritten his concluding lines, but failed to remove his note. The editor, unfamiliar with the originals, also left it in.

The following ballad is typical of the many *romances* describing the outstanding success of the Cid and his warriors in their battles against the Moors during the period of his exile. Again, a version by Gibson is placed with the original.

Por mando del rey Alfonso
El buen Cid es desterrado;
Caballeros van con él
Trescientos; son hijosdalgo.

The Cid has left Alfonso's Court,
  And by the King's command;
With him are thrice a hundred knights,
  All gentry of the land.

Ganó el buen Cid a Alcocer,
Este castillo nombrado;
Los moros en él lo cercan
Con todos sus allegados.

And he has conquered Alcocer,
  That Castle of renown,
When raging Moors in countless bands
  Laid siege unto the town.

No salen a la batalla,
Por ser muchos los paganos;
Aquese buen Alvar Fáñez
Que de Minaya es llamado,
A las compañas del Cid
Ansí les estaba hablando:

Rodrigo had but little hope
  Their battle-ranks to break,
When Alvar Fañez of Minaya
  Thus to his comrades spake:

[4] James Young Gibson, *The Cid Ballads and Other Poems and Translations from Spanish and German,* ed. Margaret Dunlop Gibson (London: Kegan Paul, Trench and Co., 1887), 1: 155.

—Amigos, salidos somos De León, ese reinado Do tenemos nuestras tierras, Y hasta aquí somos llegados;	"My friends, the kingdom of Leon Ye all have left behind, And all your good broad lands as well, Much better lands to find.
Menester es el esfuerzo De que sois tan abastados, Que a no lidiar con los moros, Comemos pan mal ganado.	For this we need stout arms and hearts, And such, I trow, are yours; Ill-earned will be our bread unless We battle with the Moors!
A ellos salgamos luego, Firámoslos denodados, Ansí ganaron la honra Los nuestros antepasados.—	So let us forth into their midst, And strike both firm and bold, For so our fathers gained renown In the good old days of old."
El Cid le dijo: —Minaya, Vos habláis como esforzado, Y como buen caballero, Que lo sois, y muy honrado:	"Thy words, Minaya!" said the Cid, "Are brave as is thy heart; Thou speakest like a gallant knight And honoured, as thou art!
Mostráis bien que descendéis De buen linaje estimado, Y que no perdieron honra, Antes siempre la han ganado,	Well dost thou show that thou hast [sprung From out of goodly line, Whose honour rose with every fight, Nor ever knew decline;
Y no temieron la muerte Ni sufrir cualquier quebranto, Por qu'ella fuese adelante De quien vos tomáis dechado.—	Who never flinched at sight of death, Nor dangers of the fray; Who placed their honour in the front, As thou hast done this day!"
Plugo a Pedro Bermúdez, La su seña le había dado: Díjole: —Pedro Bermúdez, Sois muy bueno y esforzado,	To Pedro Bermudez then he turned, To him his standard gave: "I know thee, Pedro, I know thee well, A good man and a brave;
Por esto vos doy mi seña, Como a noble hijodalgo; No aguijéis con ella mucho, Hasta ver el mi mandado.—	Bear thou my standard like a knight, As true as in the land; Advance it not too far, I pray, But wait for my command!"
Respondió Pedro Bermúdez: —Y os juro, buen Cid honrado, Por Dios trino, verdadero, Y al apóstol Santiago,	"Now by the Holy Trinity, And Santiago's name! By these, O Cid, I swear this day To give thy banner fame.

De la poner hoy en parte
Do jamás hobiera entrado,
Y que ella gane gran honra,
O morir como hidalgo. —

Where it has never been before
Thy men shall see it wave;
And I will hold it firm and fast,
Or perish with the brave!"

Y con muy crecido esfuerzo
Dió de espuelas al caballo,
Hirió por medio los moros,
Por medio d'ellos fué en salvo:

With this he gathered up his force,
And spurred his steed of war,
And charged with might the Moorish [ranks,
And bore the banner far.

El Cid también los firió,
El campo les ha ganado.

Whene'er the crimson Cross was seen,
The Moorish ranks gave way;
Right through their squadrons rode the [Cid
And won the field that day.

Gibson's translation, showing the Scotsman's usual regard for fidelity to ideas and spirit, matches the original well in all respects. Some slight compression of verses is noted, as for example in the introduction of Alvar Fáñez, but there is little addition or diminution of thought. The spirited, warlike qualities of the Cid's knights and the atmosphere of comradeship suffer no loss in translation, and the ballad is as pleasing in the English as in the Spanish.

One of the oldest and most interesting of the Cid ballads describes the champion's frustrating encounter with a proud and arrogant Moorish king. Gibson's translation is typical of his best style.

Helo, helo por do viene
El moro por la calzada,
Caballero a la gineta
Encima una yegua baya;

He comes, he comes, the Moorman comes
Along the sounding way;
With stirrup short, and pointed spur,
He rides his gallant bay.

Borcequíes marroquíes
Y espuela de oro calzada;
Una adarga ante los pechos,
Y en su mano una azagaya:

His spurs are of the beaten gold,
His socks of leather gay;
He bears his buckler on his arm,
In his hand an assegay.

Mira y dice a esa Valencia:
— ¡De mal fuego seas quemada!

He looks upon Valencia's towers,
And mutters in his ire:
"Valencia, O Valencia,
Burn thou with evil fire!

Primero fuiste de moros
Que de cristianos ganada.

Although the Christian holds thee now,
Thou wert the Moor's before;

Si la lanza no me miente	And if my lance deceive me not,
A moros serás tornada,	Thou'lt be the Moor's once more!
Y a aquel perro de aquel Cid	That cursed dog they call the Cid,
Prenderélo por la barba:	His beard I'll pluck and tear,
Su mujer Doña Jimena	And to my tent I'll captive lead
Será de mi captivada,	His wife Ximena fair!
Y su hija Urraca Hernández	His daughter Urraca Hernando
Será la mi enamorada:	Shall be my leman then;
Después de yo harto d'ella	And when I've had my will of her,
La entregué a mis compañas. —	I'll hand her to my men!"
El buen Cid no está tan lejos	Thus spake the angry Moorman,
Que todo no lo escuchara.	And gave his fury vent;
	The Cid was near, and heard him,
	And to his daughter went.
— Venid vos acá, mi fija,	"Come hither now, Urraca,
Mi fija Doña Urraca;	My daughter I love best;
Dejad las ropas continas,	Take off thy homely garments,
Y vestid ropas de pascua,	And be thou gaily dressed!
A aquel moro hi-de-perro	Beguile that dog the Moorman
Detiénemelo en palabras,	With many a civil word,
Mientras yo ensillo a Babieca,	While I saddle Bavieca,
Y me ciño la mi espada. —	And buckle on my sword!
La doncella muy fermosa	The bonnie maiden busked herself,
Se paró a una ventana;	And to the window hied;
El moro desque la vido	The Moorman when he saw her
D'esta suerte le fablara;	With courteous greeting cried:
— ¡Alá te guarde, señora,	"May Allah keep thee, lady,
Mi señora Doña Urraca!	Urraca, lady dear!"
— ¡Así faga a vos, señor,	"The same I wish for thee, Señor,
Buena sea vuestra llegada!	Thou'rt very welcome here!
Siete años ha, Rey, siete,	For seven years, O King, for seven,
Que soy vuestra enamorada.	My lover dear thou art!"
— Otros tanto ha, señora,	"As many more, Señora,
Que os tengo dentro en mi alma.—	I hold thee in my heart!"
Ellos estando en aquesto,	While thus they stood and answered,
El buen Cid ya se asomaba.	With many a word and sweet,
	The good Cid on his charger
	Came riding up the street.

— Adiós, adiós, mi señora,
La mi linda enamorada,
Que del caballo Babieca
Yo bien oigo la patada. —

"Farewell, farewell, Señora,
I may not tarry here;
For Bavieca's pattering hoofs
Are sounding in my ear!"

Do la yegua pone el pie
Babieca pone la pata.

Away the Moorman gallops off,
The Cid holds not aloof;
For where the good mare strikes the [ground
Bavieca plants his hoof.

El Cid fablara al caballo,
Bien oiréis lo que fablaba:
— ¡Reventar debía la madre
Que a su hijo no esperaba! —

Spake the Cid unto his charger,
Ye will hear his words each one:
"Now shame be on the mother
That waits not for her son!"

Siete vueltas la rodea
Al derredor de una jara;
La yegua que era lijera
Muy adelante pasaba

Through bush and brake full seven times
He tracked her round and round;
The nimble mare, so light of limb,
Passed onward with a bound!

Fasta llegar cabe un rio
Adonde una barca estaba.
El moro desque la vido
Con ella bien se folgaba;

A river lay before them,
A bark was on the stream;
And when the Moorman saw it,
With joy his eyes did gleam!

Grandes gritos da el barquero
Que le allegase la barca:
El barquero es diligente
Túvosela aparejada;

"Ho! bring thy bark, good boatman,
And bring it quick to me!"
The boatman heard his shouting,
And rowed right lustily.

Embarcóse presto en ella,
Que no se detuvo nada.
Estando el moro embarcado
El buen Cid se llegó al agua,

The Moorman leapt within it,
Nor made the least delay;
And when the good Cid galloped up,
He saw him sail away.

Y por ver al moro en salvo
De tristeza reventaba;
Mas con la furia que tiene
Una lanza le arrojaba,

Right angry was the Cid, I ween,
And fire was in his glance;
And with the fury that he had
He launched at him his lance!

Y dijo: — ¡Coged, mi yerno,
Arrecogedme esa lanza,
Que quizá tiempo verná
Que os será bien demandada!

"Pick up my lance, good son-in-law,
And keep it firm and fast;
I'll maybe ask it back from thee
Ere many days are past!"

Most of the variations used in the popular four- and three-stress pattern are found in this translation and contribute to its undeniable effectiveness. The merit of Gibson's translations often closely parallels the merit of the models, thus revealing not only his fidelity to the material but also, in the case of the better originals, a mark of his poetic ability. An excellent original inspired his best efforts and the resulting translation is almost always highly satisfactory. The above poem seems to be a good example. The poetry is pleasant and unconstrained, suffering neither from monotony nor highly irregular lines, the spirit of the *romance* is duplicated exactly, and the correspondence of ideas is exact.

Thomas Rodd, one of the first authors to become interested in the *romances,* also did a translation of this ballad which is quite representative of his technique and which may be compared with Gibson's.

Look, look, on the causey yonder
  Rides the Moorish King this way;
Like a trim light horseman mounted
  On his mare, a glossy bay.

Round his legs Morocco buskins,
  On his heels gold spurs he wears;
On his breast a shining target;
  In his hand a lance he bears.

At Valencia is he looking,
  How 'tis strongly circled round.
"O Valencia, O Valencia,
  "Fire consume thee to the ground!

"Once to valiant Moors belong'st thou,
  "Now the Christians o'er thee reign;
"If my lance doth not deceive me,
  "Moors shall be thy Lords again.

"That vile dog the Cid I'll take him
  "By the beard, though ne'er so brave;
"And his wife, Ximena quickly
  "Shall she bow my humble slave.

"But his daughter, fair Urraca,
  "For my mistress I intend;
"When I have enough enjoy'd her,
  "Then I'll give her to my friend."

All this heard the Cid, who, list'ning,
  Stood behind the city wall.
"Hither, hither, my Urraca;
  "Daughter, 'tis your father's call.

"Off your daily robes, and quickly
  "Put your Sunday garments on;
"Keep this haughty Moor in converse,
  "Whilst I arm myself anon.

"I must saddle my Babieca,
  "And my sword about me gird."
To the window came Urraca,
  When her father's voice she heard.

When the gallant Moor perceiv'd her,
  You shall soon hear what he said:
"Alla guard thee, fair Urraca!
  "Alla guard thee, lovely maid!"

"Welcome! welcome! cry'd the lady;
  "Glad am I to see you here:
"Seven long years have I esteem'd you,
  "Seven long years have held you dear.

"Just so many, lovely lady,
  "In my loyal breast you reign."
Whilst the Moorish King was parleying,
  Came the noble Cid again.

"Farewell, my true love," she answer'd;
  "I must go, adieu! adieu!
"Hark! it is Babieca's master,
  "Loud doth he inquire for you."

Where the mare her foot sets nimbly,
  There Babieca sets his own;
Thus the Cid, with sorrow grieving,
  Made his deep vexation known:

"May the mother burst that will not
  "Wait her loving son's embrace!"
Sev'n times doth he nearly catch him,
  Swiftly as he holds the chase.

But the mare was young and active;
  To the river side she came,

Where a boat was moor'd, rejoicing,
  Thus the King did loud exclaim;

"Boatman! boatman! hither, hither!
  "Time admits of no delay."
Leaps the King in haste within it,
  And the boatman rows away.

When the Cid came nigh the river,
  And perceived the Moor was safe,
Fury, in his bosom rising,
  Did his noble spirit chafe;

But he whirl'd his sharp lance at him
  And exclaimed, with high disdain,
"Son-in-law, expect me shortly
  "To demand the lance again."

The outstanding characteristics of Rodd's work are the literalness of his translation and the almost mechanical regularity. His verse is in the four-stress, trochaic lines of eight and seven syllables which is perhaps the closest parallel to the rhythmic pattern of the *romances* and which would be quite effective if it were occasionally varied with other meters. Placed side by side, the translations of Gibson and Rodd point up both the similarities and differences of the two most popular short-line ballad meters. This also gives some idea of their comparative advantages and disadvantages, as well as suggesting the relative skill of the two men who are most representative of each type.

Certain references in the preceding poems suggest that fortune smiled on the Cid during his exile, and indeed, as is well known to readers of the *Poema,* such was the case. He won many battles against the Moors, established himself as lord of the rich and beautiful city of Valencia, had his devoted wife, Ximena, and his two daughters brought there from Castile, and in due course was reconciled with King Alfonso. These and other events told in the ancient epic, such as the marriage of the Cid's daughters to the ignoble Infantes de Carrión, the mistreatment of the daughters, and the ultimate happy outcome after the trials in Alfonso's court, are all treated in ballads which were translated in characteristic fashion by Gibson. It was necessary for the Cid to defend his conquests almost constantly, however, and danger was ever-present, as is suggested by the following ballad describing his instructions to Ximena prior to one of his battles.

— Si de mortales feridas
Fincare muerto en la guerra,
Llevadme, Jimena mía,
A San Pedro de Cardeña:

If in the strife of battle
Of mortal wounds I die;
O carry me, Ximena,
To the church where I shall lie!

Y así buena andanza hayades
Que me fagades la huesa
Junto al altar de Santiago,
Amparo de lides nuesas.

In San Pedro de Cardeña
Let my sepulchre be made:
By the shrine of Santiago,
Our champion and our aid.

Non me curedes plañir,
Porque la mi gente buena
Viendo que falta mi brazo
Non fuya y deje mi tierra.

No sound be heard of wailing,
For fear my gallant band,
When they shall miss this arm of mine,
Lose heart and leave the land!

Non vos conozcan los moros
En vuestro pecho flaqueza,
Sino que aquí griten armas,
Y allí me fagan obsequias:

Be bold before the Moormen
Nor show the least despair;
Nor let them raise the shout, To arms:
While I am buried there.

Y la Tizona que adorna
Esta mi mano derecha,
Non pierda de su derecho,
Ni venga a manos de fembra.

Nor let the pride of this right arm,
Tizona, my good brand,
Be e'er defrauded of its rights,
Or found in woman's hand!

Y si permitiere Dios
Que el mi caballo Babieca
Fincare sin su señor,
Y llamare a vuesa puerta,

And should my Bavieca,
If his be such a fate,
Return without his master,
And clamour at thy gate;

Abridle y acariñadle
Y dadle ración entera,
Que quien sirve a buen señor,
Buen galardón dél espera.

Then open it and fondle him,
And feed him well for me;
Who serves an honest master
Expects an honest fee!

Ponedme de vuesa mano
El peto, espaldar y grevas,
Brazal, celada y manoplas,
Escudo, lanza y espuelas;

Now bring my greaves and buckler,
And dress me for the field,
My morion and my gauntlets,
My spurs and lance and shield.

Y puesto que rompe el día
Y me dan los moros priesa,
Dadme vuesa bendición
Y fincad enhorabuena. —

For now the day is dawning,
And the Moors they will not rest;
Bestow on me thy blessing,
And be thou also blessed!"

Con esto salió Rodrigo	With this he left Valencia,
De los muros de Valencia	And rode with all his men
A dar la batalla a Búcar.	To battle with King Bucar;
¡Plegue a Dios que con bien [vuelva!	God bring him safe again!

Gibson's translation is a close copy of the Spanish, maintaining in excellent fashion the words and sentiments of the Cid. As in many of his shorter translations, there is a predominance of three-stress lines which imitate well the rhythm of the original.

This ballad was also translated by Edward Maturin, whose version offers an interesting contrast to that of Gibson. Maturin's usual technique was to focus on the tone and mood of the original, following only the bare outline of the narrative and using his imagination to fill in the details. Like Lockhart, he usually preferred the long line, as illustrated below:

"Should the God of battles lay me low in the field whereto I'm bound,
Should I fall beneath the Moorish foe, and bite in death the ground.
Ximena! let thy husband's grave be in San Pedro's shrine;
Above me let no banner wave, save Jesus' holy sign!

"I charge thee, let no woman's tear bewail thy husband dead;
Let warrior-hands, upon the bier, compose my pillow'd head.
I would not have my soldiers weep upon their leader's pall,
Nor grief her lightless vigil keep, where'er I chance to fall.

"As knight of Christ, I charge thee, yet, should sorrow dim thy lid,
Let not the hordes of Mahomet see thee weeping for thy Cid;
I charge thee further, by the sword Bivar in battle wore,
Let it not own a second lord or fell another Moor!

"It may be that my gallant steed, with loose and dangling rein,
(True as e'er served a knight at need, or trod the soil of Spain)
May stand without his master's gate, with low and drooping head,
And the empty saddle where I sate will tell thee I am dead!

"Open the gate, as though I yet bestrode my courser brave,
And prythee let his bones be laid within his master's grave;
For they who've fought in bloody field should still be one in death —
The spear should lie upon the shield, and the sword within its sheath!

"Soon as the parting soul is sped, and leaves to earth her spoil,
Ximena, — thou anoint my head with myrrh and holy oil;
Then buckle harness on my breast, and helmet on my head,
And leave Bivar to take his rest among Spain's gallant dead!"

Maturin's version is more faithful to the model than most of his ballads, although he has shifted the ideas considerably and in the last two stanzas has departed from the text. He seems to have been influenced by other ballads on the Cid which describe his burial and the ultimate disposition of the bones of his noble horse, Babieca. Aside from the questionable procedure of introducing outside material, his translation could be commended for its unity and compactness and for the favorable way in which it reflects the pervading spirit of the model. He omitted, of course, the last few lines of the original.

The Cid's affection for Babieca, evident in the preceding ballad, is matched by his generosity as he attempts to show his regard for King Alfonso in the following composition. Gibson's work is again with the original.

<table>
<tr><td>Ya se parte de Toledo
Ese buen Cid afamado,
Y acabáronse las cortes
Que allí se habían celebrado.
Aquese buen rey Alfonso,
Muy gran derecho le ha dado
De los Infantes, los condes
De Carrión el condado.</td><td>The Cid has left Toledo
The good Cid of renown;
The King to show his courtesie
Rides with him from the town.</td></tr>
<tr><td>Don Rodrigo va a Valencia,
Que a los moros la ha ganado:
Novecientos caballeros
Lleva todos fijosdalgo,
Que de la rienda le llevan
A Babieca, el buen caballo.</td><td>Nine hundred men are round him,
A brave and gallant train;
With Bavieca in their midst,
Led onward by the rein.</td></tr>
<tr><td>Despidióse el Rey del Cid,
Que le había acompañado:
Lejos van uno de otro,
El Cid envió un recaudo
Pidiendo merced al Rey
Le aguarde para hablallo.</td><td>The King has scarcely left him
When back he sends his men,
And prays the King would wait a space,
To speak with him again.</td></tr>
<tr><td>El Rey aguardara al Cid,
Como a bueno y leal vasallo,
Y el Cid le dijo: —Buen Rey,
Yo he sido muy mal mirado
En llevarme yo a Babieca,</td><td>"Good King!" he said on meeting,
"My heart is full of shame,
To bear my Bavieca back,
That horse of wondrous fame!</td></tr>
<tr><td>Caballo tan afamado,
Que a vos, señor, pertenece</td><td>For such a steed befits a king,
And I have done thee wrong;</td></tr>
</table>

Como mas aventajado.
Non le merece ninguno,
Vos sí solo a vueso cabo:

To none on earth except my liege
May such a steed belong.

Y porque veáis cual es
Y si es bien el estimallo,
Quiero facer ante vos
Lo que no he acostumbrado,
Si non es cuando hube lides
Con enemigos en campo. —

And if thou wilt I'll show thee what
Thou hast not seen before;
How Bavieca quits himself
When trampling down the Moor."

Cabalgó el buen Cid en él,
De piel de armiño arreado,
Firióle de las espuelas,

They bring the steed before the King
Beclad with whitest fur;
The Cid leaps lightly on his back,
And chafes him with the spur.

El Rey se quedó espantado:
En mirar cuan bien lo face,
A ambos está alabando;

Anon they wheel, anon they bound,
And o'er the plain they thunder;
The King and all his nobles round,
Stand rooted there in wonder!

Alababa a quien lo rige,
De valiente y esforzado,
Y al caballo por mejor,
Que otro no es visto ni hallado.

And now they praise the gallant knight,
His courage cool and keen
And now they praise the gallant horse,
Whose like was never seen.

Con la furia de Babieca,
Una rienda se ha quebrado,
Paróse con una sola
Como si estuviera en prado.

While Bavieca charges
In fury round the spot
One bridle rein is snapped in twain,
The Cid regards it not.

El Rey y sus ricos homes
De verlo se han espantado,
Diciendo que nunca oyeron
Fablar de tan buen caballo.

With one alone he gallops on,
And guides him round and round;
At topmost speed he checks the steed,
And lights upon the ground.

El Cid le dijo: — Buen Rey,
Suplícoos queráis tomallo.
— Non lo tomaré yo, el Cid,
El Rey por respuesta ha dado:

"I pray thee, take him!" cries the Cid,
"He is thine own, O King!"
"I will not do it!" he replies,
"Far from me such a thing!

Si fuera, buen Cid, el mío
Yo vos lo diera de grado,
Que en vos mejor que en ninguno
El caballo está empleado.

"If he were mine, I'd give him thee,
"He would be mine no more;
"For better knight with better horse
"Was never matched before.

Con él honrades a vos,
Y a nos en extremo grado,
Y a todos los de mis tierras,
Por vuesos fechos granados;

"He does thee honour, noble Cid,
"He honours us as well;
"And all my folk in all my lands
"Thy daring deeds will tell;

Mas yo lo tomo por mío
Con que vos queráis llevarlo,
Que cuando yo lo quisiere
Por mí vos será tomado.—

"Yet, by my sooth, he shall be mine,
"But take him with thee now;
"And when I wish to have him back,
"I'll send to thee, I vow!"

Despidióse el Cid del Rey,
Las manos le había besado,
Y fuese para Valencia,
Donde le están aguardando.

The Cid then bade the King farewell,
And kissed the royal hand;
And onward to Valencia
He rode with all his band.

Some editing on the part of the translator is evident in this ballad, especially in the first ten lines, and all superfluous information is cut out. The thought of the remainder is adhered to carefully, although there is some rearrangement and some amplification, particularly in the description of the Cid's ride. The alteration is not excessive, however, and the development of the rather bare details of the Spanish seems quite excusable.

This ballad was also translated by Maturin and Lockhart, and again it may be worthwhile to compare Gibson's work with that of another poet. As may be expected, Lockhart's version is superior to Maturin's, but does not come off so well when placed with Gibson's. It omits all the preliminary material and begins at the point of highest interest — the offer of the horse to the king.

The King looked on him kindly, as on a vassal true;
Then to the King Ruy Diaz spake after reverence due,
"O King, the thing is shameful, that any man beside
The liege lord of Castile himself should Bavieca ride:

"For neither Spain nor Araby could another charger bring
So good as he, and certes, the best befits my King.
But that you may behold him, and know him to the core,
I'll make him go as he was wont when his nostrils smelt the Moor."

With that, the Cid, clad as he was in mantle furred and wide,
On Bavieca vaulting, put the rowel in his side;
And up and down, and round and round, so fierce was his career,
Streamed like a pennon on the wind Ruy Díaz' minivere.

And all that saw them praised them, — they lauded man and horse,
As matched well, and rivalless for gallantry and force;
Ne'er had they looked on horseman might to this knight come near,
Nor on other charger worthy of such a cavalier.

Thus, to and fro a-rushing, the fierce and furious steed,
He snapped in twain his hither rein: — "God pity now the Cid! —
God pity Diaz!" cried the Lords, — but when they looked again,
They saw Ruy Diaz ruling him, with the fragment of his rein;
They saw him proudly ruling with gesture firm and calm,
Like a true lord commanding, — and obeyed as by a lamb.

And so he led him foaming and panting to the King, —
But "No!" said Don Alphonso, "it were a shameful thing
That peerless Bavieca should ever be bestrid
By any mortal but Bivar, — mount, mount again, my Cid!"

The first four stanzas, while far from a literal translation, convey all the principal ideas quite well. The fifth — the climactic one — adds considerably to the lines "El Rey y sus ricos homes / De verlo espantado," but the extension of thought is not improbable. The last twenty lines of the original are condensed into a final four-line stanza aimed, perhaps, at keeping attention on the ride itself. It is interesting to note that Lockhart puts the white fur on the Cid while Gibson has it on the horse. The antecedent of "De piel de armiño arreado" is not completely clear, but Gibson's rendition is probably the correct one inasmuch as the adjective "arreado" ("adorned" or "decorated") is placed closest to the horse. It seems fair to say that Lockhart, in somewhat typical fashion, has transcribed the essential action and the spirit or mood of the original, but his rendition is far from being a translation in the same sense that Gibson's is.

Few critics would question the statement that Gibson is the best of the translators of Cid ballads, and if the translations studied above are accepted as representative of the others in his collection, several generalizations may be permitted at this juncture. Most obvious, of course, is a definite similarity of method and technique. Gibson preferred to stay as close to the original as possible, especially in ideas and spirit. In many cases he was able to use almost the same language, and only infrequently did he choose somewhat different English expressions as a better way of communicating the thought. His translations show an excellent understanding of the underlying emotions of the *romances,* and the background for the action is carried over into English as faithfully as the dramatic events themselves. His aim with the Cid ballads was to present a unified and comprehensive picture of his hero's character, personality, and history. Consequently, he obviously selected for translation those ballads which best lent themselves to this purpose and which, it must be admitted, portray the Cid in as favorable a light as possible. Once the selection was made, however, he did very little editing of the materials, with the exception of an occasional slight change at the beginning or end of a ballad to smooth the transition from one poem to another. In no case does one find significant alterations of either thought or mood.

With regard to imitation of the verse patterns of the originals, Gibson did not try to duplicate either the assonance or the continuous verse arrangement of the Spanish. He chose, instead, a conventional English ballad meter corresponding to the Spanish only in that many of the lines are eight-syllable. Practically all his Cid ballads exhibit the familiar four- and three-stress pattern. The rhythm is somewhat similar to the Spanish, however, with the final stress falling frequently on the seventh syllable, but usually on the eighth. The choice seems a good one for the historical ballads, which are concerned with narrative and which are well suited to the quickened tempo of short lines. If the smoothness and ease of composition typical of so much of Gibson's work is also considered along with all the factors just noted, his efforts must be adjudged to compare favorably with almost any translation criteria.

Many additional details of the Cid's history and final destiny are included in other translations in Gibson's collection. Several, for example, are devoted to the circumstances surrounding the great champion's death. "Muerto yace ese buen Cid" ("The Good Cid Lies Dead") describes the departure from Valencia of Ximena and the Cid's men and their journey back to Castile with his body. There is also a short, and inadequate, version of this ballad among Maturin's translations. "En Sant Pedro de Cardeña" records the miracle at the Cid's tomb when the arm of the embalmed hero drew his sword against a Jew who tried to do what no one had been able to do when the Cid was alive: pull his beard. The ballad also appears in an anonymous translation in the *Foreign Quarterly Review,* Volume 4 (1829). The last selection in this series relates the honor paid the

Cid by King Sancho the Valiant, when he dedicated his spoils of war to the Abbey of San Pedro de Cardeña, the Cid's final resting place. Although none of the preceding need be singled out for special study, all are consistent with the high standards of translation characteristic of most of Gibson's work.

CHAPTER II

OTHER HISTORICAL BALLADS

EVEN IF ONE WERE TO LEAVE ASIDE THE ENORMOUS NUMBER of ballads devoted to the adventures of the Cid, the historical ballads would still rank as the most important, and in many ways the most interesting, of the several categories of *romances.* The themes treated run the gamut from the great events of biblical and classical history to relatively insignificant and minor incidents of a purely local and contemporary nature, but the most fully developed cycles concern the legendary figures and major episodes of national history from about the eighth century through the fifteenth. Too, certain family or personal histories, such as that of the Siete Infantes de Lara, were so filled with drama and passion that these became part of the common historical legend. The English translators of ballads, also, have shown an understandable preference for those *romances históricos* much celebrated in the popular tradition which seem to illustrate most clearly the developing Spanish character during the centuries between the Moorish invasion of 711 and the first complete unification of the nation in 1492.

There is a close connection between the historical ballads and many of the early prose chronicles, but the nature of that relationship is often obscure. In some cases it seems certain that the chroniclers incorporated into their works either ballad or epic versions of historical events, while in others, the ballads were based upon and inspired by the chronicles. In any event, the *romances históricos* should not be accepted as fact, since even those which are most accurate historically contain a large measure of legend and fancy.

One of the most colorful groups, and one which undoubtedly presents a highly fictionalized account of a tremendously important event, is the series devoted to Rodrigo, the last of the Gothic kings. These ballads offer a moral explanation for the success of the Moslems by considering it as a punishment for the sins of the king. There are three basic parts to the legend, each of which is illustrated by a sizable number of *romances*. The first part tells how Rodrigo entered the forbidden "House of Hercules" in Toledo, thereby incurring a severe curse on his head and on his kingdom. Later he became fatally enamored of the daughter of one of his nobles (usually referred to as "La Cava") and in the father's absence seduced the girl. When he learned what had happened, the offended parent, Count Julian, the governor of Ceuta on the Moroccan coast, decided to revenge himself against the king by helping the Moors to invade the country. The third element of the story concerns what happened to Rodrigo after his defeat and the loss of his realm. Although his fate is described in various ways, the most popular version has him repenting of his misdeeds and willingly accepting a punishment appropriate to his sin. An example of one of the ballads from the first part of the legend is found below, with an accompanying translation by John Oxenford, who gave his version the title of "The Omens by Which the Ruin of Spain Was Foretold." The original is a *romance viejo*.

Don Rodrigo, rey de España
Por la su corona honrar,
Un torneo en Toledo
Ha mandado pregonar:

In the city of Toledo,
Don Rodrigo, King of Spain,
Has declar'd he'll hold a tourney,
To give lustre to his reign.

Sesenta mil caballeros
En él se han ido a juntar.
Bastecido el gran torneo,
Queriéndole comenzar,

Sixty thousand noble champions
At the tournament are seen;
When the guests are all assembled,
They are anxious to begin.

Vino gente de Toledo
Por le haber de suplicar
Que a la antigua casa de Hércules
Quisiese un candado echar,
Como sus antepasados
Lo solían costumbrar.

But the people of Toledo
Come, a favour to implore,
That the king will set a padlock
Upon Hercules' old door —
'Twas an ancient, honour'd custom,
Of the kings, who reign'd before.

El Rey no puso el candado,
Mas todos los fué a quebrar,

King Rodrigo sets no padlock,
But to break them all he goes,

Pensando que gran tesoro Hércules debía dejar.	Hoping Hercules' old temple Will some hidden wealth disclose.
Entrando dentro en la casa Nada otro fuera hallar Sino letras que decían: "Rey has sido por tu mal; Que el rey que esta casa abriere A España tiene quemar."	When the house at length he enters, There is nothing he can see, But some characters that tell him, "'Tis an evil act for thee — By the king, who opes this dwelling, All the realm consum'd shall be."
Un cofre de gran riqueza Hallaron dentro un pilar, Dentro dél nuevas banderas Con figuras de espantar; Alárabes de caballo Sin poderse menear,	Then they search, and, in a column, Find a coffer, richly chas'd, Which is full of unknown banners, With dread figures on them trac'd; Forms of Arabs upon horseback, In their saddles firmly plac'd.
Con espadas a los cuellos, Ballestas de bien tirar. Don Rodrigo pavoroso No curó de más mirar.	From their necks their swords are hang-[ing, Goodly crossbows, too, they bear; Don Rodrigo looks no further, For his heart is struck with fear.
Vino un águila del cielo, La casa fuera quemar. Luego envía mucha gente Para Africa conquistar:	From the sky there came an eagle, And the house in flame was lost; But the king, to conquer Afric, Soon despatch'd a num'rous host.
Veinte y cinco mil caballeros Dió al conde Don Julián, Y pasándolos el Conde Corría fortuna en la mar:	Four and twenty thousand warriors Were to Count Don Julian sent; When Don Julian had embark'd them, On the faithless sea he went.
Perdió doscientos navíos, Cien galeras de remar, Y toda la gente suya, Sino cuatro mil no más.	And two hundred sailing vessels, With an hundred of the oar, With the total force were founder'd, Save four thousand men — no more.

Oxenford varied the length of his stanzas to conform somewhat to the sentence grouping of the original, and in other respects he tended toward a literal translation. He was careful to explain, for example, that he had deliberately deviated from the Spanish in his rendition of the line "Rey has sido por tu mal," [1] but the other lines

[1] See the footnote accompanying his translations, *New Monthly Magazine* 77 (1846): 270.

were transcribed quite faithfully. Most of his translations make use of the standard four-stress trochaic line observed above.

The next ballad, which describes how the king received the first news of Count Julian's betrayal, is considered one of the oldest of the Rodrigo cycle. The Spanish text is as follows:

Los vientos eran contrarios,
La luna era crecida,
Los peces daban gemidos
Por el tiempo que hacía,
Cuando el Rey Don Rodrigo
Junto a la Cava dormía,
Dentro de una rica tienda
De oro bien guarnecida.
Trescientas cuerdas de plata
La su tienda sostenían,
Dentro había cien doncellas
Vestidas a maravilla;
Las cincuenta están tañendo
Con muy estraña armonía,
Las cincuenta están cantando
Con muy dulce melodía.
Allí hablara una doncella
Que Fortuna se decía:
—Si duermes, buen Rey Rodrigo,
Despierta por cortesía,
Y verás tus malos hados,
Tu peor postrimería,
Y verás tus gentes muertas
Y tu batalla rompida,
Y tus villas y ciudades
Destruidas en un día.
Castillos y fortalezas
Otro señor las regía,
Si me pides quien lo ha hecho
Yo muy bien te lo diría:
Ese Conde Don Julián
Por el amor de su hija,
Porque se la deshonraste
Y más della no tenía,
Juramento viene haciendo
Que te ha de costar la vida.—
Despertó muy enojado
Con aquella voz que oía,
Con cara triste y penosa
Desta suerte respondía:
—Mercedes a ti, Fortuna,
Desta tu mensagería.—
Estando en esto llegó
Uno que nuevas traía
Como el Conde Don Julián
Las tierras le destruía,
Apriesa pide el caballo
Y al encuentro le salía;
Los enemigos son tantos
Que esfuerzo no le valía,
Que capitanes y gentes
Huía el que más podía.

There are versions in English by Thomas Rodd, W. S. Merwin, and Matthew Gregory Lewis, but the one by James Young Gibson offers an interesting contrast to his translations of Cid ballads. It reads as follows:

The winds were sadly moaning, the moon was on the change,
The fishes they were gasping, the skies were wild and strange,
'Twas then that Don Rodrigo beside La Cava slept,
Within a tent of splendour, with golden hangings deckt.

Three hundred cords of silver did hold it firm and free,
Within, a hundred maidens stood passing fair to see;

The fifty they were playing with finest harmonie,
The fifty they were singing with sweetest melodie.

A maid they called Fortuna uprose and thus she spake:
"If thou sleepest, Don Rodrigo, I pray thee, now awake;
Thine evil fate is on thee, thy kingdom it doth fall,
Thy people perish, and thy hosts are scattered one and all,
Thy famous towns and cities fall in a single day,
And o'er thy forts and castles another lord bears sway.
What traitor hand hath done it? The news to thee I'll break,
It is the Count Don Julian, and for his daughter's sake;
Because thou hast dishonoured her, and put her name to scorn
That this will cost thy life's blood, he with an oath hath sworn."

There came while thus she answered, a messenger to hand,
Who told how Count Don Julian was ravishing the land;
Up started Don Rodrigo, his face with passion white,
In haste he called his charger, and sallied to the fight;

But thousand foes are circling round, his valour has no play,
His Captains fall, his people flee, and he has lost the day.

Gibson's verse pattern is quite different from that observed in his previous work. He uses the long line of six iambs and thirteen syllables with an occasional caesura after the seventh syllable. The lines are rhymed in couplets with stanza division corresponding roughly to breaks in the narrative. The last couplet is composed of fourteen-syllable, seven-stress lines and serves not only as a distinctive ending to this translation but also as a separation between this ballad and the one that follows. There is close correspondence between much of the original and the translation, with each line of English encompassing two lines of Spanish. Several additions and changes are noted, however, and several lines are left out altogether. In the first stanza, "the skies were wild and strange" is not in the original, but the addition helps to create the desired mood of the poem and is appropriate. Rodrigo's reply to the maiden Fortuna is left out altogether, perhaps because his words and actions are not quite consistent with the haste he shows in the last stanzas and with the impression the translator wished to leave. The last phrase, "and he has lost the day," is not in the original, but it is an effective summary. The spirit of the ballad is admirably conveyed, and the overall impression of the translation is favorable.

Gibson followed this ballad with the one below, also very old, which continues the story of the king's misfortunes.

Las huestes del Rey Rodrigo
Desmayaban y huían
Cuando en la octava batalla
Sus enemigos vencían.
Rodrigo deja sus tierras
Y del real se salía:
Solo va el desventurado
Que no lleva compañía.
El caballo de cansado,
Ya mudar no se podía,
Camina por donde quiere,
Que no le estorba la vía.
El Rey va tan desmayado
Que sentido no tenía,
Muerto va de sed y hambre
Que de velle era mancilla,
Y va tan tinto de sangre
Que una brasa parecía;
Las armas lleva abolladas,
Que eran de sangre perdida;
La espada lleva hecha sierra
De los golpes que tenía;
El almete de abollado
En la cabeza se hundía,
La cara llevaba hinchada
Del trabajo que sufría.
Subióse encima de un cerro
El más alto que veía:
Desde allí mira su gente
Como iba de vencida.
De allí mira sus banderas
Y estandartes que tenía,
Como están todos pisados
Que la tierra los cubría,
Mira por los Capitanes
Que ninguno parescía;
Mira el campo tinto en sangre
La cual arroyos corría.
El triste de ver aquesto
Gran mancilla en sí tenía;
Llorando de los sus ojos
Desta manera decía:
—Ayer era Rey de España,
Hoy no lo soy de una villa;
Ayer villas y castillos,
Hoy ninguno poseía;
Ayer tenía criados
Y gente que me servía,
Hoy no tengo una almena
Que pueda decir que es mía.
¡Desdichada fué la hora,
Desdichado fué aquel día
En que nací y heredé
La tan grande señoría,
Pues lo había de perder
Todo junto y en un día!
¡Oh muerte! ¿por qué no vienes
Y llevas esta alma mía
De aqueste cuerpo mezquino,
Pues te se agradecería?

Gibson's translation of this ballad employs a verse pattern similar to that noted in the preceding poem and also reveals his usual concern for fidelity in letter and spirit. However, Lockhart's version, chosen for reproduction below, although inferior to Gibson's as far as accuracy is concerned, is unquestionably one of his best efforts and has received wide recognition.

The hosts of Don Rodrigo were scattered in dismay,
When lost was the eighth battle, nor heart nor hope had they;
He, when he saw that field was lost, and all his hope was flown,
He turned him from his flying host, and took his way alone.

His horse was bleeding, blind, and lame,—he could no farther go;
Dismounted, without path or aim, the king stepped to and fro;
It was a sight of pity to look on Roderick,
For, sore athirst and hungry, he staggered, faint and sick.

All stained and strewed with dust and blood, like to some smouldering brand
Plucked from the flame, Rodrigo showed:—his sword was in his hand,
But it was hacked into a saw of dark and purple tint;
His jewelled mail had many a flaw, his helmet many a dint.

He climbed unto a hill-top, the highest he could see,
Thence all about of that wide rout his last long look took he;
He saw his royal banners, where they lay drenched and torn,
He heard the cry of victory, the Arab's shout of scorn.

He looked for the brave captains that led the hosts of Spain,
But all were fled except the dead, and who could count the slain?
Where'er his eye could wander, all bloody was the plain,
And, while thus he said, the tears he shed run down his cheeks like rain:—

"Last night I was the King of Spain,—to-day no king am I;
Last night fair castles held my train,—to-night where shall I lie?
Last night a hundred pages did serve me on the knee,—
To-night not one I call mine own:—not one pertains to me.

"Oh, luckless, luckless was the hour, and cursed was the day,
When I was born to have the power of this great signiory!
Unhappy me, that I should see the sun go down to-night!
O Death, why now so slow art thou, why fearest thou to smite?"

A comparison of Gibson's translation with Lockhart's would reveal a similarity in both verse pattern and phraseology, indicating that Gibson, too, recognized the success achieved by his predecessor. Lockhart, although not quite as careful with the details of the original *romance,* has reproduced marvelously the spirit of the ballad. The last three stanzas of the poem are especially good, and the quatrain beginning "Last night I was the King of Spain" represents Lockhart at his best.

There is another version of the above ballad by a contemporary of Lockhart, George Moir. Somewhat freer than either Gibson's or Lockhart's rendition, it nevertheless is not a bad translation. It is arranged in quatrains of fifteen-syllable, eight-stress, trochaic lines. The most unusual feature, however, is its unchanging rhyme scheme, which the translator describes as an attempt "to imitate the effect of the continual repetition of the same rhyme."[2] Two stanzas will show the contrast it offers to the more common *aabb* patterns.

From the eighth and fatal battle, where the Moor had won the day,
Fled the hosts of Don Rodrigo, scattered round in wild dismay.—
Town and tower and royal palace soon behind him lessening lay,
When by every friend forsaken, Roderick took his lonely way.

From his weary steed dismounted, toil'd and weary where he lay,
Parched with thirst and faint with hunger, still he held his toilsome way.
Dyed from head to foot in crimson, like some brand's devouring ray,
While his soiled and bruised armour told the fortune of the fray.

Gibson has a third ballad on the theme of Rodrigo which brings this monarch's history to an end. It is based on the following rather long poem, which Menéndez Pidal terms a *romance juglaresco* from the fifteenth century.[3]

Después que el Rey Don Rodrigo
A España perdido había
Ibase desesperado
Por donde más le placía.
Métese por las montañas
Las más espesas que veía,
Porque no le hallen los moros
Que en su seguimiento iban.
Topado ha con un pastor
Que su ganado traía,
Díjole: —¿Dime, buen hombre,
Lo que preguntar quería
Es si hay por aquí poblado
O alguna casería
Donde pueda descansar,
Que gran fatiga traía?—
El pastor respondió luego
Que en balde la buscaría,
Porque en todo aquel desierto
Solo una ermita había,
Adonde está un ermitaño
Que hacía muy santa vida.
El Rey fué alegre de esto
Por allí acabar su vida.
Pidió al hombre que le diese
De comer si algo tenía:
El pastor sacó un zurrón,
Que siempre en él pan traía,
Dióle dél y de un tasajo
Que acaso allí echado había.
El pan era muy moreno,
Al Rey muy mal le sabía,
Las lágrimas se le salen,
Detener no las podía,
Acordándose en su tiempo
Los manjares que comía.
Después que hubo descansado
Por la ermita le pedía,
El pastor le enseñó luego
Por donde no erraría.

---

[2] George Moir, "Early Narrative and Lyric Poetry of Spain," *Edinburgh Review* 39 (1824): 416.

[3] Ramón Menéndez Pidal, *Flor nueva de romances viejos*, 8th ed. (Buenos Aires: Espasa-Calpe, Colección Austral, 1950), p. 58.

El Rey le dió una cadena
Y un anillo que traía:
Joyas son de gran valor
Que el Rey en mucho tenía.
Comenzando a caminar,
Cuando el sol se retraía,
A la ermita es ya llegado
Que el pastor dicho le había.
Él dando gracias a Dios
Luego de rezar se metía;
Después que hubo rezado
Para el ermitaño se iba:
Hombre es de autoridad
Que bien se le parecía.
Preguntóle el ermitaño
Como allí fué su venida;
El Rey, los ojos llorosos,
Aquesto le respondía:
—El desdichado Rodrigo
Yo soy, que Rey ser solía:
Vengo a hacer penitencia
Contigo en tu compañía;
No recibas pesadumbre
Por Dios y Santa María.—
El ermitaño se espanta,
Por consolallo decía:
—Vos cierto habéis elegido
Camino cual convenía
Para vuestra salvación,
Que Dios os perdonaría.—
El ermitaño a Dios ruega
Por si le revelaría
La penitencia que diese
Al Rey que le convenía.
Fuéle luego revelado
De parte de Dios un día,
Que le meta en una tumba
Con una culebra viva,
Y esto tome en penitencia
Por el mal que hecho había.
El ermitaño al Rey
Muy alegre se volvía,
Contóselo todo al Rey
Como pasado le había.
El Rey desto muy gozoso
Luego en obra lo ponía,
Métese como Dios manda
Para allí acabar su vida,
Y el ermitaño muy santo
Mírale al tercero día.
Dice: —¿Cómo os va, buen Rey?
¿Vaos bien con la compañía?
—Hasta ahora no me ha tocado
Porque Dios no lo quería,
Ruega por mí, el ermitaño,
Porque acabe bien mi vida.—
El ermitaño lloraba,
Gran compasión le tenía,
Comenzóle a consolar
Y esforzar cuanto podía.
Después vuelve el ermitaño
A ver si ya muerto había,
Halla que estaba rezando
Y que gemía y plañía.
Preguntóle como estaba:
—Dios es en ayuda mía,—
Respondió el buen Rey Rodrigo,
—La culebra me comía,
Cómeme ya por la parte
Que todo lo merecía,
Por donde fué el principio
De la mi muy gran desdicha.—
El ermitaño lo esfuerza,
El buen Rey allí moría.
Aquí acabó el Rey Rodrigo,
Al cielo derecho se iba.

In his translation, Gibson parallels the above throughout with one or two minor exceptions. The shepherd's words are put into direct quotations, and four of the lines following the revelation of the punishment are omitted in translation. The original is perhaps not quite as good as the first two ballads, but the translation is a very satisfactory rendition.

Soon as the King Rodrigo the crown of Spain had lost,
He travelled on despairing where'er it pleased him most;
He hied him to the mountains, the bleakest he could find,
The Moors who were pursuing he left them far behind.

A-feeding of his flocks there a shepherd he did see—
"Good man, I pray thee tell me, what I shall ask of thee;
If there be any village here, or any place of rest,
Where I can lay me down awhile, for I am sore distressed."

To this the shepherd answered: "In vain you'll seek around,
There's but a single Hermitage in all this desert ground,
There dwells a lonely hermit, who leads a life of prayer;"
The King was happy if he could but end his sad life there.

He humbly asked the shepherd, if aught to eat he had,
The shepherd from his wallet drew forth a loaf of bread,
Therewith a piece of sun-dried meat,
And gave the King to eat.

The King he scarce could touch it, the bread was very black,
The tears came downward flowing, he could not hold them back,
Remembering well the dishes sweet
That he was wont to eat.

Soon as his rest was over, he journeyed on his way,
The shepherd well directed him, lest he should go astray;
The King a chain did give, a golden ring likewise,
Most rare and precious jewels, that he was wont to prize.

The sun was beating on his head as he the road did take,
At length he reached the Hermitage of which the shepherd spake.
And first before the holy shrine he thanks to Heaven gave,
Then went to seek the Hermit, a holy man and grave.

The Hermit asked him what he sought within this desert place,
The King to him gave answer, while tears ran down his face;
"I am the wretch Rodrigo, the King that used to be,
I've come to suffer penance in company with thee.

By Heaven and blessed Mary! deny me not, I pray."
The Hermit in amazement to soothe him thus did say:
"Thow certainly hast chosen the way most sure and plain
To work out thy salvation, and Heaven's mercy gain."

The Hermit God entreated that He to light would bring
The penance he should offer most fitting for the King;

One day at length did Heaven the revelation make;
To place him in a gloomy vault, and with a living snake!

Soon as the King had heard it, nought better would he ask,
But with a light and joyful heart to set him to the task;
He went where God had ordered, to end his life of shame;
To him the holy Hermit upon the third day came:
"Good King," he said, "is't well with thee,
With thee, and with thy company?"

"As yet it hath not touched me, God wills it not to be,
That soon my wretched life may end, Hermit, entreat for me."
The Hermit wept and sorrowed, compassion in his soul,
Whate'er he could he gave him to strengthen and console.

Again the Hermit sought the vault, to see if he were dead,
But found him there absorbed in prayer with groanings loud and dread;
He questioned how it fared with him: "God sure hath heard my vow;"
Replied the King Rodrigo, "the snake doth eat me now!

It eats me in the very part, that best deserves the fate,
That was the cause of all my crime, and my misfortune great."
The Hermit stooped to succour him; he saw the good King die;
Thus ended Don Rodrigo; his soul fled to the sky.

There are also versions of the above ballad by Lockhart, Merwin, and Thomas Rodd. Lockhart's translation, like the one previously noted, is close to the Spanish in spirit and is also good poetry. The most important ideas are brought over, and although there is no attempt to parallel the model exactly, the deviations are not excessive.

One of the most notable series of *romances históricos* sprang from one of the lost Spanish epics; it concerns a hero who is probably only pseudohistorical, since many scholars believe he was created as a counterpart to the famous Roland of the *Chanson de Roland*. In any event, the history of Bernardo del Carpio was as widely known and certainly as popular as that of many another figure whose historical existence is beyond doubt. The background for the story is the eighth-century French expedition into Spain under the leadership of Charlemagne and the subsequent defeat of the army at Roncesvalles. In the Spanish version, it was Bernardo del Carpio who commanded the Spanish forces and who killed the great Roland. According to the ballads, most of which seem to be *romances eruditos* from the sixteenth century, Bernardo was the illegitimate son of a certain Don Sancho,

Count of Saldaña, and Doña Ximena, the sister of King Alfonso the Chaste. The pious king, angered at his sister's indiscretion, sent her to a convent and had the count locked up in prison. Bernardo was brought up at court and educated as a noble, but for a long time was either ignorant of his background and his father's plight or unable to do anything about it. One of the first ballads in the cycle, translated below by Caleb Cushing, describes the feelings of the count as he hears of the exploits of his son and wonders why the youth does nothing to secure his release.

Bañando está las prisiones Con lágrimas que derrama El Conde Don Sancho Díaz, Ese señor de Saldaña.	Bathing in tears his prison bars, And weeping life away, The noble Count Don Sandiaz, Saldaña's Señor, lay.
Y entre el llanto y soledad, D'esta suerte se quejaba De Don Bernardo su hijo, Del rey Alfonso y su hermana:	And thus, in solitude and wo, He mourned his hapless lot, Abandoned by his wife and King, By Don Bernardo, too, forgot.
—Los años de mi prisión Tan aborrecida y larga, Por momentos me lo dicen Aquestas mis tristes canas.	'The years that I have dragged along, 'A prisoner in this loathsome cell, 'How many and how sad they've been, 'These hairs proclaim too well.
Cuando entré en este castillo Apenas entré con barbas, Y agora por mis pecados La veo crecida y blanca.	'The down of youth was on my lips, 'When first within these walls I came; 'But now these long white locks betray 'An age of sorrow, sin, and shame.
¿Qué descuido es éste, hijo? ¿Cómo a voces no te llama La sangre que tienes mía A socorrer donde falta?	'What scorn is in thy heart, my son? 'The blood of mine, that fills thy veins, 'Should summon thee to rescue him, 'Who withers here in felon chains.
Sin duda que te detiene La que de tu madre alcanzas, Que por ser de la del Rey Juzgarás mal de mi causa.	'Or is it that thy mother's blood, 'The blood of stern Alfonso's race, 'Stifles the voice of nature thus, 'And bids thee shun thy father's face?
Todos tres sois mis contrarios. Que a un desdichado no basta Que sus contrarios lo sean, Sino sus propias entrañas.	'All, all are now Don Sancho's foes:— 'Wretch that I am! I well might pine, 'The victim of a stranger's crime; 'But not, my gallant son, of thine.

Todos los que aquí me tienen Me cuentan de tus hazañas: Si para tu padre no, Dime, ¿para quién las guardas?	'From guard and castellain I hear 'The story of thy chivalry: — 'For whom should be thy feats of arms, 'For whom, if none are wrought for [me?
Aquí estoy en estos hierros, Y pues d'ellos no me sacas, Mal padre debo de ser, O tú, mal hijo, me faltas.	'And since, to set thy father free, 'No knightly deed by thee is done, 'Or I a wicked sire must be, 'Or thou a most unworthy son.
Perdóname si te ofendo, Que descanso en las palabras, Que yo como viejo lloro, Y tú como ausente callas. —	'But thou in fields of fame afar 'Playest the valiant soldier's part: 'Forgive me, if, in age or grief, 'I wrong thy nobleness of heart.'

The majority of Cushing's translations are rather loose, the one above being perhaps somewhat more literal than the average. His favorite metrical pattern is the four- and three-stress iambic, not unlike that frequently used by Gibson.

The next important twist to the legend develops when King Alfonso, having no children of his own and not willing to recognize Bernardo as an heir, decides to invite the French king, Charlemagne, to take possession of his kingdom. Several of the ballads describe Bernardo's opposition to this move and his rallying of his countrymen to resist the invasion. The one below is typical.

Con tres mil y más leoneses
Deja la ciudad Bernardo,
Que de la perdida Iberia
Fué milagroso restauro:
Aquella cuya muralla
Guarda y dilata en dos campos
El nombre y altas victorias
De aquel famoso Pelayo.
Los labradores arrojan
De las manos los arados,
Las hoces, los azadones;
Los pastores los cayados;
Los jóvenes se alborozan,
Aliéntanse los ancianos,
Los inútiles se animan,
Fíngense fuertes los flacos,
Todos a Bernardo acuden,
Libertad apellidando,
Que el infame yugo temen
Con que los amaga el galo.
—Libres, gritaban, nacimos,
Y a nuestro Rey soberano
Pagamos lo que debemos
Por el divino mandato.
No permita Dios, ni ordene
Que a los decretos de extraños
Obliguemos nuestros hijos,
Gloria de nuestros pasados:
No están tan flacos los pechos,
Ni tan sin vigor los brazos,
Ni tan sin sangre las venas,
Que consientan tal agravio.
¿El francés ha por ventura
Esta tierra conquistado?

¿Victoria sin sangre quiere?
No, mientras tengamos manos.
Podrá decir de leoneses,
Que murieron peleando;
Pero no que se rindieron,
Que son al fin castellanos.
Si a la potencia romana
Catorce años conquistaron
Los valientes numantinos
Con tan sangrientos estragos,
¿Por qué un reino, y de leones,
Que en sangre libia bañaron
Sus encarnizadas uñas,
Escucha medios tan bajos?
Déles el Rey sus haberes,
Mas no les dé sus vasallos;
Que en someter voluntades
No tienen los reyes mando.—

Lockhart's translation of this ballad is vigorous and spirited and is another good example of his technique. The first stanza is in fifteen-syllable, eight-stress, trochaic lines, but the others illustrate his more familiar pattern of fourteen-syllable iambics. Taken as a whole, the poem is an accurate reflection of the bold and freedom-loving spirit expressed in the original.

With three thousand men of Leon, from the city Bernard goes,
To protect the soil Hispanian from the spear of Frankish foes:
From the city which is planted in the midst between the seas,
To preserve the name and glory of old Pelayo's victories.

The peasant hears upon his field the trumpet of the knight, —
He quits his team for spear and shield and garniture of might;
The shepherd hears it 'mid the mist, — he flingeth down his crook,
And rushes from the mountain like a tempest-troubled brook.

The youth who shows a maiden's chin, whose brows have ne'er been bound
The helmet's heavy ring within, gains manhood from the sound;
The hoary sire beside the fire forgets his feebleness,
Once more to feel the cap of steel a warrior's ringlets press.

As through the glen his spears did gleam, these soldiers from the hills,
They swelled his host, as mountain-stream receives the roaring rills;
They round his banner flocked, in scorn of haughty Charlemagne,
And thus upon their swords are sworn the faithful sons of Spain.

'Free were we born, 'tis thus they cry, 'though to our King we owe
The homage and the fealty behind his crest to go;
By God's behest our aid he shares, but God did ne'er command
That we should leave our children heirs of an enslaved land.

'Our breasts are not so timorous, nor are our arms so weak,
Nor are our veins so bloodless, that we our vow should break,
To sell our freedom for the fear of Prince or Paladin;
At least we'll sell our birthright dear, — no bloodless prize they'll win.

'At least King Charles, if God decrees he must be Lord of Spain,
Shall witness that the Leonese were not aroused in vain;
He shall bear witness that we died as lived our sires of old, —
Nor only of Numantium's pride shall minstrel tales be told.

'The Lion that hath bathed his paws in seas of Lybian gore,
Shall he not battle for the laws and liberties of yore?
Anointed cravens may give gold to whom it likes them well,
But steadfast heart and spirit bold, Alphonso ne'er shall sell.'

In addition to Lockhart's version above, there is an excellent translation of this ballad by Henry Wadsworth Longfellow, plus quite adequate versions by Gibson and Cushing.

Alfonso seems to have been forced to give up his plan to invite in the French, and when Roland and his troops invade anyway, the king finds it necessary to call upon Bernardo for assistance. For this and other services, Bernardo, who now knows about his father and is resolved to free him, extracts from the king a promise that the count will be released. Once the danger is past, however, the unrelenting monarch is reluctant to keep his word. The following ballad, with the translation by Oxenford, is one of several in which Bernardo is pleading for his father's liberty.

— Antes que barbas tuviese,
Rey Alfonso, me juraste
De darme a mi padre vivo,
Y nunca me das mi padre.

"Ere my beard grew, King Alfonso,
This thou vow'd'st — can'st thou forget?
Thou would'st free my noble father,
And thou hast not freed him yet.

Cuando nací de tu hermana,
Que nunca fuera mi madre,
Le metiste en la prisión,
Y aun dicen que meses antes.

"When thy sister, *not my mother,*
(Speak that word I never may)
Gave me birth, then thou confined'st him, —
Nay, 'twas months before, they say.

Acuérdate, Alfonso rey,
Ya que no dél, por mi parte,
Que es tu hermana sangre tuya,
Y que es mi padre mi sangre.

"Oh! bethink thee, King Alfonso,
Not for his sake, but for mine,
That my blood is still my father's,
That thy sister's blood is thine.

Si yerros fueron los suyos,
Bien de hierros le cargaste;
Que los que son por amor
Alcanzan perdón de balde.

"Though his trespass has been heavy,
He has suffer'd heavy chains,
And a sin, through love committed,
Ready pardon, sure, obtains.

Prometido me lo tienes,
No de tu palabra faltes,
Que no es oficio de reyes,
Que de lo dicho se extrañen.

"Bear in mind what thou hast promised,
Oh thy promise do not break,
For 'tis conduct most unkingly,
A deceitful vow to make.

A tu cargo es la justicia,
Y a mi cargo el libertarle;
Pero si yo soy mal hijo
No debo, Rey, de culparte.

"'Tis thy duty to do justice,
Mine to set my father free,
If I am a son unworthy,
King I may not censure thee.

Todos mis amigos dicen
Que soy guerrero cobarde,
Sabiendo que padre tengo,
Y que no conozco padre.

"With the scornful name of craven
By my friends I am beset,
For they know I have a father,
And I have not seen him yet.

Después que espada me ciño
La he puesto por ti en mil lances,
Y cuanto más la ejercito,
Menos mercedes me haces.

"Since my sword I girded on me,
I have used it for thine aid,
And the more has been my service,
I have been the less repaid.

Si de mi padre te extrañas,
No es justo d'ella te extrañes;
Que algún galardón merece
Quien buenos servicios hace.

"If thou hat'st my noble father,
Still be grateful to my sword,
For the man who well has served thee
Surely merits some reward.

Si en premio d'ello merezgo
El premio que el mundo sabe,
Tiempo es ya que me le dés,
Buen Rey, o me desengañes.

"If I have deserved a guerdon,
That which all the world must know,
Now 'tis time to undeceive me,
Or the guerdon to bestow."

— Calledes vos, Don Bernardo,
No temáis que yo vos falte.
Que la merced de los reyes,
Si se cumple, nunca es tarde;

"Nay, be silent, Don Bernardo,
I deceive not, be it known,
That when kings display their mercy
It can ne'er too late be shown.

Que antes que mañana oiga
Misa en San Juan de Letrane,
Veréis vuestro padre libre
De su persona y mi cárcel. —

"Mark, your sire shall quit his prison,
This, I swear shall come to pass,
Ere I go to John of Latrans
To attend to-morrow's mass."

Cumplióle el Rey la palabra,
Mas fué con engaño grande,
Porque sin ojos y muerto
Mandó que se le entregasen.

And the king fulfill'd his promise,
But 'twas done in artful wise,
For, before he freed the pris'ner
He had put out both his eyes.

There are varying accounts in the *romances* as to how Bernardo's father died (some say that he died in prison from the wounds received when his eyes were put out, others that he was released but lived only a short time), but at any rate, he was never able to see his son, and Bernardo understandably felt that he had been betrayed. He decides to leave the service of the king and renounce his loyalty to the crown. Among several ballads which describe the resultant power struggle between vassal and lord, the following, translated by Cushing, is representative.

Con solos diez de los suyos Ante el Rey, Bernardo llega, Con el sombrero en la mano Y acatada reverencia:	With only ten of his picked men, With hat in hand, with gentle word,— In guise of seeming reverence, Bernardo stands before his Lord.
Los demás, hasta trescientos, Hacia palacio enderezan De dos en dos divididos, Porque el caso no se entienda.	The rest, some good three hundred more, Divided two by two with care, That none their purpose may suspect, Straight to the palace court repair.
—Mal venido seáis, le dice, Alevoso, a mi presencia, Hijo de padres traidores. Y engendrado entre cautelas,	'False wretch,' the angry King exclaims, 'Thy presence here we welcome not, 'Base offspring of a traitor sire, 'In fraud and perfidy begot.
Que con el Carpio os alzastes Que dado os había en tenencia; Mas fiad de mi palabra, Que de vos tomaré enmienda; Aunque no haya que admirarse, Si el traidor traidor engendra. No hay que procurar disculpa, Pues ninguna tienes buena.—	'Ye held El Carpio's battlements 'Against the banner of your lord; 'But trust me, I'll repay the deed; 'I swear it by my knightly word.'
Bernardo, que atento estaba, Respondió con faz siniestra: —Mal os informaron, Rey, Y con relación mal hecha;	Bernardo, who impatient stood Fiercely responded to the King: 'They who inform Alfonso thus, 'False tidings to his hearing bring.
Que mi padre fué tan bueno, Que a la antigua estirpe vuestra En bondad no debía nada, Y esto es cosa manifiesta.	'I dare avouch with sword and lance, 'My father's old ancestral line 'Could gain, whate'er thy royal boast, 'No added purity from thine,—

Y en decir que fué traidor,
Miente quien lo dice o piensa,
De vuestra persona abajo,
Que como a Rey se os reserva.

'The name of traitor to my sire
'Whoe'er in thought or word applies,
'Prince or hidalgo, whatsoe'er
'His rank, I say the villain lies.

¡Muy bien mis grandes servicios
Con este nombre se premian!
De los cuales fuera justo
Que noticia se tuviera:
Mas es propio del ingrato;
Su propiedad, Rey, es esta,
Olvidar el beneficio,
Por negar la recompensa.

'My service you reward right well,
'Branding me with insulting terms: —
'Ungrateful lord, unworthy king,
'Who thus his plighted faith confirms.

Una os debiera obligar,
Si de otra no se os acuerda,
Cuando en la del Romeral,
En la dudosa contienda
Os mataron el caballo,
Quedando en notable afrenta:

'Bethink thee how, at Romeral,
'Thy horse was slain, thyself wast [down,
'And I rushed in to save thy life,
'At deadly peril of my own.

Y yo, como soy traidor,
Os di el mío con presteza,
Sacándoos, como sabéis,
De aquella mortal refriega.

'I dragged thee senseless from the press,
'I held the Saracens at bay,
'I placed thee on my charger's back: —
'And this the traitor's part I play.

Por ello me prometistes
Con razones halagüeñas
De darme a mi padre libre,
Sin lesión y sin ofensa.

'For which I had thy solemn pledge,
'With words of constancy full store;
'Thou wouldst in all good faith, my sire
'To freedom and to fame restore.

Pero mal vuestra palabra
Cumplistes y real promesa;
Que para ser rey, por cierto,
Tenéis muy poca firmeza,
Pues que murió en la prisión,
Cual sabéis, con pasión vuestra.

'Nobly, Lord King, thy royal word,
'Thy knightly pledge, thou hast ful- [filled,
'Since in the prison where he lay
'My father thou hast basely killed,

Mas si yo fuera el que debo,
Si el hijo que debo fuera,
Su muerte hubiera vengado
En cosas que os ofendiera.
Pero yo la vengaré,
En algunas donde entienda,
Para más os deservir,
Que notable daño os venga.

'And here stand I, Don Sancho's son,
'Defiance at thy beard to fling; —
'Here mid thy vassals, in thy hall,
'I swear to be avenged, Lord King.'

— Prendedle, prendedle, dice, Mis caballeros, y muera El loco desacatado Que mi deshonra desea. —	'Seize on the frantic wretch, my knights, 'Seize him,' Alfonso cries: 'Dares he defy me on my throne? 'The base-born caitiff-miscreant dies.
Prendedle, gritaba el Rey; Pero ninguno lo intenta, Porque vieron que Bernardo El manto al brazo rodea,	'Seize him,' still shouts the furious King: But none in all that presence stand, Who dare Bernardo's rage to brave. — Folding his cloak around his hand,
Poniendo mano a la espada, Diciendo: — Nadie se mueva, Que soy Bernardo, y mi espada	He half unsheathed his falchion's blade, And shouted: 'Touch me ye who dare; 'I am Bernardo, and to none 'Homage or fealty do I bear.
A ninguno se sujeta, Y sabéis muy bien que corta, De que tenéis experiencia. —	'My sword is mine: its point obeys 'Nor king nor conde high or low; 'And when Bernardo wields it well, 'The temper of its edge ye know.'
Los diez, visto el duro trance, A la contienda se aprestan: Meten mano a los estoques; Del hombro los mantos sueltan,	Whereat Bernardo's chosen men, Watching their time with eager eye, Put hand to sword, and flinging back Their cloaks upon their shoulder, fly
Y a los lados de Bernardo Con feroz saña se aprietan, Avisando a los demás Con una acordada seña;	Promptly to bold Bernardo's side, Marshalled in grim array. A blast upon his bugle horn Summons their fellows to the fray.
Los cuales del fuerte alcázar Toman las herradas puertas, Diciendo: — ¡Viva Bernardo, Y quien le ofendiere muera! —	They seize upon the alcazar gates; Their shouts ring loud and clear; 'Viva Bernardo,' still they cry, 'Del Carpio's valiant cavalier.'
Vista la resolución, Dijo el Rey con faz serena: — Lo que de burlas os dije, ¿Tomado lo habéis de véras?	His taunting speech and hasty threats Sorely Alfonso then did rue: With smothered rage he smiles, and says, 'Ye take my merry jests for true.'
— Burlando lo tomo, Rey, — Bernardo le respondiera; Y de la sala se sale, Haciéndole reverencia. Con él vuelven los trescientos, Con bella y gallarda muestra,	Scornfully turning on his heel, Bernardo quick and short replied, 'I give you jest for jest, Lord King, 'And sharper ones may yet betide.'

Y derribando los mantos,
Ricas armas manifiestan,
De que el Rey quedó espantado
Y su injuria con enmienda.

The enmity between King Alfonso and Bernardo lasted a long time and inspired many other intriguing stories, but the ultimate fate of this hero is not described in the *romances*. Cushing's rendition of the preceding ballad, although not outstanding, perhaps, seems quite adequate. The same comment could be made about others which he has in this series (he translated nine from the Bernardo del Carpio legend), and it seems to apply equally well to the translations of John Oxenford. Both authors are represented again in the next cycle.

The story of the Siete Infantes de Lara is almost a classic tale of insult, family feud, treachery, and vengeance, although it is based on real events. The moving details of certain of the *romances* from this group easily explain the story's popularity. It begins when the seven sons of Gonzalo Bustos (or Gustios, in some versions), the lord of Salas, attend the wedding of their mother's brother, the proud Ruy (Rodrigo) Velázquez. The opening lines of one of the old ballads, translated below by Oxenford, set the stage for what is to come later.

¡Ay Dios, qué buen caballero Fue Don Rodrigo de Lara, Que mató cinco mil moros Con trescientos que llevaba!	What a knight was Ruy Velasquez, Oh, how great was his renown, When his army of three hundred Cut five thousand Arabs down!
Si aqueste muriera entonces, ¡Qué gran fama que dejara! No matara sus sobrinos Los siete Infantes de Lara, Ni vendiera sus cabezas Al moro que las llevara.	On that day he should have perish'd, He had died without a stain, For his seven gallant nephews, He had never basely slain; And the seven heads of Lara, By the Moor had ne'er been ta'en.
Ya se trataban las bodas Con la linda Doña Lambra: Las bodas se hacen en Burgos, Las tornabodas en Salas:	Ruy Velasquez now will marry Doña Lambra, proud and fair, And the wedding is at Burgos, There is noble feasting there. When the nuptials all are ended, Then to Salas they repair.

Las bodas y tornabodas Duraron siete semanas; Las bodas fueron muy buenas, Las tornabodas muy malas.	And at Burgos and at Salas, Seven weeks in feasts were past; They began with nought but pleasure, But it changed to grief at last.

Exactly what happened at the wedding celebration is not clear, but at any rate, a quarrel developed between Ruy Velázquez's bride, Doña Lambra, and his nephews, the Siete Infantes. The high point of this part of the narrative comes when Doña Lambra instructs one of her servants to throw a blood-filled object on one of the brothers, and they retaliate by dragging the unfortunate wretch from beneath his mistress's skirts and killing him. The husband takes his wife's side in the quarrel and concocts a treacherous plan to dispose of not only the seven youths but also their father. One of the Moorish kings, Almanzor, a friend of Ruy Velázquez, is to be the agent in the affair, as explained in the following portion of another ballad translated by Oxenford.

Ruy Velázquez el de Lara Gran maldad obrado había, Que al bueno Gonzalo Gustios Para Córdoba lo envía Para que luego lo mate Almanzor, que ahí residía.	Ruy Velasquez, he of Lara, On an evil work is bent; For the good Gonzalo Bustos He to Cordova has sent; That Almanzor there may kill him, — 'Tis a villanous intent!
A los Infantes de Lara, Hijos dél, que no debía, Con palabras engañosas Gran engaño les hacía.	And the seven sons of Lara, Though his kin he has betray'd, And his language was deceitful, When with honied words he said:
Díjoles: — Los mis sobrinos, Mientras mi hermano volvía, Quiero hacer una entrada Hasta Almenar, esa villa.	"Ere my brother, dearest nephews, From the Moorish king comes back; Yonder city of Almenar, 'Tis my purpose to attack.
Si vos habedes por bien De ir en mi compañía Habré gran placer convusco; Y si en placer no os venía Quedad a guardar la tierra, Que solo por mí lo haría. —	"In this gallant expedition, If you wish to join, ye may, For your presence would delight me. If you choose to answer 'Nay,' I will lead it unassisted, While to guard the land you stay."
Los Infantes respondieron Que todos con él irían,	Then the seven Infants answer'd, They would gladly with him go,

Y que yendo él contra moros Bien guisado non sería Quedar ellos en la tierra Y él aventurar su vida.	And that if at home they tarried, While he march'd against the foe, And expos'd his life to danger, 'Twould a craven spirit show.

The uncle leads the sons of Gonzalo Bustos into a trap prearranged with the Moorish monarch, and all seven are quickly captured and beheaded. For some reason, though, Almanzor decides only to imprison Bustos, rather than kill him. This cannot be interpreted completely as an act of kindness, however, since he engages in an exquisitely refined bit of torture by asking the old man to identify the heads of seven Spanish soldiers killed in a recent battle. He has heard, he says, that the men were from the same general locality as Bustos. The scene in which the unsuspecting father finally realizes the extent of his loss as he takes up the seven heads, one by one, and identifies them to his grief, is certainly one of the most dramatic and moving episodes in Spanish literature. Although there are many *romances* which describe it, none, to my knowledge, exists in a good English translation. However, one which tells of Bustos's reaction as he begins to recover from the initial shock has been rendered by Caleb Cushing. It begins as Bustos speaks directly to Almanzor to reproach him for his cruelty.

—¡No se puede llamar Rey Quien usa tal villanía! Le dice Gonzalo Bustos Al rey Almanzor un día, Que habiéndome convidado Y héchome gran cortesía, Como mi sangre merece, Me des por sobrecomida La cosa mas dolorosa Que jamas dado se había,	'Nor king nor cavalier art thou, To do a deed so black and base, As place these gory ghastly heads In sport before Gonzalo's face.
Mostrándome las cabezas De siete hijos que tenía, Más obedientes a un padre Que jamás visto se habían, Defensa de los cristianos, Destruición de la morisma.	Oh, never sire had nobler sons Than they, whose trunkless heads I [feel,— The kindest, truest, purest hearts, The bravest champions of Castile.
Por traición, rey Almanzor, Debió de ser tal desdicha;	But well I know some treacherous wile, Has trained them to thy cruel hands:

Que tú no fueras bastante,
Ni toda tu compañía,
Si vinieran aplazados
A batalla conocida,
A traerlos d'este modo
Que ante mis ojos los vía,
Pues de éste, menor de todos,
En una batalla un día
Te vi yo, rey Almanzor,
Alejarte a más porfía
Que quisiera tu caballo,
Que volara aunque corría,
Y llevar armas más dobles,
Mil moros en compañía.
El no había veinte y un años,
Y las armas las traía
Por mil partes hechas piezas
Desmallada la loriga,
El yelmo todo abollado
De golpes que en él tenía,
Deseoso de alcanzarte
Por probar tu valentía;
Tu caballo era mejor
Que el que el Infante traía,
Y por eso te libraste
De no morir aquel día.

... ...
Acabada esta razón
A sus hijos se volvía,
Sin poder disimular
El gran dolor que sentía.
Limpia las siete cabezas
Que a la mesa le servían,
Las limpia y besa mil veces,
Y besándolas decía:
—No lloro yo vuestra muerte,
Pues se puede llamar vida,
Entendiendo la vengastes
Como el caso lo pedía;
Pero siempre queda pena,
Que la congoja la aviva,
En ver que fuese a traición
Y usando de villanía:

In challenged fight and equal field,
Nor thou, nor all thy Moorish bands,

Could conquer these my gallant sons:
I've seen thyself forsake the fight,
When young Gonzalez sought thee out, —
Gaining thy safety but in fight.

And this the famed Almansor's faith! —
My sons, in ambush ta'en, he slays,
And me, a Christian knight, he brings
In guise of courtesy, to gaze

In anguish on their bleeding brows.' —
'Twas thus to King Almansor's head,
Reckless of danger, bonds, or death,
His grief Gonzalo Bustos said.

Then turning to the gory heads,
He kissed and kissed them o'er and
[o'er: —
'I weep not for your death,' he cried,
'Since death is life forevermore.

Vengeance, I doubt not, on your foes,
Vengeance ye wreaked full deep and
[well,
Ere yielding, not to skill or strength,
But only multitudes, ye fell.

¡Hijos míos! ¡quien se hallara
En batalla tan esquiva,
Siquiera para poder
Socorrer la mayor prisa!
Muriera donde vosotros
Y si quedara con vida
Fuera por mal de Almanzor,
Como otras veces solía. —

I mourn for this, and this alone
That old Gonzalo was not there,
To sell his life as dearly too,
And with his gallant sons to dare

Estas palabras diciendo
Para un moro arremetía,
Y quitándole un alfanje,
A él, y a otros que allí había,

A hundred Moorish foes to fight:' —
And snatching, as he spoke, a sword,
From out the nearest soldier's hand,
Suiting the action to the word,

Les dio tan pesados golpes,
Que nadie se defendía
Que no quedase a sus pies,
Y el que se libraba huía;

He struck the helpless guardsman down, —
He rushed th' affrighted Moors [among, —
He cut and slew in reckless rage, —
The hall with blows and shoutings [rung, —

Y de los que le aguardaron,
Con sus hijos trece envía.
Almanzor le está mirando
Y con ruegos le decía:

Until, o'erpowered amid them all,
And spent with fury, he gave o'er;
While, seamed with gaping wounds of [death,
Lay at his feet full many a Moor.

— Aplaca, Gonzalo Bustos,
Aplaca tu grande ira,
Que me pesa haberte dado
Tal postre en esta comida,
Que aunque los Infantes eran
Destruición de mi morisma,
Si los pudiera tornar
De muertos a dar la vida,
Por ver su florida edad
Y su esfuerzo en demasía,
Lo hiciera, Gonzalo Bustos,
Aunque es cosa conocida
Que si tuvieran vida ellos
Presto quitaran la mía:

'Hold! hold! — Almansor cried: 'sir [knight,
I do repent me that I brought
These bleeding tokens of thy loss
Before thine eyes, in boastful thought.

I would, though well I know the hate
They felt for aught of Moorish name,
I would thy seven brave sons remained
Alive, for thee, for hope, for fame.

Pero por satisfacción
De tu razón conocida

It may not be; — but thou art free
To seek once more thy northern home,

Yo te concedo licencia
Para que hoy en este día,
O cada y cuando que quieras
Te puedas ir a Castilla,
Y llevar estas cabezas,
Si te place, en compañía.

And bear these relics of thy race
To place them in a Christian tomb.'

The translation is extremely loose and not one of Cushing's better efforts (much of the original is left out completely), but it transcribes fairly accurately the principal ideas. The Moorish king did seem to have repented somewhat of his past actions, since he eventually gave Bustos his freedom and allowed him to return home. Even before he was released, he was apparently allowed a good bit of liberty, since he managed to win the love of a Moorish lady who subsequently gave birth to his child. She promised that if the child were a boy she would give him a good education, tell him the story of his background, and eventually send him to his father. She kept her word, and the second part of the legend describes how the boy, whose name was Mudarra, sought revenge for the deaths of his half-brothers before going to join his father. The encounter between Mudarra and Ruy Velázquez, who had heard that he was being sought, is related in a ballad that has been translated by Gibson, Lockhart, Oxenford, and W. J. Entwistle. Gibson's version appears below with the original, a *romance tradicional.*

A cazar va Don Rodrigo,
Y aun Don Rodrigo de Lara:
Con la gran siesta que hace
Arrimádose ha a una haya,
Maldiciendo a Mudarrillo,
Hijo de la renegada,
Que si a las manos le hubiese,
Jura de sacarle el alma.

A-Hunting went the noble knight,
And Don Rodrigo he was hight,
Rodrigo, he of Lara;
The noonday heat was very great,
Beneath a shady beech he sate,
And cursed the young Mudarra;
"Thou son of Moorish maid," quoth he,
"If I should lay my hands on thee,
Thou bastard of a cursed race,
I'd tear thy heart from out its place."

El señor estando en esto
Mudarrillo que asomaba:
— Dios te salve, caballero;
Debajo la verde haya.
— Así haga a ti, escudero;
Buena sea tu llegada.
— Dígasme tú, el caballero,

Thus spoke the lordling in his pride;
A stranger youth came to his side,
And due obeisance made;
"Sir Knight, God's blessing rest on thee,
Beneath the green and shady tree;"
The Knight he bowed, and said:
"Good Squire, thy coming it is blest,

¿Cómo era la tu gracia?

Pray sit thee down awhile and rest!"
"Nay, good Sir Knight, before I go,
Thine honoured name I fain would [know."

—A mí dicen Don Rodrigo,
Y aun Don Rodrigo de Lara,
Cuñado de Gonzalo Bustos,
Hermano de Doña Sancha;
Por sobrinos me los hube
Los siete infantes de Lara.
Espero aquí a Mudarrillo
Hijo de la renegada;
Si delante lo tuviese
Yo le sacaría el alma.

Then up and spake the Knight of fame:
"'Tis Don Rodrigo is my name,
  Rodrigo, I of Lara;
My sister, Lady Sancha fair,
Wedded Gonzalo, Lara's heir;
My nephews were the youthful band,
Whose fate is known through all the [land,
  The seven sons of Lara;
I wait Mudarra in this glade,
Son of the cursed Moorish maid,
If he were now before my sight,
I'd tear his heart out to the light."

—Si a ti dicen Don Rodrigo,
Y aun Don Rodrigo de Lara,
A mí Mudarra González,
Hijo de la renegada,
De Gonzalo Bustos hijo,
Y alnado de Doña Sancha:
Por hermanos me los hube
Los siete infantes de Lara:
Tú los vendistes, traidor,
En el val de Arabiana;
Mas si Dios a mí me ayuda
Aquí dejarás el alma.

"If thou hast come from Lara's stem,
And Don Rodrigo is thy name,
  Then I'm the young Mudarra;
Born of the Moorish renegade,
Gonzalo's son by Moorish maid;
I am the Lady Sancha's heir,
And these, they were my brothers fair,
  The seven sons of Lara;
Their lives, O traitor, thou did'st sell,
In dark Arabiana's dell,
May God above be in my aid,
And I will lay thee with the dead!"

—Espérame, Don Gonzalo,
Iré a tomar las mis armas.
—El espera que tú diste
A los infantes de Lara:
Aquí morirás, traidor,
Enemigo de Doña Sancha.

"Wait here a space within this field,
Till I shall bring my sword and shield,
  I'll fight with thee, Mudarra!"
"The space thou gavest *them,* I'll give,
One moment more thou hast to live;
Go, traitor, to thy doom below,
My father's curse and Sancha's foe!"
  Struck home the young Mudarra.

This translation presents another standard ballad meter found infrequently in Gibson's work, although as is evidenced above, he uses it with notable success. This is the four-stress, iambic line, usually of eight syllables. It is generally found in quatrains, but Gibson chose here to use five longer stanzas of from eight to twelve lines, varying the meter and the rhythm with two three-stress lines placed at regular intervals in each stanza. The meter bears little resemblance to the original, but the spirit and ideas of the Spanish are faithfully reproduced even though the translation is somewhat freer than is customary with Gibson. Still, the alterations are minor, and this ballad may be justly regarded as one of his best.

The story of the *Siete Infantes* is concluded when Mudarra seeks out his aging father to bring him the proof that he is avenged. Another translation by Oxenford is placed with the original.

Después que Gonzalo Bustos
Dejó el cordobés palacio,
Y en Salas guardaba el suyo;
Entre duros simulacros

Fatigaba su memoria,
Culpaba su inútil brazo
Por los efectos del tiempo,
Archivo de sus agravios.

— ¡Oh tronco, dice, sin fruto!
Solo has quedado en el campo
Do el villano codicioso
Podó tus pimpollos caros:

¡Yo te conocí con siete
Con que fuiste un tiempo ufano,
Y ahora te contentaras
Con el más endeble y flaco!

Cada momento, mis fijos,
De nuevo os pierdo, y os hallo,
Para gozaros ausentes,
En mi mente degollados.

Fresca está la sangre en ella,
Que el traidor, que fizo el daño,
Con su presencia atormenta
La poca que en mí ha quedado.

De merced vivo con él,
Y por momentos aguardo
Cuando querrá derramarla
Si no es, por vengarse, humano.

When from Cordova to Salas
Don Gonzalo came at last,
He dwelt sadly in his palace,
'Mid the relics of the past.

In his mem'ry all his sorrows
As a mighty weight he bears,
And he blames his arm as useless —
It has lost its force by years.

"Ah, thou tree so bare and fruitless,
On the plain thou stand'st alone,
For an avaricious traitor
Lopp'd thy branches ev'ry one.

"Once in sev'n good sons rejoicing,
Now of all thou art bereft;
Yes, thou now would'st be too happy,
If the feeblest one were left.

"Ev'ry hour again I lose you,
And whene'er I try to find
Your dear forms, as headless spectres
Ye are present to my mind.

"Oh, the blood shed by the traitor,
Ever fresh to me remains;
And he tortures by his presence
That which lingers in my veins.

"I expect, too, ev'ry moment
That the last drop he will spill;
For revenge, perchance, he spares me,
Since 'twere kindness sure to kill.

¡Ay miserable dél solo,
Y más cuando el hado avaro
Viene a hacer de sus causas
Juez a su cruel contrario!

¡Mejor estaba entre moros,
Fijos, que en el suelo patrio,
Que entre ellos hallé piedad
Y quien se movió a mi llanto! —

Estas quejas esparcía
Desde un mirador Gonzalo,
Regando sus blancas canas,
Recostado en un escaño,

Cuando tendiendo la vista
Por el espacioso campo
Vió en un caballo andaluz
Venir un moro gallardo,

Jóven, hermoso y dispuesto,
De rostro agradable, manso,
Grave, compuesto, gracioso,
Apacible y despejado.

En la adarga media luna
Trae puesta en un cielo claro,
Y una roja "F" en medio
Con un letrero dorado,

Que dice: "A buscarte voy:
¡Venturoso si te alcanzo!"
En la lanza un pendoncillo
Con cruz verde en campo blanco,

Y una cabeza pendiente
En el pretal del caballo,
Destilando fresca sangre
Entre el cabello erizado.

Llegó, y bajando la suya,
El arzón casi besando,
Con el cuento de la lanza
Sobre la yerba afirmado,

Dijo: — Tú debes ser,
Según las señas que traigo,

"Oh, this solitude is wretched,
And a grievous cause is that
When the enemy who wrongs us
Is the judge assign'd by fate.

"Rather in the Moorish country
Would I live, my sons, than here;
There, at least, was one to pity —
There was one to shed a tear."

In the balcony Gonzalo
Thus his woes is mourning yet,
On a lowly bench reclining
Till his beard with tears is wet.

When by chance his sight extending
O'er the plain that lies before,
On an Andalusian courser,
He perceives a gallant Moor.

He is young — of noble stature —
Full of dignity and grace;
There's a mingled air of earnest
And of mildness in his face.

On his shield a shining crescent
In a clear blue sky appears,
In the midst an "F" in crimson,
And a motto, too, he bears, —

Writ in gold, "I try to seek thee,
If I find thee, what delight!"
From his lance there hangs a pennant,
A green cross in field of white.

On the breast-plate of his courser
A suspended head he bore,
From the locks of hair dishevell'd
There were falling drops of gore.

As he came, his lance he planted
In the grass, and bow'd so low
In saluting Don Gonzalo,
He near kiss'd the saddle-bow.

And he said, "From signs I carry,
I conclude that thou must be

El noble señor de Salas,
Que el ser que tengo me ha dado.

That most noble lord of Salas
Who has given life to me.

Recibe de Ruy Velázquez,
Vendedor de mis hermanos,
Esta prenda, que el traidor
Nunca reposa a su salvo.

"Here's the head of Ruy Velasquez,
Oh, my off'ring pray receive!
See, the wretch that sold my brothers
Could in safety never live!

Yo soy Mudarra, señor,
Y ha mucho tiempo que afano
Por hacer esta sangría
En tu tronco antiguo y claro.—

"Know, my lord, I am Mudarra,
And I labour'd long indeed
Ere the trunk of your old lineage
In this fashion I could bleed."

Grandes voces daba el viejo:
—Sube, hijo, y da a mis brazos
Lo que tanto ha deseaban,
Que hoy se acaban mis trabajos.

Then the old man shouted gladly:
"Come, embrace me, noble son;
Now my wishes all are granted,
And my sorrows all are gone."

Oxenford has a note to the above ballad explaining that it is believed that the letter "F" stood for "fijo," the old word for son, signifying that Mudarra, as a son, had a responsibility to avenge his father.[4] The translation itself is quite regular.

Although few of the historical ballad cycles are represented as extensively in translation as the ones just reviewed, there are many aspects of Spanish history illustrated by scattered or occasional renditions of *romances* in English. The better known or more colorful kings have been favorite subjects; ballads about three of them will be included here. Oxenford, for example, has three translations of ballads concerning Alfonso X of Castile, who was known as "The Learned" and who was much celebrated for his great erudition and for the impetus which he gave to the development of Spanish literature. He was less successful as a ruler, however, a fact which may be explained in part by a tendency to let his generosity and good nature override his judgment. This would seem to be one interpretation of the following poem.

De la gran Constantinopla
Su Emperatriz se partía:
A Burgos había llegado
Do está el buen rey de Castilla

Great Constantinople's empress
Has departed from her home,
And to see good King Alfonso,
Now to Burgos she has come,—

[4] *New Monthly Magazine* 76 (1846): 384.

Don Alfonso era llamado,
Hijo del rey que a Sevilla
Conquistó como valiente
Con toda el Andalucía.

Treinta dueñas trae consigo;
Todas de negro vestían:
El Rey y otros caballeros
Salieron a recibilla.

Hízole toda la honra
Que a su estado convenía,
Llevárala a su palacio
A do la Reina vivía.

Mucho le plugo a la Reina,
Con ella placer había;
La mesa mandó poner,
Y la Reina la convida.

Respondió la Emperatriz
Que a mesa no comería:
La Reina pidió la causa,
Ella luego respondía:

— Tú, Reina, estás en tu honra,
Y ésta a mí me fallecía;
Tú estás con el tu marido,
Yo triste no lo tenía;

El tuyo está en libertad,
El mío preso yacía;
Ausente de la su tierra
El Soldán me lo tenía.

Quintales cincuenta en plata
Por su rescate pedía,
El Papa me diera el tercio
Que demandado le había,

Otro tanto el rey de Francia
A mí me lo concedía.
Nuevas me dieron del Rey
Que por marido tú habías,
Loaron la gran nobleza
Y la bondad que tenía.

King Alfonso, whose brave father,
Was the hero of Castile,
For he took Andalusia,
With the city of Seville.

Thirty dames are with the empress,
All in sable garments dight;
King Alfonso goes to meet her,
In his train is many a knight.

Every tribute of high honour
Which her rank may claim he gives;
And he takes her to the palace,
Where the queen, his consort lives.

The arrival of the empress,
The Castilian queen delights,
And she bids them spread the tables,
And her royal guest invites.

"Nay, I eat not," said the empress,
"Where a festal board is spread."
Then the queen inquired the reason,
And the empress to her said:

"Thou art living, queen, in honour,
But no honour now is mine;
I am mourning for my husband,
Thou art living still with thine.

"Yes, thy husband has his freedom,
In a dungeon mine is cast;
He is absent from his country,
For the Soldan holds him fast.

"Fifty quintals weigh'd in silver,
For his liberty he claims,
And the pope a third will give me
Of the ransom which he names.

"And the King of France has granted
To my pray'rs another third;
Now they tell me of thy husband,
Of his goodness I have heard.

Véngole a pedir socorro
Como a Rey de gran valía
Para librar mi marido

"So I come to crave his succour,
Sure so good a king as he,
From the anguish which he suffers,
Will my wretched husband free, —

De la crecida fatiga
Que padece en captiverio
Como contado te había,
Y hasta que haya la respuesta
A mesa no comería. —

"From the pris'n, where, as I told you,
He is now condemn'd to sigh;
And I may not eat at table
Till I know the king's reply."

La Reina lo dijo al Rey,
Y el buen Rey le prometía
Por su fe y real corona
De cumplir lo que pedía,

Then the queen to good Alfonso
Made the lady's wishes known,
And he vow'd that he would aid her
By his faith and royal crown.

Y que comiese a manteles
Porque él lo proveería.
Entonces la Emperatriz
En los manteles comía
A la mesa de la Reina
Con gran placer y alegría,

And he bade her without scruple,
At the table take a seat;
By the queen then sat the empress,
And her happiness was great.

Y aquese buen rey Alfonso
Dende al veinteno día
Toda la suma de plata
Le diera que prometía,

Now the good king, Don Alfonso,
When some twenty days had fled,
Gave the whole amount of silver,
To the empress, as he said.

Con que al Papa y rey de Francia
Diese lo que recibía.
Con este haber fuera libre
El que captivo yacía.

All the money France had lent her,
And the pope, she might repay,
And redeem her captive husband
From the dungeon where he lay.

Publica el Emperador
La bondad que el Rey tenía
Juntamente la franqueza
Y valor que en él había;
Sonando por todo el mundo
La fama que dél corría.

When the emperor left his prison,
All this kindness he made known,
And the goodness of Alfonso,
Was to ev'ry nation shown.

Muriera el rey de Alemaña
Cuando aquesto acaecía,
Y en concordia al rey Alfonso
Para su rey lo elegían,
Porque era merecedor
D'esto y de mayor valía.

So the German people chose him
To succeed their king, who died;
For he well deserv'd the honour,
And a greater boon beside.

The other two translations by Oxenford on this theme relate some of the difficulties King Alfonso had with the Spanish peers and with his rebellious second son, Don Sancho. The handsome gift to the empress described in the above ballad seems to have been one of the factors underlying the noble king's troubles.

A second monarch who inspired many songs and legends and who is amply dealt with in the *Romancero* is Don Pedro el Cruel, king of Castile in the fourteenth century. Two of the more dramatic episodes which marked the violent reign of this ruler concern the murder of his French-born queen, Doña Blanca de Borbón, and his own death later at the hands of his brother, Don Enrique. There are a good many translations from this cycle by Lockhart and others, but the sampling here will be confined to two ballads, each based on one of these incidents. The first, translated by Gibson, has the king addressing his mistress, Doña María Padilla, whose jealousy of the queen was apparently the motivating force behind the assassination. Her jealousy was unwarranted, since the king had married for political reasons and had neither love nor regard for his wife. In general, the ballad is considered to be historically correct.

— Doña María Padilla,
N'os mostréis tan triste vos,
Que si me casé dos veces
Hícelo por vuestra pro,
Y por hacer menosprecio
A esa Blanca de Borbón,

"Lady Mary of Padilla!
Gloom not with thine eyes at me;
Though I wedded two times over,
'Twas alone for love of thee;
And my bitter hate to launch
At the Bourbon Lady Blanche.

Que a Medinasidonia envío
A que me labre un pendón.
Será el color de su sangre,
De lágrimas la labor.
Tal pendón, Doña María,
Yo lo haré hacer para vos.—

I will bid them at Medina
Weave for me a banner good,
With her burning tears bespangled,
Purpled over with her blood;
And this banner wrought for me,
Lady, 'tis a gift for thee."

Llamó luego a Iñigo Ortiz,
Un excelente varón:
Díjole fuese a Medina
A dar fin a tal labor.

Quick he called Alonso Ortiz,
He, a baron bold and true:
"Hie thee straightway to Medina,
End the work I bade thee do."

Respondiera Iñigo Ortiz:
— Aqueso no lo haré yo,
Que quien mata a su señora
Face aleve a su señor.—

Boldly spake Alonso Ortiz;
"Far from me be such a thing;
He who slays his royal Lady
Is a traitor to his King."

El Rey d'aquesto enojado A su cámara se entró, Y a un ballestero de maza El Rey su ordenanza dió.	Wild with fury rose the Monarch, Forth into the hall he went, And a fierce and trusty bowman On the deadly errand sent.
Aqueste vino a la Reina Y hallóla en oración. Cuando vido al ballestero La su triste muerte vió.	When the Queen's abode he entered, There she knelt alone in prayer; As her sad eyes met the bowman's Quick she saw that death was there:
Aquél le dijo: — Señora, El Rey acá me envió A que ordenéis vuestra alma Con aquel que la crió, Que vuestra hora es llegada, No puedo alargalla yo.	"Thy last hour has come, my Lady, 'Tis my royal lord's command; Make thy peace at once with Heaven, For I cannot stay my hand."
— Amigo, dijo la Reina, Mi muerte os perdono yo: Si el Rey mi señor lo manda, Hágase lo que ordenó. Confesión no se me niegue, Porque pida a Dios perdón. —	"Friend," replied the royal lady, "This my death I pardon thee; If the King hath so commanded, Do thy deadly work on me!"
Con lágrimas y gemidos Al macero enterneció, Y con voz flaca, temblando, Esto a decir comenzó:	Then her eyes she raised to Heaven, And to God for mercy prayed; And the bowman's heart it trembled With the melting words she said:
— ¡Oh Francia, mi noble tierra! ¡Oh mi sangre de Borbón! Hoy cumplo dezisiete años Y en los deziocho voy:	"France, O France, my lovely country! O my Bourbon blood and name! Seventeen birthdays have I witnessed, And to-day the eighteenth came.
El Rey no me ha conocido, Con las vírgenes me voy. Castilla, di, ¿qué te hice? Yo no te hice traición.	Never has my husband known me, Virgin am I, pure and whole; Castile! What have I done thee? There's no treason in my soul!
Las coronas que me diste De sangre y suspiros son; Mas otra terné en el cielo, Que será de más valor. —	Heavy was the crown thou gavest, Stained with blood and many a tear; But I'll wear a crown in Heaven, Better far than any here!"
Y dichas estas palabras El macero la hirió: Los sesos de su cabeza Por la sala los sembró.	Thus she knelt, and thus she uttered, And to Heaven for mercy cried; With his mace the bowman struck her, And the noble lady died.

There is another version of this ballad beginning "Doña María de Padilla," which is very similar to the above. Gibson had access to both copies when he made his translation, as is indicated by the reference to "Alonso Ortiz" and the phrase "for love of thee," both of which appear in the second version. Most of the translation is very literal with the greatest deviation from the text coming in the last stanza. An exact rendering of the last two lines of the Spanish — as crudely dramatic and expressive as they are — would not only have been a breach of good taste, but would have destroyed the sentiment and pathos developed by Lady Blanca's final speech. Gibson gives another proof of his poetic versatility in this translation with his switch from an iambic to a trochaic meter. The syllable count is eight and seven, with four stresses to each line. The rhythm is just as smooth and easy as in his iambic verses, and he appears equally at home with either type. The arrangement of stanzas at the beginning parallels to some extent the turns in the narrative, with the concluding couplets used in the speech to Lady Mary being abandoned as the king turns to carry out his promise.

Other bloody excesses on the part of King Pedro, many against members of his own family, alienated a large portion of his people who might otherwise have admired him for his reputed dauntless courage and strength of character. A natural brother, Enrique, who earlier had been exiled by Pedro, was able to take advantage of this sentiment and after several attempts was finally able to defeat and capture the king. According to one account, their first face-to-face encounter ended in an exchange of insults and, finally, the deadly struggle described below. The ballad was translated by Sir Walter Scott and included among those published by Lockhart.

Los fieros cuerpos revueltos	Henry and King Pedro clasping,
Entre los robustos brazos	Hold in straining arms each other;
Están el cruel Don Pedro	Tugging hard, and closely grasping,
Y Don Enrique su hermano.	Brother proves his strength with brother.
No son abrazos de amor	Harmless pastime, sport fraternal,
Los que los dos se están dando,	Blends not thus their limbs in strife;
Que el uno tiene una daga	Either aims, with rage infernal,
Y otro un puñal acerado.	Naked dagger, sharpened knife.

El Rey tiene a Enrique estrecho
Y Enrique al Rey apretado,
Uno en cólera encendido
Y otro de rabia abrasado:

Y en aquesta fiera lucha
Solo un testigo se ha hallado,
Paje de espada de Enrique
Que de afuera mira el caso.

Después de luchar vencidos
¡Oh suceso desgraciado!
Que ambos vinieron al suelo,
Y Enrique cayó debajo.

Viendo el paje a su señor
En tan peligroso caso,
Por detrás al Rey se allega,
Reciamente de él tirando,

Diciendo: —No quito Rey
Ni pongo Rey de mi mano,
Pero hago lo que debo
Al oficio de criado.—

Y dió con el Rey de espaldas
Y Enrique vino a lo alto,
Hiriendo con un puñal
En el pecho del Rey falso,

Donde a vueltas de la sangre,
El vital hilo cortando,
Salió el alma más cruel
Que vivió en pecho cristiano.

Close Don Henry grapples Pedro,
  Pedro holds Don Henry strait,
Breathing, this, triumphant fury,
  That, despair and mortal hate.

Sole spectator of the struggle,
  Stands Don Henry's page afar,
In the chase who bore his bugle,
  And who bore his sword in war.

Down they go in deadly wrestle,
  Down upon the earth they go,
Fierce King Pedro has the vantage,
  Stout Don Henry falls below.

Marking then the fatal crisis,
  Up the page of Henry ran,
By the waist he caught Don Pedro,
  Aiding thus the fallen man.

"King to place, or to depose him,
  Dwelleth not in my desire,
But the duty which he owes him,
  To his master pays the squire."—

Now Don Henry has the upmost,
  Now King Pedro lies beneath,
In his heart his brother's poniard
  Instant finds its bloody sheath.

Thus with mortal gasp and quiver,
  While the blood in bubbles welled,
Fled the fiercest soul that ever
  In a Christian bosom dwelled.

Scott's translation is another example of the use of a standard four-stress trochaic line as the basic meter. Although not a perfect transcription, it is a sufficiently literal and satisfying version of the original.

The last translation among the *romances históricos* to be considered here has been widely acclaimed. One of the two ballads rendered by John Hookham Frere, it describes the sentiments of King Alfonso V, of Aragon, as he surveys the city of Naples and contemplates the results of fifteenth-century Spanish imperialism in Italy. The original is very old.

Miraba de Campoviejo
El rey de Aragón un día,
Miraba la mar de España
Cómo menguaba y crecía;

Miraba naos y galeras,
Que unas van y otras venían:
Unas venían armadas,
Otras con mercaduría;

Unas van la vía de Flandes,
Otras las de Lombardía.
Esas que venían de guerra
¡Oh cuán bien que parecían!

Miraba la gran ciudad
Que Nápoles se decía;
Miraba los tres castillos
Que la gran ciudad tenía:

Castelnovo y Capitana,
San Telmo, que relucía;
Aquese relumbra entre ellos
Como el sol a mediodía.

Lloraba de los sus ojos,
De la su boca decía:
— ¡Oh ciudad, cuánto me cuestas
Por la gran desdicha mía!

Cuéstasme duques y condes,
Hombres de muy gran valía;
Cuéstasme un tal hermano,
Que por hijo le tenía;

D'esotra parte menuda
Cuento ni par no tenía;

Cuéstasme ventidós años,
Los mejores de mi vida;
Que en ti me nacieron barbas,
Y en ti las encanecía.

The King of Aragon look'd down
From Campo Viejo, where he stood,
And he beheld the Sea of Spain,
Both the ebb-tide and the flood.

He saw the galleys and the ships —
How some set sail and others enter;
Some were sailing on a cruise,
And others on a merchant's venture.

Some were sailing to Lombardy,
And some to Flanders, far away:
And, oh, how bright were the ships of
[war,
With swelling sails and streamers gay!

He saw the city that spread below —
Royal Naples, that noble town!
And the three castles, how they stood,
On the great city looking down:

The new castle and the Capuan,
And St. Elmo, far the best —
Like the sun at the noon-day,
It shone so bright above the rest.

The King stood silent for a while,
He gazed and wept at his own
[thought —
"Oh, Naples, thou'rt a princely purchase,
But thou hast been dearly bought!

Many brave and loyal captains
You had cost, ere you were won;
Besides a dear and valiant brother,
Whom I grieved for like a son, —

Knights and gallant gentlemen,
Whose like I ne'er shall see again,
Of soldiers and of other subjects,
Many, many thousands slain;

Two-and-twenty years you cost me,
The best of my life that are pass'd
[away;
For here this beard began to grow,
And here it has been turn'd to grey."

Frere's poem is based on the quite common four-stress iambic line with variations. It is a masterly reproduction of the ideas and emotion expressed in the *romance,* and one questions whether any improvement would be possible.

Many other stories from Spanish history could be told through judicious selection and positioning of certain related ballads, and several of the English translators have chosen their originals with this thought in mind. There is some evidence that Gibson had intended to develop other themes more fully than he actually did, and one is sorry that he did not live to finish the task. For the most part, however, the reader of English is forced to search among translations of uneven quality by sundry authors for the details needed to trace a complete picture of countless intriguing historical and legendary figures. In most instances, fortunately, he will be well rewarded for his efforts and will gain a fascinating perspective of history unlike that available through any other source.

CHAPTER III

MOORISH BALLADS

THE MOORISH BALLADS FORM A LARGE AND FASCINATING CLASS which includes some types similar to those already studied and others with characteristics peculiar to themselves. This seeming ambiguity is explained by the difficulties resulting from the attempts to classify and categorize the many different kinds of poems found in the *Romancero* and by my decision to treat in one section all ballad types in which the Moors have a key role. In general, there are two principal kinds. The *romances fronterizos,* based on events connected with the *frontera* or border between Moors and Christians, have much in common with the *romances históricos* and in many collections will be placed among the historical ballads. Some of these, especially those relating to the Spanish efforts to recapture Granada, may be a specialized type of *noticiero* or "news-bearing" ballad, composed shortly after the events described in them and popularized, perhaps, for their propaganda effect. The *romances moriscos,* on the other hand, are definitely a product of the postwar period, when the Spanish imagination, kindled by the richness and luxury of the Moorish civilization, sought to recreate the fancied exotic life and manners of the Moslem inhabitants of the South. The romantic outlook and the conscious artistic effort evident in these ballads put them in the category of *romances artísticos* or *artificiosos,* although this fact in no way diminishes their interest. Numerous examples of both types will be found in the translations studied in this chapter. The one reproduced below obviously belongs to the first group. It describes a female reaction to the maiden tribute being exacted of the Christians by one of the Moorish kings during one stage of the Moslem occupation. The original reads as follows:

En consulta estaba un día
Con sus grandes y consejo
El noble rey Don Ramiro
Varias cosas discurriendo,
Cuando sin pedir licencia
Se entró por la sala adentro
Una gallarda doncella
De amable y hermoso gesto.
Vestida toda de blanco,
A quien el rubio cabello
Bordaba de oro los hombros,
A causa de venir suelto.
Ponen los ojos en ella,
Y poniéndolos en ellos
Ella comenzó a hablar,
Y ellos a darle silencio.
—Perdóname, dice, Rey
Si tu Consejo atropello,
Aunque si te le dan malo,
Antes soy digna de premio.
No sé si de rey cristiano
Te dé nombre, porque entiendo
Que con fingida apariencia
Debes ser moro encubierto;
Que quien da a los que lo son
Las doncellas ciento a ciento,
Si ya no es moro, a ellas
Las soborna para serlo.
Si por darle muerte oculta
Vas desangrando tu reino,
Por harto mejor tuviera
De una vez pegarle fuego;
O si no en tributo y parias
Dieras hombres a lo menos,
Que era dalles enemigos,
De quien vivieran con miedo.
Pero si les das doncellas,
Allá, en dejando de serlo,
Nacerán de cada una
Cinco o seis contrarios nuestros.
Mas bien acordado está
Que tus hombres se estén quedos,
Porque puedan engendrar
Hijas que paguen en feudo:
Que solo para engendrallas
Deben de tener sugeto
De hombres, que en lo demás
Yo por mujeres los tengo.
Si te acobardan las guerras,
Las mismas doncellas creo
Que han de venírtela a dar
Por el mal que las has hecho,
Y sin duda vencerán,
Si lo ponen en efecto,
Que ellas son mujeres hombres,
Y hombres mujeres aquestos.—
Alborotáronse algunos,
Y el Rey, corrido y suspenso,
Determinó de morir
O libertar a su reino.
Juntó su gente de guerra,
Y prestándoles su esfuerzo
El glorioso Santiago,
Dió la batalla y vencieron.
Quedó medroso Almanzor,
Y el Rey con aqueste hecho
Dió libertad a Castilla,
Y a sí mesmo honroso premio.

This ballad was translated by both Gibson and Lockhart, and both renditions are satisfactory. Gibson used the basic quatrain of four- and three-stress lines, while Lockhart's version reveals the longer six-stress lines noted below.

The noble King Ramiro within the chamber sate,
One day, with all his barons, in council and debate,
When, without leave or guidance of usher or of groom,
There came a comely maiden into the council-room.

She was a comely maiden, — she was surpassing fair;
All loose upon her shoulders hung down her golden hair;
From head to foot her garments were white as white may be;
And while they gazed in silence, thus in the midst spake she.

'Sir King, I crave your pardon, if I have done amiss
In venturing before ye, at such an hour as this;
But I will tell my story, and when my words ye hear,
I look for praise and honor, and no rebuke I fear.

'I know not if I'm bounden to call thee by the name
Of Christian, King Ramiro; for though thou dost not claim
A heathen realm's allegiance, a heathen sure thou art;
Beneath a Spaniard's mantle thou hidest a Moorish heart.

'For he who gives the Moor-King a hundred maids of Spain,
Each year when in its season the day comes round again, —
If he be not a heathen, he swells the heathen's train;
'Twere better burn a kingdom than suffer such disdain.

'If the Moslem must have tribute, make *men* your tribute-money,
Send idle drones to teaze them within their hives of honey;
For when 'tis paid with maidens, from every maid there spring
Some five or six strong soldiers to serve the Moorish King.

'It is but little wisdom to keep our men at home,
They serve but to get damsels, who, when their day is come,
Must go, like all the others, the heathen's bed to sleep in;
In all the rest they're useless, and no wise worth the keeping.

'And if it is fear of battle that makes ye bow so low,
And suffer such dishonor from God our Saviour's foe,
I pray you, sirs, take warning, — ye'll have as good a fright,
If e'er the Spanish damsels arise themselves to right.

'Tis we have manly courage within the breasts of women,
But ye are all hare-hearted, both gentlemen and yeomen.' —
Thus spake that fearless maiden; I wot when she was done,
Uprose the King Ramiro and his nobles every one.

The King called God to witness, that come their weal or wo,
Thenceforth no Maiden Tribute from out Castile should go;
'At least I will do battle on God our Saviour's foe,
And die beneath my banner before I see it so.'

A cry went through the mountains when the proud Moor drew near,
And trooping to Ramiro came every Christian spear;

The blessed Saint Iago, they called upon his name; —
That day began our freedom, and wiped away our shame.

The translation is quite good and in agreement with the original down to the last two stanzas. Even there the meaning of the last ten or eleven lines of the model is transcribed, although in terms very different from those the anonymous composer used. Otherwise, the poem exhibits no unusual features.

The next ballad, like the one above, could be called just as accurately a *romance histórico,* although its *fronterizo* elements justify its consideration here. It explains the origin of an illustrious Spanish name, Garcilaso de la Vega. The original is quite long, but the intrinsic interest of the subject and a fine translation by Gibson call for its inclusion. The Spanish text is as follows:

Cercada está Santa Fe
Con mucho lienzo encerado,
Alrededor muchas tiendas
De seda, oro y brocado,
Donde están duques y condes,
Señores de grande estado,
Y otros muchos capitanes
Que lleva el rey Don Fernando,
Todos de valor crecido,
Como y habréis notado
En la guerra que se ha hecho
Contra el granadino estado;
Cuando a las nueve del día
Un moro se ha demostrado
Encima un caballo negro
De blancas manchas manchado,
Cortados ambos hocicos,
Porque lo tiene enseñado
El moro que con sus dientes
Despedace a los cristianos.
El moro viene vestido
De blanco, azul y encarnado,
Y debajo esta librea
Trae un muy fuerte jaco,
Y una lanza con dos hierros
De acero muy bien templado,
Y una adarga hecha en Fez
De un ante rico estimado.
Aqueste perro, con befa,
En la cola del caballo,
La sagrada Ave-María
Llevaba, haciendo escarnio.
Llegando junto a las tiendas
D'esta manera ha hablado:
—¿Cuál será aquel caballero
Que sea tan esforzado
Que quiera hacer conmigo
Batalla en aqueste campo?
Salga uno, salgan dos,
Salgan tres o salgan cuatro:
El alcaide de los Donceles
Salga, que es hombre afamado;
Salga ese conde de Cabra,
En guerra experimentado:
Salga Gonzalo Fernández,
Que es de Córdoba nombrado,
O si no, Martín Galindo,
Que es valeroso soldado;
Salga ese Portocarrero
Señor de Palma nombrado,
O el bravo Don Manuel
Ponce de León llamado,
Aquel que sacara el guante
Que por industria fué echado
Donde estaban los leones,
Y él le sacó muy osado;
Y si no salen aquestos,
Salga el mismo rey Fernando,

Que yo le daré a entender
Si soy de valor sobrado.—
Los caballeros del Rey
Todos le están escuchando:
Cada uno pretendía
Salir con el moro al campo.
Garcilaso estaba allí,
Mozo gallardo, esforzado;
Licencia le pide al Rey
Para salir al pagano.
—Garcilaso, sois muy mozo
Para emprender este caso;
Otros hay en el real
Para poder encargarlo.—
Garcilaso se despide
Muy confuso y enojado,
Por no tener la licencia
Que al Rey había demandado.
Pero muy secretamente
Garcilaso se había armado,
Y en un caballo morcillo
Salido se había al campo.
Nadie le ha conocido
Porque sale disfrazado;
Fuese donde estaba el moro
Y de esta suerte le ha hablado:
—¡Ahora verás, el moro,
Si tiene el rey Don Fernando
Caballeros valerosos
Que salgan contigo al campo!
Yo soy el menor de todos,
Y vengo por su mandado.—
El moro cuando le vió
En poco le había estimado
Y díjole d'esta suerte:
—Yo no estoy acostumbrado
A hacer batalla campal
Sino con hombres barbados:
Vuélvete, rapaz, le dice,
Y venga el más estimado.—
Garcilaso con enojo
Puso piernas al caballo;
Arremetió para el moro,
Y un gran encuentro le ha dado.
El moro que aquesto vió
Revuelve así como un rayo:
Comienzan la escaramuza
Con un furor muy sobrado.
Garcilaso, aunque era mozo,
Mostraba valor sobrado;
Dióle al moro una lanzada
Por debajo del sobaco:
El moro cayera muerto,
Tendido le había en el campo.
Garcilaso con presteza
Del caballo se ha apeado:
Cortárale la cabeza
Y en el arzón la ha colgado:
Quitó el Ave-María
De la cola del caballo:
Hincado de ambas rodillas
Con devoción la ha besado,
Y en la punta de su lanza
Por bandera la ha colgado.
Subió en su caballo luego,
Y el del moro había tomado.
Cargado d'estos despojos
Al real se había tornado,
Do estaban todos los grandes,
También el rey Don Fernando,
Todos tienen a grandeza
Aquel hecho señalado;
También el Rey y la Reina
Mucho se han maravillado
En ser Garcilaso mozo
Y haber hecho un tan gran caso.
Garcilaso de la Vega
Desde allí se ha intitulado,
Porque en la Vega hiciera
Campo con aquel pagano.
Y d'esta suerte le lleva
Delante al Rey su señor.

Gibson puts the above into one six-line stanza and fifteen quatrains of fourteen-syllable, seven-stress lines.

Around the walls of Sante Fe beleaguering lines were laid,
And countless tents were pitched behind of silk and gold brocade;
Full many a Duke and Count were there, the noblest in the land;
And Captains bold, that swelled the host of good King Ferdinand;
They all were men of valour proved, and now had drawn the sword,
To win Granada's kingdom fair in battle for their lord.

One morning at the hour of nine, there came a Moor in sight,
Who rode upon a charger black, with many a speck of white;
And, strange to see, its nostrils twain were severed underneath,
The Moor had trained it thus to bite the Christians with its teeth.

The Moor was clad in vesture fine, of scarlet, white and blue,
And underneath his flowing robes a coat of armour true;
He bore a double-headed lance of temper wondrous keen,
And buckler of the buffalo hide, the finest Fez had seen.

Upon his horse's tail there hung, by way of bitter jest,
The blessed Mary's rosary, such scorn was in his breast.
Soon as he reached the martial tents he spake out bold and free:
"Now who will be the hardy knight that dares to fight with me?

Come one, come two, come three or four, it matters not a jot,
Or let the Captain of the youths, he is a man of note;
Let Count de Cabra sally forth, in war a potent name,
Or Gonzalo Fernández, whom Cordova doth claim;

Or let brave Martin Galindo, a soldier few can touch,
Or the brave Portocarrero, whom Palma honours much;
Or else Don Manuel de Leon, the first of daring men,
Who boldly snatched his lady's glove out from the lions den.

Or if they shrink, let Ferdinand, the good King, sally forth,
I'll cause him soon to understand what Moorish might is worth."
The Cavaliers around the King the fierce defiance heard,
And each was burning to be first the Moorish Knight to beard.

Then up rose Garcilaso, a gallant youth of grace,
And begged permission of the King the pagan foe to face;
"O Garcilaso, thou art young, too young for such a feat,
It needs a stronger arm than thine this raging Moor to meet."

Away went Garcilaso, all angry and confused,
To think the King before the camp his prayer had refused;
He went to gird his armour on, his plan he kept concealed,
And mounted on his coal-black steed he sallied to the field.

In dark disguise he went his way, no man his errand guessed,
And when he reached the battle-ground, he thus the Moor addressed:

"Now wilt thou see, thou caitiff Moor, that good King Ferdinand
Has hosts of valiant Cavaliers thy prowess to withstand;

I am the youngest of them all, and come by his desire." —
The Moor looked down upon the youth, and said with scornful ire:
"I am not wont to take the field to fight with beardless boys,
Return, rash lad, and tell the King to send a better choice!"

Then Garcilaso, mad with rage, put spurs into his steed,
And straight against the scoffing Moor he launched with all his speed.
The Moor, who saw him coming fast, round in a circle wheeled,
And then commenced a furious fight all round the tilting-field.

Though Garcilaso was a youth, he fought with valour true,
And pierced his foe beneath the arm, and sent his lance right through.
The Moor he staggered on his seat, and on the field fell dead,
The youth alighted from his horse, and severed off his head.

He placed it on his saddle-bow; from the horse's tail he tore
The blessed Mary's rosary, dishonoured by the Moor;
He fell upon his bended knees, and kissed it long and loud,
And placed it on his lance's point, to serve as pennon proud.

He seized the Moorish charger, and with the spoils of war
He hastened to the royal camp; they saw him from afar;
The lords and nobles every one received him with applause,
They held him as a gallant Knight, to fight in such a cause.

He knelt before the King and Queen; they gave him honour meet,
And marvelled much that such a youth should do so grand a feat.
'Twas in Granada's Vega that thus he won his fame,
And Garcilaso de la Vega thereafter was his name.

The smooth flow of the narrative, the easy, unrestrained rhythm, and the harmonious expression of this poem give it the appearance of an original composition and belie its faithful adherence to the Spanish text. In reality it is almost as literal a translation as could be desired, and with very few exceptions, each line of the translation can be matched easily with two lines from the model. Judged from the standpoint of its fidelity to the word or spirit of the ballad it seeks to reproduce, or considered on its own merits as an independent composition, the poem is a success worthy of critical approval. This translation can be compared with versions by Thomas Rodd and Jeremiah Holmes Wiffen.

Many of the *fronterizo* ballads deal with besieged cities and fortresses. The next translation relates how a certain Don García unwittingly influenced the Moors to abandon a long and costly siege against his castle. The original is considered a *romance viejo*.

A tal anda Don García
Por un adarve adelante,
Saetas de oro en la mano,
En la otra un arco trae.
Maldiciendo a la fortuna
Grandes querellas le dae:
—Crióme el Rey de pequeño,
Hízome Dios barragane;
Dióme armas y caballo,
Por do todo hombre más vale,
Diérame a Doña María
Por mujer y por iguale,
Diérame a cien doncellas
Para a ella acompañare,
Dióme el castillo de Ureña
Para con ella casare;
Diérame cien caballeros
Para el castillo guardare,
Basteciómelo de vino
Basteciómelo de pane
Basteciólo de agua dulce
Qu'en el castillo no la haye.
Cercáronme los moros
La mañana de San Juane:
Siete años van pasados
El cerco no quieren quitare,
Veo morir a los míos,
No teniendo que les dare,
Póngolos por las almenas
Armados como se estane,
Porque pensasen los moros
Que podrían peleare:
En el castillo de Ureña
No hay sino un solo pane,
Y si le doy a mis hijos,
La mi mujer ¿qué harae?
Si lo como yo, mezquino,
Los míos se quejarane.—
Hizo el pan cuatro pedazos
Y arrojólos al reale:
El un pedazo de aquellos
A los pies del Rey fué a dare.
—Alá, pese a mis moros,
A Alá le quiera pesare,
De las sobras del castillo
Nos bastecen el reale.—
Manda tocar los clarines
Y su cerco luego alzare.

The English version is by Gibson:

Don García paced the Castle walls, his grief he could not smother,
One hand did hold his golden shafts, his bow was in the other;
He cursed his evil fortune, that had brought him to this day,
And as he walked he muttered, to give his sorrow play:

"The King he trained me from a boy, still firm for love and war,
He gave me horse and armour, the best of things that are,
He gave the Lady Mary to be my loving spouse,
He gave a hundred damsels to tend her in the house.

He gave Ureña's Castle to be her wedding dower,
He gave a hundred Cavaliers to watch and keep the tower;
He sent me bread, he sent me wine, he sent me water sweet,
The Castle then did nothing lack, that man could drink or eat.

But alack! the Moors beleaguered me, one morning of St. John,
And still they hold the siege as close, though seven years are gone;
My men they die of hunger, they cannot hold out long,
I place the dead armed on the walls, that the Moors may think us strong.

Our stores are all exhausted, we have the worst to dread;
For all the Castle doth contain is one small loaf of bread;
And if I give it to the boys, for my wife what shall remain?
Or if, O wretch, I eat it, my men may well complain."

He breaks the loaf in pieces four, and hurls them from the walls.
One fragment strikes the royal tent, and at the King's feet falls:
"O Allah! sorrow to my Moors, with rage they well may stamp,
When the leavings of yon Castle are sent to feed our camp."
He bids the trumpets sound retreat, through all the country round,
And having raised the weary siege, he marches from the ground.

Some slight alteration is noticeable, as for example in the last half of the first line, the beginning of the second stanza, and in the last two lines of the translation, but little fault can be found with the changes. They serve only to clarify or reinforce the principal ideas. The plan of the original is closely paralleled, and the repetition of phrases in the second and third stanzas is not only extremely effective in English but is an excellent copy of the Spanish. The last two stanzas of the translation do not quite approach the ease and smoothness of the *romance,* but are satisfactory, nevertheless.

The next ballad, also one of the *primitivos,* has attracted the attention of many students of the *romance,* because of its striking opening lines and its graphic description of a particularly fierce battle between Moors and Christians. In addition to Gibson's rendition, given below with the Spanish, there are translations of either this poem or one of its close variants by Longfellow, Rodd, and Thomas Percy. Gibson's version appeared in the first edition of his translations, but was one of the four left out of the second edition.

¡Río-Verde, Río-Verde! Tinto vas en sangre viva; Entre tí y Sierra Bermeja Murió gran caballería.	River green, O river green, Red thou runn'st with living blood; Many a Knight lies dead between Mount Bermeja and thy flood.
Murieron duques y condes, Señores de gran valía;	Many a Duke and Count have fallen, Valiant lords of noble birth;

Allí murió Urdiales, Hombre de valor y estima.	There has perished Urdiales, Man of valour and of worth;
Huyendo va Saavedra Por una ladera arriba: Tras él iba un renegado, Que muy bien le conocía.	Down the mountain Sayavedra Hastened from the bloody fray, Close pursued a Renegado, Who had known him many a day.
Con algazara muy grande D'esta manera decía: —Date, date, Saavedra, Que muy bien te conocía:	And these burning words he uttered, With a fearful voice and strong: "Yield thee, yield thee, Sayavedra, I have known thee well and long.
Bien te vide jugar cañas En la plaza de Sevilla, Y bien conocí a tus padres Y a tu mujer Doña Elvira.	Often have I seen thee tilting In Sevilla's public square; Well I know thee and thy parents, And thy wife, Elvira fair.
Siete años fuí tu cautivo, Y me diste mala vida; Ahora lo serás mío, O me costará la mía.—	Seven years was I thy captive, And a dismal life I led; Now a prisoner I'll hold thee, Or I'll lay me with the dead."
Saavedra, que lo oyera, Como un león revolvía: Tiróle el moro un cuadrillo Y por alto hizo la vía.	Sayavedra, when he heard it, Turned him like a lion fierce, From the Moor a dart came flying, Touched his breast, but could not [pierce.
Saavedra con su lanza Duramente le hería; Cayó muerto el renegado De aquella grande herida.	Sayavedra with his sabre Cleft his turban to the brain; Straightway fell the Renegado, And was numbered with the slain.
Cercaron a Saavedra Más de mil moros que había; Hiciéronle mil pedazos Con saña que dél tenían.	Round encompassed Sayavedra Thousand Moors with passion mad, Hewed him in a thousand pieces, With the fury that they had.
Don Alonso en este tiempo Muy gran batalla hacía: El caballo le habían muerto, Por muralla le tenía Y arrimado a un gran peñón Con valor se defendía.	Then alone did Don Alonso Bear the battle's fearful shock, With his charger for a rampart, With his back against a rock.

Muchos moros tiene muertos;
Pero poco le valía,
Porque sobre él cargan muchos
Y le dan grandes heridas,
Tantas que cayó allí muerto
Entre la gente enemiga,

Many a Moor he sent to Hades,
But his arm more feeble grows;
Fighting till the last, he perished
'Mid the circle of his foes.

También el conde de Ureña,
Mal herido en demasía,
Se sale de la batalla,
Llevado por una guía
Que sabía bien la senda,
Que de la sierra salía;
Muchos moros deja muertos,
Por su grande valentía.
También algunos se escapan
Que al buen Conde le seguían.

'Mid the combat Count d'Uraña,
Though his wounds were deep and [wide,
Found an outlet from the battle,
Tended by a faithful guide.

By his mighty strength and prowess
Many a Moor he left for dead;
With him many brave companions
Safely from the combat fled.

Don Alonso quedó muerto,
Recobrando nueva vida
Con una fama immortal
De su esfuerzo y valentía.

Low in death lay Don Alonso,
But he gained a better life,
Crowned himself with fame immortal
By his valour in that strife.

Gibson adopted the four-stress, trochaic meter for this translation, which closely duplicates the Spanish in its literalness. The chief differences noted are the substitution of a sabre for a lance, the amplification of the line "Duramente le hería," and some slight contraction of the lines describing Don Alonso's death.

Although Thomas Percy seems to have used a slightly different version for his translation, its importance in setting the pattern for later translators and its enhanced poetic quality warrant the inclusion of a few lines.

Gentle river, gentle river,
Lo, thy streams are stained with gore,
Many a brave and noble captain
Floats along thy willowed shore.

All beside thy limpid waters,
All beside thy sands so bright,
Moorish chiefs and Christian warriors
Joined in fierce and mortal fight.

Lords and dukes and noble princes
On thy fatal banks were slain;

Fatal banks that gave to slaughter
All the pride and flower of Spain.

Both Percy and Gibson attempted a translation of the proper name Río-Verde, but neither was completely successful. Longfellow was wiser and left it as it is in Spanish. He did not translate the whole piece, but the following portion may be compared with the corresponding lines from Percy and Gibson.

"Rio Verde, Rio Verde!
Many a corpse is bathed in thee,
Both of Moors and eke of Christians,
Slain with swords most cruelly.

"And thy pure and crystal waters
Dappled are with crimson gore;
For between the Moors and Christians
Long has been the fight and sore.

"Dukes and counts fell bleeding near thee,
Lords of high renown were slain,
Perished many a brave hidalgo
Of the noblemen of Spain.

The same meter was used, and quite successfully, by all three translators. Smooth harmonious verse would naturally be expected of Longfellow, and we find no complaints with his efforts, although he has not surpassed either Percy or Gibson.

The religious aspect of the conflict between Christians and Moors is emphasized in still another translation by Gibson. The term renegade, found in both this poem and the preceding one, usually referred to a member of either race who fraternized with the enemy. This ballad also is quite old.

Ya se salía el rey moro De Granada, en Almería, Con trescientos moros perros Que lleva en su compañía.	From Almería to Granada The Moorish King did ride; And thrice a hundred Moorish Knights Went prancing by his side.
Jugando van de la lanza, Yendo van barraganía; Cada cual iba hablando De las gracias de su amiga.	At times they sported with the lance, And then at gallantrie; And of his mistress and her charms Each one was boasting free;

Así habló un tornadizo, Que criado es en Sevilla:	When out there spake a Renegade, In Sevilla born was he:
—Porque habéis dicho las vues- [tras Deciros quiero la mía: Blanca es y colorada Como el sol cuando salía.—	"Ye all have vaunted yours, my lords, And now I'll speak of mine; Her face so fair and ruddy bright Like morning sun doth shine."
Allí hablara el rey moro, Bien oiréis lo que decía; —Tal amiga como aquesa Para mí pertenescía.	On this outspoke the Moorish King, His words were passing free: "A lovely mistress such as this Belongs of right to me."
—Yo te la daré, buen rey, Si aquí me otorgas la vida. —Dédesmela tú, el morisco, Que otorgada te sería.—	"I'll give her thee, my noble King, If thou my life wilt spare;" "Present her now," replied the King, "And I will grant thy prayer."
Echara mano a su seno, Sacó a la Virgen María; De que la vido el rey moro, A la pared se volvía.	He drew a medal from his breast, The Virgin Mary's face; The King grew pale to see it, And turned him from the place:
—Tomadme luego a ese perro, Y llevádmelo a Almería: Tales prisiones le echá, D'ellas no salga con vida.	"Away with him! This scoffing dog To Almería bear; Bestow him in a dungeon deep, To live his life out there!"

The translation is quite faithful with no outstanding or unusual characteristics. It might be argued that the tone of the ballad is altered somewhat by the substitution of "knights" for "moros perros" ("Moorish dogs") in the third line, but the change is supported by the tone of the remainder of the poem and is a more fitting expression in English than a more literal translation would have been. A device often used by Gibson—the addition of a couple of extra lines to the stanza preceding a switch to dialogue or introducing a shift in the story—may be observed in the second stanza.

The two preceding ballads suggested the captivity which was frequently the lot of soldiers from both sides during the years of the Reconquest, but one may infer from many of the *romances* that the captives often found an unexpected source of comfort during their enslavement. The following composition, sometimes called the "Cautivo cristiano," illustrates the point. Gibson's translation, which parallels the original, is interesting for its variations in rhyme and rhythm.

Mi padre era de Ronda,
Y mi madre de Antequera;
Cautiváronme los moros
Entre la paz y la guerra,
Y lleváronme a vender
A Jerez de la Frontera.
	My father was of Ronda,
	  My mother of Antequera;
	The Moors they led me captive
	  To Xeres de la Frontera;
	'Twas just between the peace and war,
	  To sell me dear they led me far.

Siete días con sus noches
Anduve en almoneda:
No hubo moro ni mora
Que por mí diese moneda,
	In the market seven days I stood,
	  God wot but they were many;
	But not a Moor or Mooress there
	  Would bid for me a penny.

Si no fuera un moro perro
Que por mí cien doblas diera,
Y llevárame a su casa,
Y echárame una cadena;
	For gold doubloons twice fifty told,
	  A Moorish dog then bought me;
	He bore me off unto his house,
	  And put a chain about me.

Dábame la vida mala,
Dábame la vida negra:
De día majar esparto,
De noche moler cibera,
	A drudging life he made me lead,
	  No rest he gave nor parley;
	By day I had to cut the grass,
	  By night to grind the barley.

Y echóme un freno a la boca,
Porque no comiese de ella,
Mi cabello retorcido,
Y tornóme a la cadena.
	He put a bridle in my mouth,
	  No meat at all he found me;
	My hair he twisted in a knot,
	  And then in irons bound me.

Pero plugo a Dios del cielo
Que tenía el ama buena:
Cuando el moro se iba a caza
Quitábame la cadena,
	But God be thanked, his mistress fair
	  Was kindlier than her betters;
	For when the Moor a-hunting went,
	  She took away my fetters.

Y echárame en su regazo,
Y espulgóme la cabeza;
Por un placer que le hice
Otro muy mayor me hiciera:
	She bade me sit upon her lap,
	  She combed my hair so finely;
	I did my best to please her well,
	  She treated me so kindly.

Diérame los cien doblones,
Y enviárame a mi tierra;
Y así plugo a Dios del cielo
Que en salvo me pusiera.
	Sent me to my ain countrie,
	  With gold doubloons twice fifty;
	And so it pleased the God of Heaven
	  That I am here in safety.

The attraction between Moorish girls and Spanish soldiers is well documented in the ballads, but the next selection hints that in this, as in every age, the male was not above using deceit when it suited his purpose. The original, placed with a good translation by George Ticknor, is an excellent example of the fragmentary nature of many of the *romances* and of the charm which can result from an abrupt beginning and an enigmatic ending. Like the preceding poem it is a *romance viejo.*

Yo me era mora Moraima,	I was the Moorish maid, Morayma,
Morilla de un bel catar;	I was that maiden dark and fair; —
Cristiano vino a mi puerta,	A Christian came, he seemed in sorrow,
Cuitada, por me engañar.	Full of falsehood came he there.
Hablóme en algarabía	Moorish he spoke, — he spoke it well, —
Como aquél que bien la sabe:	"Open the door, thou Moorish maid,
— Abrasme las puertas, mora,	So shalt thou be by Allah blessed,
Si Alá te guarde de mal.	So shall I save my forfeit head."
— ¿Cómo te abriré, mezquina,	"But how can I, alone and weak,
Que no sé quién te serás?	Unbar, and know not who is there?"
— Yo soy moro Mazote,	"But I'm the Moor, the Moor Mazote,
Hermano de la tu madre,	The brother of thy mother dear.
Que un cristiano dejo muerto;	A Christian fell beneath my hand,
Tras mí venía el alcalde,	The Alcalde comes, he comes apace,
Si no abres tú, mi vida,	And if thou open not the door,
Aquí me verás matar.	I perish here before thy face."
— Cuando esto oí, cuitada,	I rose in haste, I rose in fear,
Comencéme a levantar,	I seized my cloak, I missed my vest,
Vistiérame una almejía	And, rushing to the fatal door,
No hallando mi brial,	I threw it wide at his behest.
Fuérame para la puerta	
Y abríla de par en par.	

In some of the ballads, of course, it is the Moorish knight who is enamored of the Christian lady. Another translation by Gibson presents this side of the picture. Both the original and the English version contain an anomaly found in a good many *romances.*

Moriana en un castillo	In the tower sat Moriana
Juega con el moro Galvane;	With the Moor Galvan at play,
Juegan los dos a las tablas	Sat playing at the checker-board
Por mayor placer tomare.	To while the time away.
Cada vez qu'el moro pierde	With every game the Moor lost,
Bien perdía una cibdade;	He lost a city brave;

Cuando Moriana pierde
La mano le da a besare.

Whenever Moriana lost,
Her hand to kiss she gave.

Del placer qu'el moro toma
Adormescido se cae.
Por aquellos altos montes
Caballero vió asomare:

The Moor he sunk to slumber
In midst of his delight;
When through the lofty mountains
There came a stranger knight.

Llorando viene y gimiendo,
Las uñas corriendo sangre
De amores de Moriana
Hija del rey Moriane.

He came with tears and groaning,
With bleeding feet and bare;
For the loves of Moriana,
King Morian's daughter fair.

Captiváronla los moros
La mañana de Sant Juane,
Cogiendo rosas y flores
En la huerta de su padre.

The Moors had ta'en her captive
One morning of St. John,
While gathering flowers and roses,
In her father's fields alone.

Alzó los ojos Moriana,
Conociérale en mirarle:
Lágrimas de los sus ojos
En la faz del moro dane.

When Moriana saw him,
At a glance she knew him well;
Her tears fell fast and faster,
And on the Moor's face fell.

Con pavor recuerda el moro
Y empezara de fablare:
—¿Qu'es esto, la mi señora?
¿Quién vos ha fecho pesare?

With fear the Moor upstarted,
And thus began to say:
"What means it, O my lady,
What gives you such dismay?

Si os enojaron mis moros
Luego los faré matare,
O si las vuesas doncellas,
Farélas bien castigare;
Y si pesar los cristianos,
Yo los iré conquistare.

If my Moors have made you angry,
I'll cause them to be slain;
If your damsels have offended,
I'll make them smart with pain
Or if the Christians grieve thee,
Their lives I'll march to gain.

Mis arreos son las armas,
Mi descanso el peleare,
Mi cama, las duras peñas,
Mi dormir, siempre velare.

My dress it is my armour,
My rest it is the fight,
My bed the barren rocks,
My sleep a watch at night."

—Non me enojaron los moros,
Ni los mandedes matare,
Ni menos las mis doncellas
Por mi reciban pesare;
Ni tampoco a los cristianos
Vos cumple de conquistare;

"The Moors they have not angered me,
I would not have them slain,
Nor have my maids offended,
I would not give them pain;
Nor would I have the Christians
By you in battle ta'en.

Pero d'este sentimiento
Quiero vos decir verdade;
Que por los montes aquellos
Caballero vi asomare,
El cual pienso qu'es mi esposo,
Mi querido, mi amor grande. —

I'll tell what deeply moves me,
  I'll tell the truth to you;
For coming through the mountains
  I see a knight in view;
It is my spouse, I know it,
  My dear, my lover true."

Alzó la su mano el moro,
Un bofetón la fué a dare;
Teniendo los dientes blancos
De sangre vuelto los hae,

The Moor his hand uplifted,
  And smote her on the face;
The blood o'er all her white teeth
  Came flowing down apace.

Y mandó que sus porteros
La lleven a degollare,
Allí do viera a su esposo,
En aquel mismo lugare.

He bade his watchmen seize her,
  And there upon the spot
Where first she saw her lover
  To let her life's blood out.

Al tiempo de la su muerte
Estas voces fué a fablare.
— Yo muero como cristiana,
Y también sin confesare
Mis amores verdaderos
De mi esposo naturale.

When there she cried: "A Christian, I
  With my life's blood do part;
Because I told my true love
  For the husband of my heart."

The four lines beginning "Mis arreos son las armas" ("My dress it is my armour") are the first verses of another well-known ballad and obviously are out of place here. They seem even more inappropriate in the translation, and one immediately wonders why Gibson left them in. It is not uncommon for folksongs to borrow from each other, and this is certainly true of the ballads. Many popular lines and even whole stanzas are repeated in *romances* of greatly differing origin and theme. In his work with the ballads, however, Gibson, in spite of his desire to transcribe faithfully, usually edited out those passages which did not fit. It is possible, of course, that the above version is an early draft which did not receive final revision before his death. Several halting lines and the last stanza, which also misses the mark, lend support to such a theory. In spite of these defects, the translation retains the spirit and with minor exceptions the ideas of the ancient original.

Many of the *romances moriscos* portray the lighter side of Moorish life: the games, festivities, or revels, but the amorous intrigues of the lords and ladies and the passions aroused by love are favorite themes. The one which follows is typical of this type. Its enhanced lyrical qualities, plus a somewhat unexpected dramatic ending, have made it quite well known. Menéndez Pidal believes it may have been written by Lope de Vega when he was twenty-one years old.[1]

Sale la estrella de Venus
Al tiempo que el sol se pone,
Y la enemiga del día
Su negro manto descoge,
Y con ella un fuerte moro
Semejante a Rodamonte
Sale de Sidonia airado;
De Jerez la vega corre
De donde entra Guadalete
Al mar de España, y por donde
De Santa María el puerto
Recibe famoso nombre.
Desesperado camina,
Que siendo en linaje noble,
Le deja su dama ingrata
Porque se suena que es pobre,
Y aquella noche se casa
Con un moro feo y torpe,
Porque es alcaide en Sevilla
Del alcázar y la torre.
Quejábase tiernamente
De un agravio tan enorme,
Y a sus palabras la vega
Con dulces ecos responde:
—¡Zaida, dice, más airada
Que el mar que las naves sorbe,
Más dura e inexorable
Que las entrañas de un monte!
¿Cómo permites, cruel,
Después de tantos favores,
Que de prendas de mi alma
Ajena mano se adorne?
¿Es posible que te abraces
A las cortezas de un roble,
Y dejes el árbol tuyo
Desnudo de fruta y flores?
¿Dejas tu amado Gazul,
Dejas tres años de amores,
Y das la mano a Albenzaide
Que aun apénas le conoces?
Dejas un pobre muy rico,
Y un rico muy pobre escoges,
Pues las riquezas del cuerpo
A las del alma antepones.
Alá permita, enemiga,
Que te aborrezca y le adores,
Y que por celos suspires,
Y por ausencia le llores;
Y que de noche no duermas,
Y de día no reposes,
Y en la cama le fastidies,
Y que en la mesa le enojes;
Y en las fiestas y las zambras
No se vista tus colores,
Ni aun para verlas permita
Que a la ventana te asomes;
Y menosprecie en las cañas,
Para que más te alborotes,
El almaizar que le labres
Y la manga que le bordes,
Y se ponga el de su amiga
Con la cifra de su nombre,
A quien le dé los cautivos
Cuando de la guerra torne;
Y en batalla de cristianos
De velle muerto te asombres,
Y plegue Alá que suceda
Cuando la mano le tomes;
Y si le has de aborrecer,
Que largos años le goces
Que es la mayor maldición
Que pueden darte los hombres.—
Con esto llegó a Jerez
A la mitad de la noche;

[1] Ramón Menéndez Pidal, *De primitiva lírica española y antigua épica* (Buenos Aires: Espasa-Calpe Argentina, Colección Austral, 1951), p. 77.

Halló el palacio cubierto
De luminarias y voces,
Y los moros fronterizos
Que por todas partes corren
Con sus hachas encendidas
Y con libreas conformes.
Delante del desposado
En los estribos alzóse,
Y arrojándole la lanza
De parte a parte pasóle.
Alborotóse la plaza,
Desnudó el moro el estoque,
Y por mitad de la gente
Hacia Sidonia volvióse.

This ballad was especially popular with the early translators, and it has been put into English at least five times. The version chosen here is by George Moir.

Softly rose the Star of Evening, soft the twilight waned away,
Shadowed by the darker mantle of the dusky foe of day.
There 'twas from Sidonia's city rode a young and gallant Moor,
Down by Xeres' flow'ry valley, by the long and sounding shore —
There where Guadalete wanders with his waters thro' the plain,
And our Lady's harbour rises o'er the waste and stormy main.
Noble name and lofty lineage nought avail to sooth despair;
She, his faithless lady, leaves him — he was poor as she was fair —
Leaves her young and gallant lover — leaves her father's halls to wed
Wrinkled brow and craven spirit — Seville's rich and proud Alcayde.
To the silent air around him thus he told his tale of pain,
While a deep and wailing echo murmured back the sound again:
"Cruel as the stormy waters of yon dark engulphing sea,
Ruder than the rocky bosoms of the barren mountains be.
Zayda! can'st thou still bethink thee of our loves, and yet resign
To another lord's embrace charms which I have clasped in mine?
Round a trunk so old and rugged weave those clasping arms of thine,
And the plant thy love had cherished leave to wither and decline?
Six long years of love and duty will thou cast at once away,
Wedding thus with Abenzaydé — him the friend of yesterday?
Wilt thou chuse him, rich in treasure, poor, indeed, in all beside —
Shall the spirit's nobler riches by the body's be outvied?
Allah grant that he may hate thee — grant that thou may'st love again —
Know the weariness of absence — prove the pangs of jealous pain —
And the night her balm deny thee, and the day no rest afford —
And thy presence still be hateful, in the chamber, at the board —
At the banquet, in the dances, ne'er may he thy colours wear,
Nor permit thee, at the lattice, even to sit and see him there —
In the tourney or the battle slight the tokens of thy love —
Wear no robe that thou hast broidered, wear no scarf thy fingers wove —
But another's love's devices blazoned be upon his shield,
And another greet his captives home returning from the field.
Should'st thou hate him, grant thy penance weary years may linger on,
Darker fate I cannot wish thee, nor a deeper malison."

Speaking thus, he came to Xeres at the middle hour of night;
There he found the bridal palace blazing all with festive light.
Crowding Moors with eager paces, here departing, there returning,
All with liv'ries gaily broidered, all with torches brightly burning.
In the middle path he placed him as the bridegroom nearer drew,
In his stirrups firmly raised him, poised his lance and pierced him through.
Then arose the cry of terror, then the Moor unsheathed his sword,
And through all the crowd around him safely to Medina spurred.

Moir's translation reproduces extremely well the measured pace and poetic tenor of the Spanish, and even though it is not a literal rendition, it conveys accurately every important particular and nuance of the original. Among the other versions in English, that of John Bowring is quite good also.

The *romances moriscos* reflect almost every facet of Moorish life, and several cycles are devoted to the pleasures and sorrows of certain eminent families and personages among the Moorish aristocracy of Granada. Celín Audalla, whose funeral is described in the following ballad, was one of the latter. The original composition is somewhat unusual, featuring an *estribillo,* or refrain, which is not common to the *romance,* but of greatest interest here is the extremely different treatment accorded it by Lockhart and Gibson. Gibson's rendition accompanies the Spanish.

Por la puerta de la Vega	Through the gateway of the Vega
Salen moros a caballo,	Ride the Moors at dead of night,
Vestidos de raso negro,	Clad in robes of deepest mourning,
Ya de noche al primer cuarto,	Tis a sad and fearful sight;
Con hachas negras ardiendo,	In their midst they bear a coffin,
Un ataúd acompañando.	Torches cast a lurid light:
¿A dó va el mal logrado	"Reft of life and love together,
Celín, del alma y vida despojado?	Whither goes poor Celin, whither?"
Matóle el pasado día	'Twas but yesterday he tilted
Sin razón un moro airado	With the knights of high renown;
En una fiesta solemne	When a fierce and furious Moorman
De que hubo presto el pago:	Without reason struck him down;
Llóralo toda Granada,	Tears were flowing in Granada,
Porque en estremo es amado.	Loved was he by all the town;
¿A dó va el desdichado	"Reft of life and love together,
Celín, del alma y vida despojado?	Whither goes poor Celin, whither?"

Con él van sus deudos todos,
Y un alfaquí señalado,
Y cuatro moras hermanas,
Con muchos en su resguardo;
Y dicen al son funesto
De un atambor destemplado:
¿A dó va el desdichado
Celín, del alma y vida despojado?

March behind him all his vassals,
And an aged seer and wise;
All his sisters four are round him,
Tears are streaming from their eyes
And the tambour's solemn beating
Mingles with their sobs and cries:
"Reft of life and love together,
Whither goes our Celin, whither?"

Mesan los rubios cabellos
Que enlazan a un libertado,
Y de entre ellos va saliendo
Un licor claro y salado,
Y sobre rostros de nieve
Vierten el color rosado.
¿A dó va el desdichado
Celín, del alma y vida despojado?

Deep in sorrow stand the Moormen,
As they see the funeral go;
Hoarse and quivering are their voices,
Though the sound be hushed and low.
Hark! from every Moor and Mooress
Comes the throbbing cry of woe:
"Reft of life and love together,
Whinther goes poor Celin, whither?"

Y los moros que más sienten
Ver tan espantoso caso,
Llevan roncas las gargantas;
Y aunque en son callado y bajo,
Dicen los moros y moras,
Mil suspiros arrojando:
¿A dó va el desdichado
Celín, del alma y vida despojado?

Una mora, la más vieja,
Que de niño lo ha criado,
Sale llorando al encuentro,
Mil lágrimas derramando,
Y con furia y accidente
Pregunta al bando enlutado:
¿A dó va mi hijo amado
Celín, del alma y vida despojado?

Breaks the ranks an ancient Mooress,
She had nursed him when a child,
Tears her hair and beats her bosom,
Crying out in accents wild:
"Tell me, all ye standers-by,
Whither goes my darling child? —
Life and love and all together,
Whither goes my Celin, whither?"

It is obvious that this translation is not completely faithful to the text, and one of the stanzas has been left out completely. There are also four stanzas in the original following those given here which Gibson chose to omit. In spite of this, and in spite of the fact that his translation is not slavishly literal, he has given us an excellent picture of the scene described by the original and has actually increased the effect of grief and sorrow which it conveys. He was able to concentrate and heighten the emotion of the event, whereas inclusion of the extra stanzas would have weakened it.

Lockhart's translation, as seen below, is different in practically all respects, making it a fascinating contrast to the one above.

At the gate of old Granada, when all its bolts are barred,
At twilight, at the Vega gate, there is a trampling heard;
There is a trampling heard, as of horses treading slow,
And a weeping voice of women, and a heavy sound of woe.
What tower is fallen, what star is set, what chief come these bewailing? —
"A tower is fallen, a star is set! — Alas! alas for Celin!"

Three times they knock, three times they cry, and wide the doors they [throw;
Dejectedly they enter, and mournfully they go;
In gloomy lines they mustering stand beneath the hollow porch,
Each horseman grasping in his hand a black and flaming torch;
Wet is each eye as they go by, and all around is wailing,
For all have heard the misery. — "Alas! alas for Celin!"

Him, yesterday, a Moor did slay, of Bencerraje's blood, —
'Twas at the silemn jousting, — around the nobles stood:
The nobles of the land were by, and ladies bright and fair
Looked from their latticed windows, the haughty sight to share;
But now the nobles all lament, — the ladies are bewailing, —
For he was Granada's darling knight. — "Alas! alas for Celin!"

Before him ride his vassals, in order two by two,
With ashes on their turbans spread, most pitiful to view;
Behind him his four sisters, each wrapped in sable veil,
Between the tambour's dismal strokes take up their doleful tale;
When stops the muffled drum, ye hear their brotherless bewailing,
And all the people, far and near, cry, — "Alas! alas for Celin!"

Oh! lovely lies he on the bier, above the purple pall,
The flower of all Granada's youth, the loveliest of them all;
His dark, dark eyes are closed, his rosy lip is pale,
The crust of blood lies black and dim upon his burnished mail;
And ever more the hoarse tambour breaks in upon their wailing, —
Its sound is like no earthly sound, — "Alas! alas for Celin!"

The Moorish maid at the lattice stands, — the Moor stands at his door;
One maid is wringing of her hands, and one is weeping sore;
Down to the dust men bow their heads, and ashes black they strew
Upon their broidered garments, of crimson, green, and blue;
Before each gate the bier stands still, — then burst the loud bewailing
From door and lattice, high and low, — "Alas! alas for Celin!"

An old, old woman cometh forth, when she hears the people cry,—
Her hair is white as silver, like horn her glazed eye:
'Twas she that nursed him at her breast,—that nursed him long ago:
She knows not whom they all lament, but soon she well shall know!
With one deep shriek, she through doth break, when her ears receive their [wailing:—
"Let me kiss my Celin ere I die!—Alas! alas for Celin!"

The variety in the meter used by Lockhart is immediately evident, although the basic pattern is iambic with a liberal sprinkling of anapests. Syllable count ranges from twelve to sixteen. The atmosphere created by the translation is very different and much less restrained than that accompanying Gibson's poem, and the emphasis is on the description rather than the emotional content. This description is largely from Lockhart's imagination, since most of it is not in the original, and much of it is not even suggested by it. Still, one must admire Lockhart's ability to recreate an impressive and very authentic-appearing scene from the sparse details provided by the *romance*. One feels that this is the way the scene should have looked, regardless of whether it really did or not. His poem is a fine one; the only fault is that it is not a good translation. It is a good original poem based on the ideas of the *romance* and imitating its characteristic spirit. Regarded in this light, it may not be fair to compare the composition with Gibson's, since obviously the two men had different objectives. This difference is exemplified, among other ways, by the treatment of the refrain. Lockhart regarded it only as a lament, the words of which were unimportant, and did not translate it at all, substituting instead a common conventional phrase. Gibson, however, accepted its philosophical implications and attempted to convey its meaning with a literal rendition, even though these particular lines are difficult to translate poetically. If the basic criterion for judging a translation is fidelity to the original insofar as possible, there can be little doubt that Gibson has given us the best translation, but one must still praise Lockhart's ability to express poetically the images evoked in his mind by the Spanish narrator.

One of the most remarkable things about the Moorish ballads is their reflection of the Moorish point of view. In many instances, the description of Moorish behavior and the expression of the Moorish outlook and sentiments are so authentically sincere, with no trace of irony, sarcasm, or contempt, that many early critics believed that such ballads must have been translated into Spanish from Arabic originals. There is no evidence to support such a belief, however, and we must assume that the often profound comprehension of an alien, although neighboring, people is a tribute to the anonymous poets and singers who composed the *romances*.

The understanding of Moorish feeling is nowhere better displayed than in the ballads based on the struggles for, and the ultimate capture of, the territory of Granada, the last of the Moorish strongholds in Spain. One of these is the old and justly famous ballad of "Abenámar," which beautifully symbolizes the intense desire of both races to possess this ancient and opulent seat of Moorish power. The speakers are King John II of Castile and Abenámar, Moslem pretender to the throne of Granada, as the two presumably converse on a hill overlooking the city, and finally the city itself, as the personification of the bride of the conquerer. The ballad was first translated by Thomas Rodd, but there are also versions by Gibson, Robert Southey, Georgiana King, and Epiphanius Wilson. Gibson's rendition is with the Spanish.

—¡Abenámar, Abenámar,
Moro de la Morería,
El día que tú naciste
Grandes señales había!

Estaba la mar en calma,
La luna estaba crecida:
Moro que en tal signo nace
No debe decir mentira.—

Allí respondió el moro,
Bien oiréis lo que decía:
—Yo te la diré, señor,
Aunque me cueste la vida.

Porque soy hijo de un moro
Y una cristiana cautiva;
Siendo yo niño y muchacho
Mi madre me lo decía,

Que mentira no dijese,
Que era grande villanía:
Por tanto pregunta, Rey,
Que la verdad te diría.—

"Abenamar, Abenamar,
Moor of Moors, and man of worth!
On the day when thou wert cradled,
There were signs in heaven and earth.

Hushed in slumber was the ocean,
And the moon was at its full;
Never Moor should tell a falsehood,
Whom the ancient planets rule."

Up and spoke the Moorish Ancient,
Listen to the words he said:
"I will tell the truth, my lord,
Though it cost me now my head;

I'm the son of Moorish father,
Of a Christian captive born,
Well she nursed me, well she taught me,
Lying words to hold in scorn.

Well she nursed me, well she taught me,
When I was a tender youth;
Ask me, King, and I will answer,
Nothing will I tell but truth."

—Yo te agradezco, Abenámar,
Aquesa tu cortesía:
¿Qué castillos son aquellos?
¡Altos son, y relucían!

"Abenamar, Abenamar,
With thy words my heart is won!
Tell me what these castles are,
Shining grandly in the sun!"

—El Alhambra era, señor,
Y la otra la mezquita;
Los otros los Alixares,
Labrados a maravilla.

"That, my lord, is the Alhambra,
This the Moorish Mosque apart,
And the rest the Alixares,
Wrought and carved with wondrous [art.

El moro que los labraba,
Cien doblas ganaba al día,
Y el día que no los labra
Otras tantas se perdía.

For the Moor who did the labour
Had a hundred crowns a day;
And each day he shirked the labour
Had a hundred crowns to pay.

El otro es Generalife,
Huerta que par no tenía;
El otro Torres-Bermejas,
Castillo de gran valía.—

Yonder stands the Generalife,
Ne'er was garden half so grand;
And below, the tower Bermeja,
Stronger none in all the land."

Allí habló el rey Don Juan,
Bien oiréis lo que decía:
—Si tú quisieses, Granada,
Contigo me casaría;
Daréte en arras y dote
A Córdoba y a Sevilla.

Up and spake the good King John,
To the Moor he thus replied:
"Art thou willing, O Granada,
I will woo thee for my bride,
Cordova shall be thy dowry,
And Sevilla by its side."

—Casada soy, rey Don Juan,
Casada soy, que no viuda;
El moro que a mí me tiene
Muy grande bien me quería.

"I'm no widow, good King John,
I am still a wedded wife;
And the Moor who is my husband,
Loves me better than his life!"

This translation would certainly seem to be one of Gibson's best, since not only are the mood and spirit of the model carefully reproduced, but with few exceptions, it is also a literal reproduction of the words of the text. In addition to this, the trochaic movement, as one critic has pointed out in commenting on this particular translation and others of its type, "imitates the rhythm of the originals as closely as could be expected, in view of the fundamental differences between English and Spanish versification."[2]

[2] George W. Umphrey, "Spanish Ballads in English, Part I—Historical Survey," *Modern Language Quarterly* 6 (1945): 493.

Any one of the other translations mentioned above might be chosen to compare with Gibson's without finding one to equal it in excellence, but the version by Robert Southey is without doubt the most interesting. Although it was done sometime before 1808, it was not published until Erasmo Buceta discovered it and another ballad translation in some manuscripts bequeathed by George Ticknor to the Boston Public Library. Buceta published both ballads, with an account of how the manuscripts reached Ticknor, in the June 1919 issue of *Modern Language Notes.*[3] The one with which we are presently concerned is as follows. Note Southey's use of the first line of the original as a title for his translation.

Abenamar, Abenamar

O thou Moor of Moreria,
There were mighty signs and aspects
On the day when thou wert born;
Calm and lovely was the ocean
Bright and full the moon above.
Moor, the child of such an aspect
Never ought to answer falsely.
Then replied the Moorish Captive
(You shall hear the Moor's reply).
Nor will I untruly answer,
Tho' I died for saying truth.
I am son of Moorish sire,
My mother was a Christian slave.
In my childhood, in my boyhood,
Often would my mother bid me
Never know the lyar's shame.
Ask thou therefore, King! thy question
Truly will I answer thee.
Thank thee, thank thee, Abenamar,
For thy gentle answer thanks
What are yonder lofty castles,
Those that shine so bright on high?
That, O King, is the Alhambra,
Yonder is the Mosque of God,
There you see the Alixares,
Works of skill and wonder they;
Ten times ten dobloons the builder
Daily for his hire received;
If an idle day he wasted
Ten times ten dobloons he paid.
Farther is the Generalife,
Peerless are its garden groves.
Those are the vermilion towers,
Far and wide their fame is known.
Then spake up the King Don Juan
(You shall hear the Monarch's [speech).
Wouldst thou marry me, Granada,
Gladly would I for thy dowry
Cordoba and Seville give.

I am married, King Don Juan,
King! I am not yet a widow.
Well I love my Moorish husband,
Well my wedded Lord loves me.

Southey's disparaging remarks concerning the Spanish ballads were mentioned earlier, but he liked the one above and considered it the finest example of its type. Consequently, it might be expected that

[3] Erasmo Buceta, "Two Spanish Ballads Translated by Southey," *Modern Language Notes* 34 (1919): 329-36.

he would have given it his best efforts, and in fact, his translation is quite good. However, in spite of the familiar four-stress, trochaic beat, the lack of rhyme is disturbing since, as George Umphrey notes in his study of *romance* translations, "if any kind of poetry needs rime, it is surely the ballad." [4] Umphrey explains Southey's technique as a consequence of his experiments with unrhymed metrical forms during this period, and he adds the following comment: "His translation of 'Abenamar' . . . conveys adequately the content and rhythm of the original; had he used some kind of rime, consonantal or assonant, and smoothed out two or three halting lines, he might have given us an ideal translation." [5]

In addition to the towns and cities being lost as the Spanish moved inexorably toward the south, the Moors were suffering other casualties of a more personal nature, as evidenced in another ballad translated by Gibson.

Suspira por Antequera El Rey moro de Granada: No suspira por la villa, Que otra mejor le quedaba,	In Antequera sighed the Moor, Granada's King was sad; But 'twas not for the town itself, Far better towns he had.
Sino por una morica Que dentro en la villa estaba; Blanca, rubia a maravilla, Sobre todas agraciada:	He sighed but for a Moorish maid, That lived a captive there, With bonnie face and rosy cheeks, The fairest of the fair.
Deziseis años tenía En los dezisiete entraba; Crióla el Rey de pequeña, Más que a sus ojos la amaba,	Her sixteenth year had come and gone, Her seventeenth now smiled; More than his eyes he loved her well, Had loved her from a child.
Y en verla en poder ajeno Sin poder ser remediada, Suspiros da sin consuelo, Que el alma se le arrancaba.	To see her thus in stranger hands, Whose power he could not shake, Made thousand sighs escape the King, As if his heart would break;
Con lágrimas de sus ojos Estas palabras hablaba: — ¡Ay Narcissa del alma!	His words were mingled with the tears That down his cheeks did roll: "Alas! Narcissa of my life, Narcissa of my soul!

[4] Umphrey, "Spanish Ballads in English," p. 486.
[5] Ibid., p. 487.

Enviéte mis cartas yo Con el alcaide de Alhambra, Con palabras amorosas Salidas de mis entrañas, Con mi corazón herido De una saeta dorada.	I've sent thee letters full of love, That burns within my heart, Red with the wounds that pain my breast, Pierced with a golden dart.
La respuesta que le diste: Que escribir poco importaba. Daría por tu rescate Almería la nombrada.	Thou gavest me this answer sad: That writing could not save — Then Almeria I will give To be thy ransom brave.
¿Para qué quiero yo bienes Pues mi alma presa estaba? Y cuando esto no bastare Yo me saldré de Granada;	Oh what are towns and lands to me? My soul in prison lies; I'll leave Granada's throne and crown, If less will not suffice.
Yo me iré para Antequera Donde estás presa, alindada Y serviré de captivo Solo por mirar tu cara.	To Antequera I will go, And take a captive's place; If but to live where thou dost live, And look upon thy face."

The translation is a fine reproduction of the tone and sentiment of the original and is also extremely faithful to the text. Two minor exceptions are noted, one in the third stanza where the translator substituted "loved her" for "reared her" ("crióla"), the second being the omission of the reference to the messenger, the "alcaide de Alhambra." The iambic verse pattern is quite regular.

Few of the old Spanish ballads have been put into English as often as the one next presented, and Gibson is only one of at least ten authors who have translated it. The subject is the despair of the Moorish king as the Spanish forces draw closer to Granada. Alhama was a small but rich town, much prized by the Moorish rulers and located only a short distance to the southwest of Granada. Since the translation attempts to imitate the earliest form of the *romances* — that is, sixteen-syllable rather than eight-syllable lines — the original is given in that style instead of in the later and more conventional arrangement of eight-syllable lines.

Paseábase el rey moro — por la ciudad de Granada,
desde la puerta de Elvira — hasta la de Vivarambla.
(¡Ay de mi Alhama!)
Cartas le fueron venidas — que Alhama era ganada:

las cartas echó en el fuego, — y al mensajero matara.
(¡Ay de mi Alhama!)
Descabalga de una mula, — y en un caballo cabalga;
por el Zacatín arriba — subido se había al Alhambra.
(¡Ay de mi Alhama!)
Como en el Alhambra estuvo, — al mismo punto mandaba
que se toquen sus trompetas, — sus añafiles de plata.
(¡Ay de mi Alhama!)
Y que las cajas de guerra — apriesa toquen al arma,
porque lo oigan sus moros, — los de la Vega y Granada.
(¡Ay de mi Alhama!)
Los moros que el son oyeron — que al sangriento Marte llama,
uno a uno y dos a dos — juntado se ha gran batalla.
(¡Ay de mi Alhama!)
Allí habló un moro viejo, — de esta manera hablara:
— ¿Para qué nos llamas, rey, — para que es esta llamada?
(¡Ay de mi Alhama!)
— Habéis de saber, amigos, — una nueva desdichada:
que cristianos de braveza — ya nos han ganado Alhama.
(¡Ay de mi Alhama!)
Allí habló un alfaquí — de barba cruda y cana:
— ¡Bien se te emplea, buen rey, — buen rey, bien se te empleara!
(¡Ay de mi Alhama!)
Mataste los Bencerrajes, — que eran la flor de Granada;
cogiste los tornadizos — de Córdoba la nombrada.
(¡Ay de mi Alhama!)
Por eso mereces, rey, — una pena muy doblada:
que te pierdas tú y el reino, — y aquí se pierda Granada. —
(¡Ay de mi Alhama!)

Gibson's translation of the above is as follows:

Slowly rode the Moorish Monarch through Granada's city great,
From the bastion of Elvira to the Bibarambla gate.
Alas for my Alhama!

Letters brought the fatal tidings, that Alhama had been ta'en,
In the fire he tossed the letters, bid the messenger be slain.
Alas for my Alhama!

From his mule he quick alighted, rode on horseback through the town,
Up the Zacatin he galloped, at the Alhambra lighted down.
Alas for my Alhama!

Through the palace rang his summons, all his people gathered round,
Bade his martial trumpets blare, bade his silver clarions sound.
Alas for my Alhama!

Bade them beat his drums of war, sounding forth the dread alarm,
Through the Vega and Granada, summoning the Moors to arm.
Alas for my Alhama!

When the Moors had heard the clamour, calling to the bloody fight,
One by one, and two by two, forth they come in all their might.
Alas for my Alhama!

Then spake out a Moorish Ancient, these the words he had to say,
"Why this summons, O my King, why this summons to the fray?"
Alas for my Alhama!

"Friends, it is a new disaster meets us to our bitter cost
By the Christians fierce assault, proud Alhama we have lost."
Alas for my Alhama!

Then spake out a grave Alfaqui, with dishevelled beard and grey,
"Well it serves thee, noble King, and will serve for many a day!
Alas for my Alhama!

Thou hast slain the Abencerrages, fair Granada's flower and pride,
And from Cordova hast gathered base deserters to thy side.
Alas for my Alhama!

For this deed thou well deservest yet to bear a double pain,
That Granada taken should be, thou and thine in battle slain."
Alas for my Alhama!

In a study of this ballad and several outstanding renditions in English, Luella Thurston Little concluded that Gibson's version was superior in almost every respect.[6] The many other translations include those by Lord Byron, Robert Southey, Matthew Lewis, Thomas Rodd, Edward Maturin, W. J. Entwistle, John Bowring, W. S. Merwin, and John Masefield.

With respect to Granada, the worst fears of the Moors were soon realized, and the city was taken by the Spaniards in 1492, thus bringing to an end the more than seven hundred years of Moslem occupation. The grief of the Moorish monarch is aired in the following lament, which is typical of several *romances* based on this event.

---

[6] Luella Thurston Little, "English Translation of Spanish Ballads" (Master's thesis, University of Washington, 1937), p. 16.

En la ciudad de Granada
Grandes alaridos dan;
Unos llaman a Mahoma,
Otros a la Trinidad:
Por un cabo entraban cruces,
De otro sale el Alcorán;
Donde antes oían cuernos,
Campanas oyen sonar.
El *Te Deum laudamus* se oye
En lugar del Alha-alha.
No se ven por altas torres
Ya las lunas levantar:
Mas las armas de Castilla
Y de Aragón ven campear.
Entra un rey ledo en Granada,
El otro llorando va;
Mesando su barba blanca,
Grandes alaridos da.
—¡Oh mi ciudad de Granada,
Sola en el mundo, sin par,
Donde toda la morisma
Se solía contigo honrar!
Bien ha setecientos años
Que tienes cetro real
De mi famoso linaje,
Qu'en mí se vino acabar.
Madre fuiste venturosa
De gente muy singular,
De valientes caballeros,
Amigos de pelear,
Enemigos de Castilla,
Daño de la Cristiandad,
Madre de gentiles damas
De gran valor y beldad,
Amigas de caballeros
En armas dignos de honrar,
Por quien los galanes de Africa
Se venían a señalar;
Por quien se vencían batallas
Por ellas las desear,
Y se honraban los galanes
Por sus señales llevar.
En ti se acabó Mahoma,
Más que dios de allén d'el mar;
En ti estaba la milicia,
La gentileza y bondad;
De soberbios edificios
Solías mucho ilustrar.
A jardines, huertas, campos
De la tu vega real
Secas las veo sus flores,
Arboles altos no hay.
Rey que tal corona pierde
No se tiene de acatar,
Ni cabalgar en caballo,
Ni hablar en pelear;
Mas do no le vean las gentes
Su vida en llanto acabar
Con esto el rey de Granada
En una fusta se va
La vía de Berbería
Y estrecho de Gibraltar,
Do a la Reina su mujer
Halló con tan gran pesar,
Qu'en velle se ha levantado,
Y con él se fué abrazar,
Diciendo a muy grandes gritos
Que el cielo hacía temblar:
—¡Oh desventurado Rey,
Que hace tal poquedad,
Que a Granada dejar pueda
Y no se quiere ahorcar!
Por el bien que te deseo,
Yo, Rey, te quiero matar,
Que quien tal reino ha dejado,
Poco es la vida dejar.—
Y con sus airadas manos
Al Rey procuraba ahogar:
El Rey, de desesperado,
A ello le fué ayudar.

Gibson and Lockhart both translated this ballad, using the same meter and the same general technique, and both translations are quite good. Lockhart has an especially good first stanza, but, overall, Gibson's version is better. It is reproduced below, as the final sampling from the *romances fronterizos.*

Within Granada's city there are sounds of woe and glee,
Some pray aloud to Mahomet, some bless the Trinity;
The Cross comes in with shouting, the Koran goes out with scorn,
And the merry bell is chiming, where once they blew the horn.

Where "Allah! Allah!" sounded, "Te Deum" now is chaunted,
Castile and Aragon's proud flag waves where the Crescent flaunted;
One King rides in with triumph, the other weeping goes,
He tears his white beard in his grief, and tells aloud his woes:

"O my city of Granada! that never had a peer,
The pride of every Moorish land, to all the Moslems dear;
For seven hundred years has the crown been worn by thee
Of the famous line of monarchs, that now must end with me!

Thou were the fruitful mother of a noble race of men,
Whose like the land saw not before, and ne'er may see again;
Who loved to be the foremost in war and chivalry,
The bitter foemen of Castile, the scourge of Christendie!

Thou wert the happy mother of maidens bright with charms,
Whose glance inflamed our cavaliers, and made them strong in arms;
For them the pride of Afric's sons were fain to cross the sea,
For them they gained their battles all, to them they bowed the knee.

Sure never braver gentler Knights did ladies' colours wear,
Nor live in nobler palaces, so costly and so rare;
But now the race with all its grace must pass away with thee!
For Mahomet has fallen here, who rules across the sea.

I see thy fields and meadows, thou Vega of renown,
But thy fragrant flowers are withered, thy stately trees are down;
O woe betide the luckless King that such a crown has lost!
'Tis his to feel the bitter shame; 'tis his to pay the cost;
No more to ride a horse of war, or rank amongst his peers,
But live where none can see his shame, and end his life in tears!"

Granada's King has left it for his bark upon the sea,
To sail across Gibraltar's strait, and on to Barbary;
The Queen is there to meet him, with anger in her eyes,
She grasps his trembling hands and gives her clamour to the skies:

"O luckless King and coward! that only thinks to fly,
Who leaves Granada to its fate, and will not rather die;
Had I my will I'd slay thee now, although I be thy wife,
Who cannot keep a crown like this should scorn to keep his life!"

Gibson used Lockhart's favorite meter for this translation — the seven-stress, iambic line of fourteen syllables — achieving almost as much success with it as with the shorter measures. An occasional trochee or anapest was substituted for the conventional iambic foot to avoid monotony. The translation is quite close to the model in the first five stanzas, each long line encompassing two of the short ones of the *romance*, but the remaining stanzas are somewhat freer. The last four lines of the original were omitted in translation in order to end the ballad at its most climactic point — the impassioned outburst of the queen.

The translations included in this chapter are only a limited introduction to the exotic world described in the Moorish ballads, and many other fine examples are available. Most of the major translators, from Thomas Percy on, have transcribed at least a few from this category. The only large assortment in one place, however, that of Epiphanius Wilson, is quite disappointing, and a really adequate collection of Moorish ballads in English is yet to be compiled.

Chapter IV

BALLADS OF CHIVALRY, LOVE, AND ADVENTURE

THE FINAL SAMPLING FROM THE *Romancero* will consist mainly of ballads which belong to the *romance juglaresco* or *romance artístico* categories. The use of either term designates a composition of relatively late origin, somewhat more personal in tone than the *romances viejos* or *tradicionales,* and one which reveals evidence of individual, rather than collective authorship. [1] The artistic ballads, especially, show signs of conscientious workmanship and are more polished in form and more regular in meter than the older ballads. They also tend to be lyric in nature rather than narrative, with a great variety of themes. Most of the ballads of chivalry are *romances juglarescos,* with some of the oldest and best coming from the Carolingian cycle. Others of this type, in which the narrative element is paramount, could be considered as *romances novelescos,* since they are based on themes from folklore or isolated tales of adventure.

The first translations to be discussed are three versions by James Young Gibson of ballads from the legends of the French knight Gayferos (Gaifers in the *Chanson de Roland*). All three have long been popular, with the first two reputedly remaining in the oral tradition of the people of Asturias down to the present time. [2] Like many of the Carolingian ballads, these are quite long, and only representative portions will be reproduced.

---

[1] Some of the ballads considered in the past to be *romances artísticos* may be quite old. See José F. Montesinos, "Algunos problemas del Romancero nuevo," *Romance Philology* 6 (1953): 231-47.

[2] S. Griswold Morley, *Spanish Ballads* (New York: Henry Holt and Company, 1924), p. 154.

The first poem relates how Gayferos as a child learns from his mother the story of his father's murder by his stepfather and how he subsequently escapes to the home of an uncle after the stepfather overhears the mother and son talking. The first three stanzas of Gibson's translation correspond to the following lines from the *romance*:

Estábase la Condesa
En el su estrado asentada,
Tijericas de oro en mano
Su hijo afeitando estaba.
Palabras le está diciendo,
Palabras de gran pesar,
Las palabras tales eran
Que al niño hacen llorar.
— Dios te dé barbas en rostro
Y te haga barragane,
Déte Dios ventura en armas
Como al paladín Roldane,
Porque vengases, mi hijo,
La muerte de vuestro padre:
Matáronlo a traición
Por casar con vuestra madre.
Ricas bodas me hicieron
En las cuales Dios no ha parte;
Ricos paños me cortaron,
La Reina no los ha tales. —
Maguera pequeño el niño
Bien entendido lo hae.
Allí respondió Don Gayferos,
Bien oiréis lo que dirae:
— Ruégolo así a Dios del cielo
Y a Santa María su madre. —

Within her tiring-chamber sat the Countess and her son
With golden scissors in her hand, to trim his locks each one;
And as she trimmed his flowing hair, she told a tale of woe,
That made his boyish heart to beat, and made his tears to flow:

"God send thee soon a manly beard, and manly strength to wield
A sword that like Orlando's wins honour in the field;
Thy father's death thou must avenge, thou, son, and not another,
A traitor pierced him to the heart, that he might wed thy mother.

They made for me a wedding grand, God's blessing was not there,
Though cloths of gold they cut for me, the Queen herself might wear;"
To this the young Gayferos said, no word did he forget:
"By God above and Mary blessed, I will avenge thee yet!"

The remainder of the translation is just as faithful to the spirit and thought of the original. Nothing is added or deleted, and the only major change is the occasional transposition of lines. There are twelve stanzas in the entire composition, all quatrains of rhyming couplets with the exception of two which have six lines each.

Lockhart also translated this ballad, his first three stanzas being the following:

Before her knee the boy did stand, within the dais so fair,
The golden shears were in her hand, to clip his curled hair;
And ever, as she clipped the curls, such doleful words she spake,
That tears ran from Gayferos' eyes, for his sad mother's sake.

"God grant a beard were on thy face, and strength thine arm within,
To fling a spear, or swing a mace, like Roland Paladin!
For then, I think, thou wouldst avenge thy father that is dead,
Whom envious traitors slaughtered within thy mother's bed.

"Their bridal gifts were rich and rare, that hate might not be seen;
They cut me garments broad and fair, — none fairer hath the Queen."
Then out and spake the little boy: "Each night to God I call,
And to his blessed Mother, to make me strong and tall."

This translation is in the same meter as Gibson's, and like the latter's, it is a good rendition. It is not quite as accurate, however, and the second stanza in particular omits an important idea in the Spanish. The meaning of "Por casar con vuestra madre" is not completely clear here, but it seems to suggest the reason the boy's father was killed. Lockhart apparently failed to recognize that a motive for the slaying was being given, and he converts the line into an unwarranted statement about where the incident took place. A few other small liberties are taken in translation, but none serious enough to merit comment.

After Gayferos reaches the safety of his uncle's home, he remains for several years until he is old enough to undertake vengeance against his stepfather. The next ballad begins with his words to his uncle, as the two prepare to set out for Paris.

— Vámonos, dijo, mi tío,
A París esa ciudade
En figura de romeros
No nos conozca Galvane.
Que si Galván nos conoce
Mandaríanos matare:
Encima ropa de seda
Vistamos las de sayale,
Llevemos nuestras espadas
Por más seguros andare,
Llevemos sendos bordones
Por la gente asegurare. —
Ya se parten los romeros,
Ya se parten, ya se vane,
De noche por los caminos,
De día por sus jarales.

"Come, Uncle, let us leave this place, and take the road to Paris,
And let us wear the pilgrim's garb for fear our plan miscarries;
For if Galvan should find us out, to death we'll quickly go,
So let us cover our silken robes with sorry weeds of woe;

And in our hands the pilgrim's staff, that we may pass as strangers,
But underneath our trusty swords, to serve us in our dangers."
In sackcloth dress, with palmer's staff, they travelled on the way,
By night along the open roads, and through the woods by day.

Gibson's translation, the only one known, continues in this vein, giving a very faithful and pleasing transcription of the arrival at Paris, the encounter with the stepfather, whom Gayferos slays, and the recognition of the youth by his mother. The style and technique are similar to the specimens just seen, and no further commentary is necessary.

The third ballad from the Gayferos series is the longest translation in Gibson's collection. It consists of some thirty stanzas and a total of almost three hundred lines. Most of the stanzas are from eight to twelve lines, although some have as few as six, and one as many as nineteen. The story it tells is how Gayferos released his captive wife from her imprisonment by the Moors. The opening lines from the original, and Gibson's translation, are as follows:

Asentado está Gayferos
En el palacio reale,
Asentado está al tablero
Para las tablas jugare.
Los dados tiene en la mano
Que los quiere arrojare,
Cuando entró por la sala
Don Carlos el Emperante:
De que así jugar lo vido
Empezóle de mirare;
Hablándole está hablando
Palabras de gran pesare:
— Si así fuésedes, Gayferos,
Para las armas tomare,
Como sois para los dados
Y para tablas jugare,
Vuestra esposa tienen moros,
Iriádesla a buscare:
Pésame a mí por ello
Porque es mi hija carnale.
De muchos fué demandada,
Y a nadie quiso tomare:
Pues con vos casó por amores,
Amores la han de sacare;
Si con otro fuera casada
No estuviera en catividade. —

Within the royal palace-hall Gayferos sat one day,
Sat playing at the checker-board, to while the time away;
He held the dice within his hand, they were about to fall,
When the Emperor Don Carlos came marching up the hall;
He stood aghast to see him thus sit playing at the game,
And, taking speech, he spoke to him these bitter words of shame:
"Gayferos, had you been as quick to arm you for the fray,
As you have been to throw the dice, and at the tables play,
Then had you gone to seek your wife enslaved by Moorish art,
She is the daughter of my house, it cuts me to the heart;
By many she was courted, but no one would she take,

She banished all her lovers, resigned them for your sake;
She married you for love alone, 'tis love must set her free,
Oh, had she been another's wife, no captive wife were she!"

The translation closely parallels the model throughout, and it is easy to match the two almost line for line. Twenty-six lines from the original describing Gayfero's refusal of a plea by his uncle that he take companions with him are omitted in translation. All the remaining lines are rendered in the characteristic manner illustrated above.

Gibson's translation makes such smooth and pleasant reading and yet conveys so well the ideas of the model that it invites comparison with the only other version known, that of Thomas Rodd. Since Rodd's translations are known for their literal qualities, an additional check on Gibson's faithfulness to the text is thus obtained. The lines from Rodd's version corresponding to those above should be sufficient for this purpose.

In the royal palace sitting,
Ere he had begun to play,
As before the Prince Gayferos
Wide the tables open lay,

In his hand the dice retaining,
Just upon the point to throw,
To the Knight the King approaching,
Did his royal person show.

With a scornful look he ey'd him,
Utt'ring with a taunt severe,—
"O Gayferos, how it shames me
To behold you idling here!

Were you but in arms as dext'rous
As at tables and the dice,
You would hold your honor surely
At a far more worthy price;

And your spouse, to Moors a captive,
This would lead you to regain.
Much I'm grieved to think my daugh- [ter
Should a hapless slave remain.

Many another Chieftain gladly
Would have call'd the maid his [own:
Since for love she chose to wed you,
Love must be her friend alone.

But if other Knight possess'd her,
There, forsooth, she wou'd not stay;
By immortal deeds of valour
He would bring his spouse away."

Contrary to what might have been expected in view of Rodd's reputation, Gibson's is actually the more literal version. It seems also to have preserved the mood and temper of the original somewhat better than Rodd's, in addition to showing more felicity of expression.

Attention should be directed, in passing, to another, much shorter, version of Gayfero's rescue of his wife, the fair Melisendra. As the second of two ballads from this cycle, Lockhart includes in his collection a quite adequate rendition of "El cuerpo preso en Sansueña."

Several of the *romances carolingios* feature the exploits of the famous Montesinos and his friend Durandarte. Readers of Cervantes are familiar with this pair through Don Quixote's description of the strange events he witnessed in the Cave of Montesinos (Chapters 22 and 23 of the second part of *Don Quixote*). The following ballad, translated by Gibson, relates an offer of love made to Montesinos by an attractive and bold young lady. Menéndez Pidal says it is without doubt very old. [3]

En Castilla está un castillo
Que se llama Rocafrida,
Al castillo llaman Roca
Y a la fuente llaman Frida.
El pie tenía de oro
Y almenas de plata fina;
Entre almena y almena
Está una piedra zafira;
Tanto relumbra de noche
Como el sol a mediodía.
Dentro estaba una doncella
Que llaman Rosaflorida:
Siete Condes le demandan,
Tres Duques de Lombardía,
A todos los desdeñaba,
Tanta es su lozanía:
Enamoróse de Montesinos
De oídas, que no de vista.
Una noche estando así
Gritos da Rosaflorida:
Oyérala un camarero,
Que en su cámara dormía.
—¿Qué es aquesto, mi señora?
¿Qué es esto, Rosaflorida?
O tenedes mal de amores,
O estáis loca sandía.
—Ni yo tengo mal de amores,
Ni estoy loca sandía,
Mas llevásesme estas cartas
A Francia la bien guarnida,
Diéseslas a Montesinos,
La cosa que más quería.
Dile que me venga a ver
Para la pascua florida,
Daréle yo este mi cuerpo,
El más lindo de Castilla,
Si no es el de mi hermana,
Que de fuego sea ardida.
Y si de mí más quisiere
Yo mucho más le daría,
Darle he siete castillos
Los mejores de Castilla.

In Castile there stands a Castle, and its name is Rosa-florida,
'Tis the Castle they call Roca, and the fountain they call Frida;
Solid gold are its foundations, and its towers of silver fine,
In the space 'twixt every turret there a sapphire stone doth shine,
Shines as clear amid the night
As the sun in broad daylight.

[3] Ramón Menéndez Pidal, *Flor nueva de romances viejos,* 8th ed. (Buenos Aires: Espasa-Calpe, Colección Austral, 1950), p. 96.

In the Castle dwells a maiden, Rosa-florida is she,
Seven Earls have sought to wed her, and three Dukes of Normandie,
Such her pride and her disdain, she has put them all to flight,
For her love to Montesinos, love by hearsay not by sight.

Being so one night it happened, Rosa-florida groaned and wept,
And her chamberlain he heard it in the chamber where he slept,
"Rosa-florida, what is this? What is this, my Lady dear?
Either thou art sick of loves, or becoming mad, I fear!"

"Neither am I sick of loves, nor becoming mad, perchance,
Take these letters now and bear them to the lovely land of France;
Give them there to Montesinos, 'tis the thing I hold most dear,
Tell him he must come and see me, at the Easter time of year;

This my body I will give him, none fairer in Castile, I know,
Be it not my lovely sister's, that with luring fire doth glow;
And if more he ask of me, much more I will give him still,
I will give him seven castles, better none in all Castile."

The rendition is literal, but nonetheless, sufficiently poetic. There is a great deal of lyrical interest which could have evaporated easily in translation, but which Gibson consciously sought to retain. He was not quite as much at ease here with the long eight-stress, trochaic lines, however, and this ballad lacks a little of the naturalness and spontaneity of expression which he seemed to achieve so readily in iambic verse. In spite of the unfamiliar appearance of the first stanza, there is nothing unusual about the structure of the poem, and the two short lines are simply a rearrangement on the page of one long line.

Montesinos appears again in the following translation, which is Gibson's version of the *romance* describing the death of Durandarte. Actually, both these French heroes are fictional characters, the personage of Durandarte having derived from the name given to Roland's sword, Durendal. There are also versions of this ballad by Lockhart and Matthew Lewis.

¡Oh Belerma! ¡oh Belerma!
Por mi mal fuiste engendrada,
Que siete años te serví
Sin de ti alcanzar nada.
Agora que me querías
Muero yo en esta batalla:
No me pesa de mi muerte

"O Belerma! O Belerma!
Thou wert born to give me pain;
Seven years I served thee truly,
Never could thy favour gain;
Though thou love me now I perish,
Perish on this battle-plain.

Aunque temprano me llama,
Mas pésame que de verte
Y de servirte dejaba,

¡Oh mi primo Montesinos!
Lo que agora yo os rogaba,
Que cuando yo fuere muerto
Y mi ánima arrancada,

O my cousin Montesinos,
Bear in mind my old behest;
That when Death should take my body,
And my soul have gone to rest,

Vos llevéis mi corazón
Adonde Belerma estaba,
Y servidla de mi parte
Como de vos yo esperaba,

You my heart would straightway carry
Where Belerma then might be;
And would serve her well and truly
For the love you bear to me;

Y traedle mi memoria
Dos veces cada semana,
Y diréisle que se acuerde
Cuan cara que me costaba,

And would twice in every week
Bring my memory to her thought;
And would bid her well remember
With what price her love I bought;

Y dadle todas mis tierras
Las que yo señoreaba;
Pues que yo a ella pierdo,
Todo el bien con ella vaya.

And would give her all my lands,
Where I reigned as lord alone;
For since now I lose herself,
All my wealth with her is gone.

¡Montesinos, Montesinos!
¡Mal me aqueja esta lanzada!
El brazo traigo cansado
Y la mano del espada:

Montesinos! Montesinos!
What a thrust this lance hath made!
Now my arm is growing powerless,
And the hand that wields my blade.

Traigo grandes las heridas,
Mucha sangre derramada,
Los estremos tengo fríos,
Y el corazón me desmaya,
Que ojos que nos vieron ir
Nunca nos verán en Francia.

All my wounds are wide and gaping,
And in streams my blood doth flow;
All my lower parts are freezing,
And my heart is beating low;
Never shall those eyes behold us,
That from France did see us go.

Abracéisme, Montesinos,
Que ya se me sale el alma.
De mis ojos ya no veo,
La lengua tengo turbada;

Now embrace me, Montesinos,
For my soul is taking flight,
And my voice is low and quivering,
And my eyes have lost their light.

A vos doy todos mis cargos,
En vos yo los traspasaba.
—El Señor en quien creéis
Él oiga vuestra palabra.—

I have given my last commands,
Act in all things in my stead."
"May the Lord in whom you trusted
Hear the words you now have said!"

Muerto yace Durandarte
Al pie de una alta montaña,
Llorábalo Montesinos
Que a su muerte se hallara:

Cold in death lay Durandarte,
Underneath a green beech-tree
Montesinos stood bewailing,
And his tears were falling free.

Quitándole está el almete,
Desciñéndole el espada,
Hácele la sepultura
Con una pequeña daga.

From his head he took the helmet,
From his side the sword unbound,
Made for him a sepulchre
With his dagger in the ground.

Sacábale el corazón,
Como él se lo jurara,
Para llevarlo a Belerma,
Como allí se lo mandara.
Las palabras que le dice
De allá le salen del alma:

By the oath that he had given,
He the heart cut from his breast,
For to bear it to Belerma,
By his cousin's last request;
Words that he could not control
Now came gushing from his soul:

— ¡Oh mi primo Durandarte!
¡Primo mío de mi alma!
¡Espada nunca vencida!
¡Esfuerzo do esfuerzo estaba!
¡Quien a vos mató, mi primo,
No sé por qué me dejara!

"O my cousin Durandarte,
Cousin to my heart most dear,
Sword that never yet was conquered,
Valour high without a peer;
He who slew you, O my cousin,
Wherefore did he leave me here?"

Again Gibson has used a trochaic meter, but the short lines skip along freely in a translation which captures exceedingly well the spirit and ideas of the original. Four lines from the model are deleted, but the artistic effect is improved by having the second stanza start with an invocation similar to that in the first. Another minor alteration is the substitution of the "green beech-tree" for the "alta montaña." The change is not unwarranted, however, since several of the ballads describing the death of Durandarte mention the "verde haya." The translation presents a strikingly clear and vivid picture of the scene and is even more impressive when we consider that our visualization of what is taking place comes primarily from the words spoken by the dying knight. The clarity of the situation is a tribute to Gibson's skill in rendering dialogue, although this translation is only one of several which illustrate this ability.

The next example from the Carolingian ballads of chivalry has drawn praise from all quarters. Lockhart called it "one of the most admired of all Spanish ballads,"[4] and George Ticknor termed it "full of the spirit of a chivalrous age, and of a simple pathos which is of all ages and all countries."[5] It relates the prophetic dream of Lady Alda at the time Roland is killed at Roncesvalles and dates back to at least the first half of the sixteenth century.

En París está Doña Alda
La esposa de Don Roldán,
Trescientas damas con ella
Para la acompañar:
Todas visten un vestido,
Todas calzan un calzar,
Todas comen a una mesa,
Todas comían de un pan,
Sino era sola Doña Alda,
Que era la mayoral:
Las ciento hilaban oro,
Las ciento tejen cendal,
Las ciento instrumentos tañen
Para Doña Alda holgar.
Al son de los instrumentos
Doña Alda adormido se ha,
Ensoñada había un sueño,
Un sueño de gran pesar.
Recordó despavorida
Y con un pavor muy grande,
Las gritos daba tan grandes,
Que se oían en la ciudad.
Allí hablaron sus doncellas,
Bien oiréis lo que dirán:
— ¿Qué es aquesto, mi señora?
¿Quién es él que os hizo mal?
— Un sueño soñé, doncellas,
Que me ha dado gran pesar,
Que me veía en un monte
En un desierto lugar:
Bajo los montes muy altos
Un azor vide volar,
Tras dél viene una aguililla
Que lo afincaba muy mal.
El azor con grande cuita
Metióse so mi brial,
El aguililla con grande ira
De allí lo iba a sacar,
Con las uñas lo despluma,
Con el pico lo deshace. —
Allí habló su camarera,
Bien oiréis lo que dirá:
— Aquese sueño, señora,
Bien os lo entiendo soltar:
El azor es vuestro esposo
Que viene de allende el mar,
El águila sedes vos,
Con la cual ha de casar,
Y aquel monte es la iglesia
Donde os han de velar.
— Si así es, mi camarera,
Bien te lo entiendo pagar. —
Otro día de mañana
Cartas de fuera le traen,
Tintas venían de dentro,
De fuera escritas con sangre,
Que su Roldán era muerto
En la caza de Roncesvalles.

Both Gibson and Lockhart translated this ballad, the former with considerable success, but the version by Sir Edmund Head is the best to date. Ticknor reproduced it for his *History of Spanish Literature,*

[4] John Gibson Lockhart, *Ancient Spanish Ballads* (New York: Wiley and Putnam, 1842), p. 163.

[5] George Ticknor, *History of Spanish Literature* (Boston: Ticknor and Fields, 1863), 1: 121.

describing it as a "beautiful translation . . . much better than the one by Lockhart, which though spirited, is diffuse and unfaithful."[6] It reads as follows:

In Paris Lady Alda sits, Sir Roland's destined bride,
With her three hundred maidens, to tend her, at her side;
Alike their robes and sandals all, and the braid that binds their hair,
And alike the meal, in their Lady's hall, the whole three hundred share.
Around her, in her chair of state, they all their places hold:
A hundred weave the web of silk, and a hundred spin the gold,
And a hundred touch their gentle lutes to sooth that lady's pain,
As she thinks on him that's far away with the host of Charlemagne.
Lulled by the sound, she sleeps, but soon she wakens with a scream,
And, as her maidens gather round, she thus recounts her dream:
"I sat upon a desert shore, and from the mountain nigh,
Right toward me, I seemed to see a gentle falcon fly;
But close behind an eagle swooped and struck that falcon down,
And with talons and beak he rent the bird, as he cowered beneath my gown."
The chief of her maidens smiled, and said: "To me it doth not seem
That the Lady Alda reads aright the boding of her dream.
Thou art the falcon, and thy knight is the eagle in his pride,
As he comes in triumph from the war and pounces on his bride."
The maidens laughed, but Alda sighed, and gravely shook her head.
"Full rich," quoth she, "shall thy guerdon be, if thou the truth has said."
'Tis morn: her letters, stained with blood, the truth too plainly tell,
How, in the chase of Ronceval, Sir Roland fought and fell.

Head's translation is, indeed, very good and shows greater variety of meter than Gibson's version, although in other respects, the two poems are quite comparable. Head's rendition is somewhat less accurate, but the admirable way in which it presents the essence of the original tends to reduce greatly the importance of this criticism. It is a satisfying translation and will not easily be surpassed.

The last illustration from the Carolingian ballads is another excessively long poem, only part of which will be reproduced here. The subject is the escape of Don Guarinos from Moorish captivity after many long years of imprisonment. There are several versions, taken from *pliegos sueltos* of the early sixteenth century. The first part is as follows:

---

[6] Ibid.

¡Mala la visteis, franceses,
La caza de Roncesvalles!
Don Carlos perdió la honra,
Murieron los doce Pares,
Cativaron a Guarinos
Almirante de las mares,
Los siete reyes de moros
Fueron en su cativare.
Siete veces echan suertes
Cual dellos lo ha de llevare,
Todas siete le cupieron
A Marlotes el Infante:
Más lo preciaba Marlotes
Que Arabia con su ciudade.
Dícele desta manera,
Y empezóle de hablare:
—Por Alá te ruego, Guarinos,
Moro te quieras tornar,
De los bienes deste mundo
Yo te quiero dar asaz;
Las dos hijas que yo tengo
Ambas te las quiero dare,
La una para el vestir,
Para vestir y calzare,
La otra para tu muger,
Tu muger la naturale.
Darte he en arras y dote
Arabia con sus ciudades;
Si más quisieres, Guarinos,
Mucho más te quiero dare.—
Allí hablara Guarinos,
Bien oiréis lo que dirá:
—No lo mande Dios del cielo
Ni Santa María su madre
Que deje la fe de Cristo
Por la de Mahoma tomar,
Que esposica tengo en Francia,
Con ella entiendo casar.—
Marlotes con gran enojo
En cárceles lo manda echar
Con esposas a las manos
Porque pierda el pelear,
El agua hasta la cintura
Porque pierda el cabalgar,
Siete quintales de fierro
Desde el hombro al calcañal.

There are translations of this ballad by Rodd, Matthew Lewis, and Lockhart, but as in so many instances, the best version is by Gibson:

At the chase of Roncesvalles, Frenchmen, bitter was your fall,
There Don Carlos lost his honour, died the twelve peers one and all;
There they captured Don Guarinos, he the Admiral of the seas,
Seven Moorish kings were round him, like a swarm of angry bees.

Seven times they drew the lot, who should have the noble knight;
Seven times Marlotes won it, seized his prize with great delight,
For he prized him better far, to give lustre to his crown,
Than the kingdom of Arabia, and its city of renown.

"Now by Allah, Don Guarinos, would you but become a Moor,
Riches you shall have in plenty, though you now be wondrous poor;
Both my daughters I will give you, one to dress and deck you fine,
And the fairer one to wed you, and upon your breast recline.
All Arabia and its city I will give you as her dower,
And if more you wish to ask, more by far is in your power."

When Guarinos heard the offer, firm his answer was expressed:
"Now may God in Heaven forbid it, and His mother Mary Blessed,
Moorish faith shall ne'er be mine, I'm a Christian born and bred,
I've a lovely bride in France, 'tis with her I mean to wed."

Like a fury rose Marlotes, thrust him in a dungeon drear,
Gyves were fastened on his hands, never more to grasp the spear,
Water flowed up to his hips, ne'er to press his charger's seat,
Seven loads of irons bound him, from the shoulder to the feet.

The rest of the ballad describes how Don Guarinos remained in prison for seven years, but finally gained access to his horse and armor by means of an incredible boast. He makes good his boast and also escapes from his captors. Several lines in the last portion are omitted in translation, although none of the thought is left out, and the sample above is a good representation of the whole.

Although there are not a large number of translations of ballads from the Arthurian or Breton cycles (in spite of the relative frequency of these legends in the *Romancero*), Gibson has two interesting translations based on the adventures of Lancelot. The first one, reportedly a very old ballad, relates an incident in which the English knight unwittingly incurs great danger in a search for an enchanted deer.

Tres hijuelos había el Rey, Tres hijuelos, que no más; Por enojo que hubo de ellos Todos malditos los ha.	Three tender striplings had the King, Three striplings and no more; And for the wrath he bore to them He cursed them loud and sore.
El uno se tornó ciervo, El otro se tornó can, El otro, que se hizo moro, Pasó las aguas del mar.	The first of them became a deer, The next a dog turned he, The last he turned a Moorish man, And sailed across the sea!
Andábase Lanzarote Entre las damas holgando, Grandes voces dió la una: — Caballero, estad parado:	Upon a time Sir Lancelot Among the dames did play; "Sir Knight," quoth she, the boldest one, "Be on your guard this day!
Si fuese la mi ventura, Cumplido fuese mi hado Que yo casase con vos, Y vos conmigo de grado, Y me diésedes en arras Aquel ciervo del pie blanco.	For were't my luck to wed with thee, And thine to wed with me, I'd ask the bonnie white-foot deer As wedding-gift from thee!"

— Dároslo he yo, mi señora,
De corazón y de grado,
Si supiese yo las tierras
Donde el ciervo era criado. —

"With all my heart, my lady fair,
I'd bring him safely here,
Gif I but knew the far countrie
Where herds that bonnie deer!"

Ya cabalga Lanzarote,
Ya cabalga y va su vía,
Delante de sí llevaba
Los sabuesos por la traílla.

Sir Lancelot he rode along
For many a weary day;
His boots hung at his saddle-bow,
And all to hunt the prey.

Llegado había a una ermita,
Donde un ermitaño había:

He clambered up among the hills,
And there he found a cell,
Where far from any living man
An Eremite did dwell.

— Dios te salve, el hombre bueno.
— Buena sea tu venida:
Cazador me parecéis
En los sabuesos que traía.

"God keep thee!" quoth the Eremite,
"Thou'rt welcome here to me;
And by the boots thou bearest there
A huntsman thou mayst be."

— Dígasme tú, el ermitaño
Tú que haces santa vida,
Ese ciervo del pie blanco,
¿Dónde hace su manida?

"Now tell to me, good Eremite,
Thou holy man austere,
Now tell to me where I may find
The bonnie white-foot deer."

— Quedaos aquí, mi hijo,
Hasta que sea de día,
Contaros he lo que vi
Y todo lo que sabía.

"Come take thy rest with me, my son,
Until the night hath flown;
I'll tell thee all that I have seen,
And all that I have known."

Por aquí pasó esta noche
Dos horas antes del día,

And as they talked the live-long night,
And whiled the time with cheer,
There passed, two hours before the light,
The bonnie white-foot deer.

Siete leones con él
Y una leona parida:
Ciete Condes deja muertos,
Y mucha caballería.

And with him seven lions, and
A lioness with young;
Full seven counts had she laid low,
And many a knight and strong.

Siempre Dios te guarde, hijo,
Por dó quier que fuera tu ida,
Que quien acá te envió
No te quería dar la vida.

"Wherever be thy home, my son,
God shield thee with His arm!
Whoever sent thee here this day
Had thought to do thee harm!

¡Ay dueña de Quintañones,
De mal fuego seas ardida,
Que tanto buen caballero
Por tí ha perdido la vida!

Shame, Lady Quintañona, shame,
Hell-fire thy portion be!
If such a brave and gallant knight
Should lose his life for thee!"

The translation conveys nicely the aura of mystery and impending danger which surrounds the original, in addition to providing a quite literal transcription of the words. One wonders, though, at the curious rendition of the word "sabuesos" ("hounds"), which Gibson translates as "boots." Otherwise, the apt choice of expression is equal, if not superior, to the poetic level of the model, and the verse is harmonious and agreeable. Gibson has improved the last two lines in translation (in the original a lament for the knights who have previously met death because of Lady Quintañona) by altering the meaning slightly and by keeping attention focused on Lancelot rather than allowing it to shift to the unnamed knights who went before him. The essential idea remains unchanged, however, and the judgment passed on the lady is just as severe.

Two anonymous translations of this ballad exist, one in the April issue of the *Foreign Quarterly Review* of 1829 and the other in *Fraser's Magazine* of 1832. The latter translates the two lines in question above in a manner which suggests that Lancelot actually was killed in this adventure. Several other errors in translation are more puzzling and are much less justified than this one. For example, the translator puts "daughters" in place of "sons," he has Lancelot knowing exactly where the deer is to be found, and he reduces the number of lions to six. Nevertheless, as a whole, the translation is quite good and compares favorably with Gibson's. It is included in its entirety below.

Three daughters had the royal king, three daughters and no more,
And for the life he led with them against their life he swore;
The one was changed into a hind, the next became a hound,
The third a Mooress turned, and pass'd the ocean waves beyond.
Laughing walks Sir Lancelot the laughing dames among;
Aloud cries one, "Sir Knight, prepare your steed and hunting throng;
For if it be the will of Heaven to rule your lot and mine,
And in the bands of married love, our hands together join,
Then give to me, in earnest first, the hind with the snow-white feet."
"That will I give with right good-will to thee, my lady sweet!
Right well I know the lands wherein the hind was born, they say."
Now mounts Sir Lancelot the bold, now mounts and rides away;
And by his side to track the hind two fleetest greyhounds run;
And he hath come to a hermit's bower as slowly sinks the sun.
"God save thee, father!" "Welcome, son, right welcome wilt thou be!
As, from thy stately hounds, thou seem'st a hunter bold and free."
"O tell me, hermit, tell me true, thou man of holy life,

Where lives the hind with the snow-white feet that causeth all this strife?"
"Tarry with me, my son, I pray, until the daylight dawn,
And I will tell what I saw and heard regarding the snow-white fawn;
This night, two hours before the day, she passes the hoary wood,—
Six bearded lions all by her side, a lioness red with blood;
Six paladins bold she has reft of life, the flower of chivalry.
God shield thee ever, my son, I pray, wherever thy journey be!
For whosoe'er hath sent thee, son, no gentle love has learned.
Ah, Duenna de Quintanyona! with evil fire be burned,
That for thy sake so brave a knight untimely death has earned!"

The second of Gibson's Lancelot ballads portrays the knight avenging an insult to Guinevere. The original is quite well known because of its mention in Chapter 13 of Part 1 of the *Quixote*. Lockhart, the only other author to render it into English, placed his translation in the notes he made for Motteux's edition of Cervantes's classic and did not include it in his *Ancient Spanish Ballads*. Gibson's version is the following:

Nunca fuera caballero De damas tan bien servido, Como fuera Lanzarote Cuando de Bretaña vino,	Never was a gallant knight Served by damosel or dame As the good Sir Lancelot, When from Britain forth he came.
Que dueñas curaban dél, Doncellas del su rocino. Esa dueña Quintañona, Esa le escanciaba el vino,	Ladies took his armour off, Damsels waited on his steed, And the Lady Quintañona Poured him out the foaming mead.
La linda Reina Ginebra Se lo acostaba consigo; Y estando al mejor sabor, Que sueño no había dormido,	Sweet and fair Queen Guinivere Took him to her secret bower, Being in the better humour, That she had not slept an hour;
La Reina toda turbada Un pleito ha conmovido. —Lanzarote, Lanzarote, Si antes hubieras venido,	There the Queen with beating breast Told her sorrow in his ear: "Lancelot, Sir Lancelot! Hadst thou but been sooner here!
No hablara el orgulloso Las palabras que había dicho, Que a pesar de vos, señor, Se acostaría conmigo.—	Never had that shameless knight Said to me the words he said: That in spite of thee, Señor, He would come to me in bed!"
Ya se arma Lanzarote De gran pesar conmovido,	Furious rose Sir Lancelot, Armed himself with double speed;

Despídese de su amiga,	To his lady bade adieu,
Pregunta por el camino,	Took the road upon his steed;
Topó con el orgulloso	Underneath the shady pine
Debajo de un verde pino,	There he found the knight he sought;
Combátense, de las lanzas	First they couched and broke the lance,
A las hachas han venido.	Then with battle-axe they fought.
Ya desmaya el orgulloso,	Lancelot with heavy stroke
Ya cae en tierra tendido,	Laid the caitiff on the green;
Cortárale la cabeza,	Cut his head from off his shoulders,
Sin hacer ningún partido;	Fairer stroke was never seen;
Volvióse para su amiga	Homeward rode Sir Lancelot,
Donde fué bien recibido.	"Welcome, welcome!" quoth the [Queen.

The rendition is accurate and quite literal, except that the translator has described the rendezvous with Guinevere somewhat more discreetly than the original and has changed the last line into a direct quotation from the queen. The verse pattern shows a variation from the normal trochaic lines of eight and seven syllables, as all of the above lines are seven.

The fairy-tale quality of the preceding poems, much more common in the English than in the Spanish ballads, is prominent in another *romance novelesco,* a very old ballad which presents a theme frequently found in European folklore. It relates the story of the enchanted lady. The Spanish text is as follows:

A cazar va el caballero,
A cazar como solía;
Los perros lleva cansados,
El falcón perdido había,
Arrimárase a un roble,
Alto es a maravilla.
En una rama más alta,
Viera estar una Infantina;
Cabellos de su cabeza
Todo aquel roble cubrían.
— No te espantes, caballero,
Ni tengas tamaña grima,
Hija soy yo del buen Rey
Y la Reina de Castilla:
Siete fadas me fadaron
En brazos de un ama mía,
Que andase los siete años
Sola en esta montiña.
Hoy se cumplían los siete años
O mañana en aquel día:
Por Dios te ruego, caballero,
Llévesme en tu compañía,
Si quisieres por muger,
Si no, sea por amiga.
— Esperáisme vos, señora,
Hasta mañana aquel día,
Iré yo a tomar consejo
De una madre que tenía. —
La niña le respondiera
Y estas palabras decía:
— ¡O mal haya el caballero
Que sola deja la niña! —

El se va a tomar consejo
Y ella queda en la montiña.
Aconsejóle su madre
Que la tome por amiga.
Cuando volvió el caballero
No hallara la Infantina,
Vídola que la llevaban
Con muy gran caballería.
El caballero que la vido
En el suelo se caía;
Desque en sí hubo tornado
Estas palabras decía:
— Caballero que tal pierde,
Muy gran pena merescía:
Yo mesmo seré el Alcalde,
Yo me seré la Justicia:
Que me corten pies y manos
Y me arrastren por la villa.

Gibson, who is one of four translators of this ballad, arranged his version in quatrains of fourteen-syllable, seven-stress lines with caesura after the eighth syllable. The rhythm will be seen to be quite regular.

The Cavalier a-hunting went, and hunted all the day,
His hounds were worn and wearied out, his falcon went astray;
He sat him down beneath an oak, an oak of wondrous height,
And as he sat and rested there, he saw a wondrous sight;

For there upon a lofty branch, amid the foliage green,
There perched a maid, whose beauty rare no mortal eyes had seen;
The clustering hair that crowned her head fell rippling down below,
Her eyes shown out like burning suns and made the forest glow.

"Fear not, Sir Knight, nor let the sight thine eyes with horror fill,
For I'm the daughter of the King and Queen of all Castile,
Seven witches they enchanted me, when in my nurse's arms,
To keep me here for seven years they brewed their hellish charms;

To-night the seven years are gone, or with the rising sun,
For God's sake stay with me this night, until the spell be done;
And bear me safely to thy home, I'll be thy loving wife,
Or if thou wilt, thy dearest friend, to serve thee all my life."

"I'll come, sweet maid, at early morn, I cannot stay tonight,
I go to ask my mother dear to counsel what is right."
"Now shame on thee, false cavalier, thy courtesy is small,
To leave a lonely maiden here and night about to fall."

At break of day he rode in haste, to free the maiden fair,
He went to find the wondrous oak, but not an oak was there;
He sought for her, and called for her, through all the forest glade,
When lo! advancing he beheld a stately cavalcade;

A troop of gallant Knights and Lords came prancing o'er the green,
And in the midst the lady rode majestic as a queen;
And when his senses came again, these fatal words he said:
"The Knight who such a prize has lost, has honour lost and fame,"
With that he fell upon his sword, and died for very shame.

The translation has caught the mood of the ballad quite well and has stayed close to the thought, but it is further from the actual wording of the model than is customary in Gibson's work. It expands the description of the princess considerably, adds the description of the knight's search for her, and describes in greater detail the approaching procession in whose midst she rides. The ending is changed also, to make it more readily acceptable to English readers.

The other translators of this ballad are Lockhart, Merwin, and John Bowring. Lockhart rendered it as follows:

The knight had hunted long, and twilight closed the day,
His hounds were weak and weary, — his hawk had flown away;
He stopped beneath an oak, an old and mighty tree,
Then out the maiden spoke, and a comely maid was she.

The knight 'gan lift his eye the shady boughs between,
She had her seat on high, among the oak-leaves green;
Her golden curls lay clustering above her breast of snow,
But when the breeze was westering, upon it they did flow.

"Oh, fear not, gentle knight! there is no cause for fear;
I am a good king's daughter, long years enchanted here;
Seven cruel fairies found me, — they charmed a sleeping child;
Seven years their charm hath bound me, a damsel undefiled.

Seven weary years are gone since o'er me charms they threw;
I have dwelt here alone, — I have seen none but you.
My seven sad years are spent; — for Christ that died on rood,
Thou noble knight, consent, and lead me from the wood!

Oh, bring me forth again from out this darksome place!
I dare not sleep for terror of the unholy race.
Oh, take me, gentle sir! I'll be a wife to thee, —
I'll be thy lowly leman, if wife I may not be."

"Till dawns the morning, wait, thou lovely lady! here;
I'll ask my mother straight, for her reproof I fear."
"Oh, ill beseems thee, knight!" said she, that maid forlorn,
"The blood of kings to slight, — a lady's tears to scorn!"

He came when morning broke, to fetch the maid away,
But could not find the oak wherein she made her stay;
All through the wilderness he sought in bower and tree;
Fair lordlings, well ye guess what weary heart had he!

There came a sound of voices from up the forest glen,
The King had come to find her with all his gentlemen;
They rode in mickle glee — a joyous cavalcade —
Fair in the midst rode she, but never word she said.

Though on the green he knelt, no look on him she cast —
His hand was on the hilt ere all the train were past.
"Oh, shame to knightly blood! Oh, scorn to chivalry!
I'll die within the wood: — No eye my death shall see!"

Each of the translations has a good opening stanza, although the last line of Lockhart's seems a rather abrupt introduction to the presence of the lady. He, too, amplifies the story in several places and alters the ending, but the changes in both translations are reasonable ones and should be permissible. Lockhart's verse is in twelve-syllable, iambic lines which read quite well. Taken altogether, his version compares favorably to Gibson's.

The same three translators, Gibson, Lockhart, and Bowring, also translated the next ballad, another *romance novelesco,* although its theme of lovers separated by death puts it in the subcategory of *romances amorosos.* Gibson's version, which shows an interesting variety of verse forms, including both iambic and trochaic meters, is the best of the three. It accompanies the original.

En los tiempos que me vi Más alegre y placentero, Yo me partiera de Burgos Para ir a Valladolid:	When I sallied forth from Burgos, I was happy as the May; When I rode on to Valladolid I was merry all the way.
Encontré con un palmero Quien me habló, y dijo así: — ¿Dónde vas tú, el desdichado? ¡Dónde vas triste de ti!	But I met a holy Palmer, And he stopped me for to say: "Why ridest thou so merrily? Thou child of sorrow, stay!
¡O persona desgraciada, En mal punto te conocí! Muerta es tu enamorada, Muerta es, que yo la vi.	My heart for thee is bleeding, It is a bitter day; For thy lady-love is lying, Cold, cold in the clay!

Las andas en que la llevan
De negro las vi cubrir,
Los responsos que le dicen
Yo los ayudé a decir.

I met her bier advancing,
And black was the array;
I heard the friars chanting,
I sang as sad as they.

Siete Condes la lloraban,
Caballeros más de mil,

Seven noble Counts were round it,
Their solemn dues to pay;
A thousand knights did follow
In mourning all the way.

Llorábanla sus doncellas,
Llorando dicen así:
"¡Triste de aquel caballero
Que tal pérdida pierde aquí!"

I heard her damsels wailing,
I heard what they did say:
'Alas! alas for the Cavalier,
Who hath lost his love this day!' "

Desque aquesto oí, mezquino,
En tierra muerto caí,
Y por más de doce horas
No tornara, triste, en mí.

The Palmer's tale was ended,
My senses went away;
Twelve weary hours passed o'er me,
As on the ground I lay.

Desque hube retornado
A la sepultura fuí,
Con lágrimas de mis ojos
Llorando decía así:
— Acógeme, mi señora,
Acógeme a par de ti. —

I went to seek her sepulchre,
And sobbing there did pray:
"Let me rest with thee, dear lady;
Let me rest with thee alway!"

Al cabo de la sepultura
Esta triste voz oí:
— Vive, vive, enamorado,
Vive, pues que yo morí:

But a voice so sad and tender
From out the grave did say:
"Live, live, my darling lover,
Though thy love hath passed away!

Dios te dé ventura en armas,
Y en amor otro que sí,
Que el cuerpo come la tierra,
Y el alma pena por ti. —

God give thee luck in battles,
And another love some day;
For my heart for thee is aching,
Though my bed be in the clay!"

The motif of the husband or lover returning home after long years of absence occurs in almost every literature, and the *Romancero* is no exception. The next ballad, translated by John Bowring, presents one of the standard variations of the theme. The original was first published in a *pliego suelto* in 1605.

— Caballero de lejas tierras,
Llegáos acá, y paréis,
Hinquedes la lanza en tierra,

"Knight that comest from afar,
Tarry here, and here recline;
Couch thy lance upon the floor,

Vuestro caballo arrendéis,
Preguntaros he por nuevas
Si mi esposo conocéis.
— Vuestro marido, señora,
Decid, ¿de qué señas es?
— Mi marido es mozo y blanco,
Gentil hombre y bien cortés,
Muy gran jugador de tablas,
Y también del ajedrez.
En el pomo de su espada
Armas trae de un marqués,
Y un ropón de brocado
Y de carmesí al envés:
Cabe el fierro de la lanza
Trae un pendón portugués,
Que ganó en unas justas
A un valiente francés.
— Por esas señas, señora,
Tu marido muerto es:
En Valencia le mataron
En casa de un ginovés:
Sobre el juego de las tablas
Lo matara un milanés.
Muchas damas lo lloraban,
Caballeros con arnés,
Sobre todo lo lloraba
La hija del ginovés;
Todos dicen a una voz
Que su enamorada es:
Si habéis de tomar amores,
Por otro a mí no dejéis.
— No me lo mandéis, señor,
Señor, no me lo mandéis,
Que antes que eso hiciese,
Señor, monja me veréis.
— No os metáis monja, señora,
Pues que hacello no podéis,
Que vuestro marido amado
Delante de vos lo tenéis.

Stop that weary steed of thine:
I would fain inquire of thee
News of wandering husband mine."
"Lady! thou must first describe
Him, thy husband, sign by sign."
"Knight! my husband's young and fair,
In him grace and beauty shine;
At the tablets dexterous he,
And at chess; the honour'd line
Of a marquis on his sword,
Well engraved, you might divine.
All his garments of brocade,
Felted crimson, fair and fine;
At his lance's point he bears
Flag from Tagus' banks, where shine
Victories that he won of old
From a valiant Gaul.": "That sign
Tells me, lady! he is dead:
Murder'd is that lord of thine.
In Valencia was he kill'd,
Where there lived a Genovine.
Playing at the tablets, he
There was murder'd. At his shrine
Many a noble lady wept,
Many a knight of valiant line:
One mourn'd more than all the rest,
Daughter of the Genovine;
For they said, and that was true,
She was his: so, lady mine!
Give me now thy heart, I pray,
For my heart is only thine."
"Nay, sir knight! it cannot be!
Nay! I must not thus incline.
To a convent first I'll go,
Vow me to that life divine."
"No! that cannot, cannot be,
Check that hasty vow of thine;
For I am thy husband, dear!
Thou the unstain'd wife of mine."

Bowring was able to imitate to a considerable extent the assonant form of the original through an unvarying rhyme scheme employed in a single long sequence, unbroken by stanzaic division or other interruption. The translation is quite literal, without being strained or awkward.

Another variation on the theme of the husband's return concerns the punishment of the unfaithful wife. The Spanish treatment of the topic is usually serious and dignified, in contrast to the coarse or humorous way in which it is often handled in other countries. The ballad of the ill-married lady, or "La bella malmaridada," is typical.

"La bella malmaridada
De las lindas que yo vi,
Véote tan triste, enojada:
La verdad dila tú a mí.
Si has de tomar amores
Por otro no dejes a mí.
Que a tu marido, señora,
Con otras dueñas lo vi
Besando y retozando;
Mucho mal dice de ti,
Juraba y perjuraba
Que te había de ferir."
Allí habló la señora,
Allí habló, y dijo así:
"Sácame tú, el caballero,
Tú sacásesme de aquí;
Por las tierras donde fueres
Bien te sabría yo servir;
Yo te haría bien la cama
En que hayamos de dormir,
Yo te guisaré la cena
Como a caballero gentil,
De gallinas y de capones
Y otras cosas más de mil;
Que a este mi marido
Ya no le puedo sufrir,
Que me da muy mala vida
Cual vos bien podéis oir."
Ellos en aquesto estando
Su marido hélo aquí:
"¿Qué hacéis, mala traidora?
¡Hoy habedes de morir!"
"¿Y por qué, señor, por qué?
Que nunca os lo merecí;
Nunca besé a hombre,
Mas hombre besó a mí;
Las penas que él merecía,
Señor, dadlas vos a mí;
Con riendas de tu caballo
Señor, azotes a mí;
Con cordones de oro y sirgo
Viva ahorques a mí;
En la huerta de los naranjos
Viva entierres tú a mí;
En sepultura de oro
Y labrada de marfil,
Y pongas encima un mote,
Señor, que diga así:
'Aquí está la flor de las flores,
Por amores murió aquí;
Cualquier que muere de amores
Mándese enterrar aquí,
Que así hice yo, mezquina,
Que por amar me perdí.' "

Lockhart's version of this ballad, the only one known, is reproduced below. Contrary to his usual practice he took few liberties in translation, and these are not serious. He also seems to have captured extremely well the tone and mood of the *romance*.

"Lovely lady, married ill, though fairest of the fair thou be,
Grief within thine eye is seated, well thy lonely grief I see.
If thou seek another lover, seek not farther, rest with me,
While thy faithless lord is wandering, faith and love I'll give to thee.

All the day thy husband wanders 'midst the damsels of the town,
He to play and prado squires them, while thy bosom's peace is flown;
Yesternight I heard them sporting, merry jibes on thee they threw,—
Soon, he said, thy days he'll finish, and another lady woo."

Out and spake the lovely lady, "Thou my sorrow well hast read;
Take me with thee, gentle stranger, let me quit my lonely bed;
Careless aye and cruel tongue, weary am I of them both,
Let me swear to be thy love, and faithfully I'll keep mine oath.

I will serve thee late and early, with an handmaid's humble cheer,
I will dress our capon neatly, I will pour our wine so clear;
I will deck our bed so fairly, all with sheets of Holland fine—
Take me where thou wilt, I'm weary of this faithless lord of mine."

While the stranger kissed the lady in her chamber o'er and o'er,
Hush! the husband hears their voices; ha! he open knocks the door,—
"Traitress false, and foul adulterer, have I caught ye in the deed?
Now to God commend your spirits, great of mercy is your need!"

"Husband, bright thy sword is gleaming!—must I, must I die to-day?
Save thyself, with mortal lover, till this hour I never lay.
But if blood thy sword must drink, hear my last request, I pray,
Harm not him that owed thee nothing; let me all the forfeit pay!

Though thou whip me with thy bridle, silently the pain I'll bear;
Though thou hang me in my girdle, anger shall not stain my prayer;
Let the youth go free, and slay me—grant the only boon I crave!
Lay me in the orange garden,—there I fain would have my grave.

Underneath the spreading branches, where the blossoms bright are shed,
Deeply dig for one that loved thee long and well, a peaceful bed;
Lay a marble stone above, and let its golden legend be,—
'Ladies, shrink from love unholy, warned by her whose tomb you see.'"

Still another example of the theme noted above is found in the ballad of "La Blancaniña." Of the four versions in English by W. S. Merwin, John Masefield, Sir Edmund Head, and John Bowring, that of Bowring appears below. Like the preceding poem and the one which is to follow, the original is a *romance tradicional.*

"Blanca sois, señora mía,
Más que el rayo del sol;
¿Si la dormiré esta noche
Desarmado y sin pavor?

"O gentle lady! thou art fair,
Fair as the sunny ray is bright;
And fearless and disarm'd at last,
In sweetest sleep I'll sleep to-night.

Que siete años había, siete,
Que no me desarmo, no;
Más negras tengo mis carnes
Que un tiznado carbón."
"Dormidla, señor, dormidla
Desarmado sin temor,
Que el conde es ido a la caza
A los montes de León."
"¡Rabia le mate los perros
Y águilas el su halcón,
Y del monte hasta casa
A él arrastre el morón!"
Ellos en aquesto estando
Su marido que llegó:
"¿Qué hacéis, la Blancaniña,
Hija de padre traidor?"
"Señor, peino mis cabellos,
Péinolos con gran dolor,
Que me dejáis a mí sola
Y a los montes os vais vos."
"Esa palabra, la niña,
No era sino traición:
¿Cúyo es aquel caballo
Que allá abajo relinchó?"
"Señor, era de mi padre,
Y envióoslo para vos."
"¿Cúyas son aquellas armas
Que están en el corredor?"
"Señor, eran de mi hermano,
Y hoy os las envió."
"¿Cúya es aquella lanza,
Desde aquí la veo yo?"
"¡Tomadla, conde, tomadla,
Matadme con ella vos,
Que aquesta muerte, buen conde,
Bien os la merezco yo!"

For full seven years I bear my arms,
And I have never put them down,
And, lady, now my skin as black,
Black as the smutty coal is grown."
"Sleep, soundly sleep, thou valiant knight,
Unarm'd and fearless sleep; the count
Is gone to hunt, as he is wont,
Is gone to hunt on Leon's mount:
Let madness there destroy his hounds,
An eagle on his falcon pounce,
And from the mountain to his home
Remove the helmet from his sconce."
While thus they spoke the count return'd,
And thus in furious tones he said:
"O what is this, white maiden, now,
Of treacherous father, treacherous [maid?"
"I comb'd my hair, O count beloved,
I comb'd my hair in grief and woe,
Because my lord had left his love,
And would to yonder mountain go."
"O maiden! no such cheating words,
No more perfidious language say!
Whose is that proud and noble horse
I heard within the stable neigh?"
"My lord! my father sent the steed
An homage of his love to thee."—
"Whose, lady, are those shining arms,
Which 'gainst the corridor I see?"
"My lord! they were my brother's arms,
Which he has sent for thee to wear."
"And whose, fair lady! is the lance
Whose sharpen'd point is moving [there?"
"O count! O count! take thou that lance,
And pierce my guilty body through;
For O! I have deserved it all,
And shame and death are now my [due."

Again the translator has conveyed extremely well the essence of the original without taking undue liberties. The *romance* itself is another fine example of ballad technique, and it has enjoyed a long popularity. Menéndez Pidal has been quoted as saying that in spite of its very adult theme, it is one of the ballads most often sung by children.[7]

Bowring has one other translation from the group of ballads depicting the penalties of illicit love. It is a remarkable example of the ability of the *romance* to concentrate in a few lines of dialogue a familiar and poignant story.

— Tiempo es, el caballero,
Tiempo es de andar de aquí,
Que me crece la barriga,
Y se me acorta el vestir.
Vergüenza he de mis doncellas,
Las que me dan el vestir,
Míranse unas a otras,
Y no hacen sino reír.
Si tenéis algún castillo
Donde nos podamos ir.
Si sabéis de alguna dueña
Que me lo ayude a parir.
— Paridlo vos, mi señora,
Que así hizo mi madre a mí,
Hijo soy de un labrador
Que el cavar es su vivir. —

"Knight! I must go from hence — must go, —
  The world will all divine:
My girdle is too narrow now, —
  They'll see my shame — and thine.
I cannot look upon my maids,
  When they my garments bring;
I see them wink, and nod their heads,
  I hear them tittering.
So bring me to thy castle home —
  Come, thither let us go,
And bid some trusty woman come
  To help me in my woe!"
"O lady! I'm a peasant lad,
  And born to guide the plough —
The woman that my mother had,
  When I was born, have thou."

Not all the ballads dealing with love have implications as tragic as those examined above. The ones which follow, for example, suggest other less serious, although in certain cases, still painful, situations arising from the relations between the sexes. The first two have a long history of publication, since they came into print several years before the earliest collection of *romances* was assembled. They were printed for the first time in the *Cancioneros generales* compiled by Fernando del Castillo in Valencia in 1511. This work was essentially a collection of courtly poetry of the period, but it included some thirty-seven ballads, nineteen of which are by known authors. These two are anonymous, however, and are generally regarded as being very old. The smooth technique and graceful lyrical qualities give evidence of considerable refining and polishing. The first, with a translation by Bowring, is as follows:

---

[7] C. Colin Smith, *Spanish Ballads* (Oxford: Pergamon Press, 1964), p. 199.

Rosa fresca, rosa fresca,
Tan garrida y con amor,

Cuando y'os tuve en mis brazos,
Non vos supe servir, non;
Y agora que vos servía
Non vos puedo yo haber, non.
— Vuestra fué la culpa, amigo,
Vuestra fué, que mía non;
Enviásteme una carta
Con un vuestro servidor,
Y en lugar de recaudar
El dijera otra razón:
Qu'érades casado, amigo,
Allá en tierras de León;
Que tenéis mujer hermosa
Y hijos como una flor.
— Quien vos lo dijo, señora,
Non vos dijo verdad, non;
Que yo nunca entré en Castilla
Ni allá en tierras de León,
Sino cuando era pequeño,
Que non sabía de amor. —

"Lovely flow'ret, lovely flow'ret,
O! what thoughts your beauties [move —
When I prest thee to my bosom,
Little did I know of love;
Now that I have learnt to love thee,
Seeking thee in vain I rove."
"But the fault was thine, young warrior;
Thine it was — it was not mine:
He who brought thy earliest letter
Was a messenger of thine:
And *he* told me — graceless traitor —
Yes! *he* told me — lying one —
That thou wert already married
In the province of León:
Where thou hadst a lovely lady,
And, like flowers too, many a son."
"Lady! he was but a traitor,
And his tale was all untrue —
In Castille I never enter'd —
From León, too, I withdrew
When I was in early boyhood,
And of love I nothing knew."

There are translations of the above ballad by Gibson, Merwin, George Ticknor, and Ruth Matilde Anderson, but Bowring's version comes closest to capturing the lyricism and charm of the original. Gibson's and Ticknor's renditions convey the thought of the Spanish in a simple, straightforward manner, however, and Ticknor's poem, especially, has much to recommend it. It is reproduced below for comparison with Bowring's.

"Rose, fresh and fair, Rose, fresh and fair,
That with love so bright dost glow,
When within my arms I held thee,
I could never serve thee, no!
And now that I would gladly serve thee,
I no more can see thee, no!"

"The fault, my friend, the fault was thine, —
Thy fault alone, and not mine, no!
A message came, — the words you sent, —
Your servant brought it, well you know.

And naught of love, or loving bands,
  But other words, indeed, he said:
That you, my friend, in Leon's lands
  A noble dame had long since wed; —
A lady fair, as fair could be;
  Her children bright as flowers to see."

"Who told that tale, who spoke those words,
  No truth he spoke, my lady, no!
For Castile's lands I never saw,
  Of Leon's mountains nothing know,
Save as a little child, I ween,
  Too young to know what love should mean."

The next ballad, even more of a *romance lírico* than the preceding, has attracted the attention of many translators. The five mentioned above, Merwin, Bowring, Gibson, Anderson, and Ticknor, also rendered this one, as did W. J. Entwistle, George Umphrey, Georgiana King, and Yvor Winter. Bowring's version is quoted here.

Fonte-frida, Fonte-frida,
Fonte-frida y con amor,
Do todas las avecicas
Van tomar consolación,
Sino es la tortolica
Qu'está viuda y con dolor.

Fount of freshness! fount of freshness!
  Fount of freshness and of love!
Where the little birds of spring-time
  Seek for comfort as they rove;
All except the widow'd turtle —
  Widow'd, sorrowing turtle-dove.

Por ahí fuera a pasar
El traidor del ruiseñor:
Las palabras que le dice
Llenas son de traición:
— Si tu quisieses, señora,
Yo sería tu servidor.

There the nightingale, the traitor!
  Linger'd on his giddy way;
And these words of hidden treachery
  To the dove I heard him say:
"I will be thy servant, lady!
  I will ne'er thy love betray."

— Véte de ahí, enemigo,
Malo, falso, engañador,
Que ni poso en ramo verde,
Ni en prado que tenga flor;
Que si el agua hallo clara,
Turbia la bebía yo;
Que non quiero haber marido,

"Off! false-hearted! — vile deceiver!
  Leave me, nor insult me so:
Dwell I, then, midst gaudy flowrets?
  Perch I on the verdant bough?
Even the waters of the fountain
  Drink I dark and troubled now.
Never will I think of marriage —
  Never break the widow-vow.

Porque hijos non haya, non;
Non quiero placer con ellos,

"Had I children they would grieve me,
  They would wean me from my woe:

Ni menos consolación.
¡Déjame, triste enemigo,
Malo, falso, mal traidor,
Que non quiero ser tu amiga
Ni casar contigo, non!

Leave me, false one! — thoughtless trai- [tor! —
Base one! — vain one! — sad one — [go!
I can never, never love thee —
I will never wed thee — no!"

The subject for this ballad came from the medieval bestiaries in which the turtle dove is described as monogamous. When in mourning for a lost mate, it reputedly "seeks the solitary places of the earth for its habitation, rests upon no green branch, and drinks from no clear spring, but chooses the dead limb for its home and muddies with beak or feet the water which is to satisfy its thirst." [8] Although the theme occurs widely in other European folk songs, the nightingale does not appear as a villain in any except the Spanish and Portuguese. [9]

With the exception of the second stanza, Bowring's rendition is quite literal, yet sufficiently fresh and poetic. It is typical of the compositions which have given him a reputation as one of the better translators of the lyrical ballads.

Of many other good translations of this ballad, George Umphrey's is the one which seems to me the most successful in conveying the elusive qualities of the original. The first two lines were adapted from the translation by Ticknor.

Cooling fountain, cooling fountain,
Fount of pleasure and of love,
Where the birds in mating season
Seeking consolation come;
All except the widowed turtle,
Grieving for her turtle-dove.
Nightingale, the traitor, passing,
Vainly tried to win her trust;
With false words he would deceive her
And supplant the one she loved:
"If it be your will, fair lady,
You alone I'd gladly serve."
"Leave me, you deceiver, leave me,
False one, hold your wicked tongue;
Rest not I on verdant branches,
Flower-strewn meadows now I shun.
Not for me the cooling fountain;
Muddied water slakes my thirst.
I'll not have another husband;
And for children, I want none
To console me with their prattle
And my thoughts of him disturb.
Leave me, then, you false deceiver;
Say no more; begone! enough!
I refuse your vows of marriage
And disdain your words of love."

[8] Phillip S. Allen, "Turteltaube," *Modern Language Notes* 19 (1904): 175.

[9] Morley, *Spanish Ballads*, p. 144.

The poetic form of Umphrey's translation is obviously a close imitation of the eight — and seven-syllable assonating lines of the *romance,* and comparison of his poem with the original indicates how closely the words of the model were followed. In addition, the lyric simplicity and personal feeling are retained to a considerable extent, although the translation does not quite equal the original in this regard. The last few lines of the *romance* give difficulty to all the translators, and Umphrey has not solved the problem much better than any of the others.

It was noted earlier that some of the ballad collections contain compositions which deviate not only in tone but also in form from the typical *romance.* Such deviations are especially common among the lyrical ballads and in the *romances amorosos.* Two of the more frequent variations are the use of a refrain and the reduction in the number of syllables in each line from eight to six. (These short-line *romances* are often referred to as *romancillos.*) The ballad of "La niña morena," translated by both Lockhart and Gibson, furnishes an illustration of both phenomena. Gibson's version is with the Spanish.

¡La niña morena,
Que yendo a la fuente
Perdió sus zarcillos,
Gran pena merece!
Diérame mi amado,
Antes que se fuese,
Zarcillos dorados,
Hoy hace tres meses.

Dos candados eran
Para que no oyese
Palabras de amores
Que otros me dijesen.
Perdílos lavando:
¿Qué dirá mi ausente,
"Sino que son unas
Todas las mujeres?"

Dirá que no quise
Candados que cierren,
Sino falsas llaves,
Mudanza y desdenes;
Dirá que me hablan
Cuantos van y vienen,

What ails the bonnie maiden,
  What grief hath she to tell?
What grief, but that her ear-rings
  Have dropped into the well!
"Alas, my golden ear-rings!
  Three months this very day
My darling lover gave them,
  When he went far away.

He meant them to be padlocks,
  That I might never hear
What other stranger lovers
  Should whisper in my ear!
I dropped them as I washed me,
  But he will think it shame;
He'll say I'm but a woman,
  And all women are the same!

He'll say I was so restless
  With locks so true as these,
And wished false keys to turn about
  As often as I please,
That I might flirt and chatter
  With any lad that came;

<table>
<tr><td>"Y que somos unas
Todas las mujeres."</td><td>He'll say I'm but a woman,
And all women are the same!</td></tr>
<tr><td>Dirá que me huelgo
De que no parece
El domingo en misa
Ni el mercado en jueves;
Que mi amor sencillo
Tiene mil dobleces
"Y que somos unas
Todas las mujeres."</td><td>He'll say I was so idle,
And so I did not care
To go to mass on Sundays,
On Thursdays to the fair;
He'll say my love so tender
Hath falsehood for its name;
He'll say I'm but a woman,
And all women are the same!</td></tr>
<tr><td>Diráme: —Traidora,
Que con alfileres
Prendes de tu cofia
Lo que mi alma prende!—
Cuando esto me diga
Diréle que miente,
"Y que no son unas
Todas las mujeres."</td><td>He'll say to me: 'False maiden,
O, traitress that thou art,
The pins from thy cofia
Go pricking through my heart!'
If such and such he tells me,
I'll tell him to his shame,
That, though I'm but a woman,
We are not all the same!</td></tr>
<tr><td>Diré que me agrada
Su pellico el verde
Muy más qu'el brocado
Que visten marqueses;
Que su amor primero
Primero fue siempre;
"Que no somos unas
Todas las mujeres."</td><td>I'll say that I love better
His jacket green of skin,
Than all the coats of Marquises,
Though broidered out and in!
I'll tell him that his first love
Hath still an honest name;
That, though I'm but a woman,
We are not all the same!</td></tr>
<tr><td>Diréle qu'el tiempo
Qu'el mundo revuelve,
La verdad que digo
Verá si quisiere.
¡Amor de mis ojos,
Burlada me dejes
"Si yo me mudare
Como otras mujeres!"</td><td>I'll say, be not too hasty,
For rolling time will show
If all my loving speeches
Be very truth or no.
I give thee leave to scorn me,
My only love and true,
If I should ever turn and change
As other women do."</td></tr>
</table>

Gibson's translation was studied by Luella Thurston Little, who analyzes it as follows: "Gibson divides the ballad into seven eight-line stanzas, all except the first closing with the refrain. He uses seven and six-syllable lines in iambic meter, accented on the sixth syllable and rimed alternately on the short lines. The arrangement is similar to that of the ballad, and the translation is almost literal line by line. The language beautifully interprets the spirit and thought of the ballad; nothing is overdone nor over dramatized, and the poetry flows along with ease and simple grace." [10] The admirable qualities of Gibson's version would be even more evident in a comparison with the translation by Lockhart, which is greatly inferior.

One of the interesting themes in Spanish lyric poetry, especially the popular poetry, is the lament of a maiden for an absent lover. The following ballad, translated in characteristic fashion by John Bowring, illustrates one treatment of the motif in the *Romancero* and is another good example of the *romance lírico.* Although faithful to the model, the translation has all the ease of an original composition.

Yo me levantara, madre,
Mañanica de Sant Joan:
Vide estar una doncella
Ribericas de la mar:
Sola lava y sola tuerce,
Sola tiende en un rosal:
Mientras los paños s'enjugan,
Dice la niña un cantar:
"¿Dó los mis amores, dó los?
¿Dó los andaré a buscar?"

Mar abajo, mar arriba,
Diciendo iba el cantar,
Peine de oro en las sus manos
Por sus cabellos peinar.
"Dígasme tú, el marinero,
Sí, Dios te guarde de mal,
Si los viste, mis amores,
Si los viste allá pasar."

Mother! I woke at early morn,
Upon San Juan's festal day,
And on the sandy shore, forlorn,
Saw a lone, silent maiden stray:
Alone she had wash'd, and strain'd, and [spread
Her garments on the rose-tree grove;
And while they dried, the maiden said,
"Where shall I go to seek my love?
Where shall I go? — O tell me where?"

And the tide it sunk, and the tide it [swell'd;
For thus her song flow'd sweetly there —
And with a comb of gold in her hand [she held,
With which she comb'd her raven hair.
"Tell me, thou busy mariner,
And so may God thy helper prove,
Tell me if thou have seen my love —
Say, hast thou seen him wandering here?"

A representative cross section of the ballads of love and adventure must necessarily include two other *romances novelescos,* both quite old, which have won universal praise. Each is adequately represented in translation, and both furnish excellent examples of ballad technique, although they differ greatly in theme and mood.

---

[10] Luella Thurston Little, "English Translation of Spanish Ballads" (Master's thesis, University of Washington, 1937), p. 33.

The first of these presents an unusual exposition of a not-uncommon story. Poems based on the experiences of captives are numerous in the *romancero,* but the one below has acquired a special place among the lyrical ballads because of the artistry of the poet in eliminating prosaic details and in reducing the prisoner's narrative to a single outburst of great emotional and lyrical intensity. It is usually called the "Song of the Captive Knight." The English version is by W. J. Entwistle.

—Por el mes era de mayo
Cuando hace la calor,
Cuando canta la calandria
Y responde el ruiseñor,
Cuando los enamorados
Van a servir al amor,
Sino yo, triste cuitado,
Que vivo en esta prisión,
Que ni sé cuando es de día
Ni cuando las noches son,
Sino por una avecilla
Que me cantaba el albor.
Matóla un ballestero,
¡Déle Dios mal galardón!

Oh 'tis May, the month of May,
when the season's heat is high,
and the larks above are singing
and the nightingales reply,
and all lovers are a-running
on love's errands far and nigh;
all but me, afflicted, wretched,
that in prison-house do lie;
neither know I when day cometh,
nor when night is passing by,
were it not for one wee birdie,
singing when the dawn is nigh:
but an archer slew my birdie—
may he earn God's curse thereby!

There are several variants of this ballad, the most common being "Que por mayo era, por mayo," and there is another longer version that goes beyond the situation revealed above to include other details which amplify the description of the prisoner's condition and which suggest a happy ending. The abbreviated version is greatly superior, however, with its deceptive simplicity and poignancy being almost unequaled in ballad literature. The rhythmic subtleties and the cumulative impact of successive evocative images are not easily put into English, but Entwistle's rendition, while not as lyrical as the original, accurately conveys its essence. Gibson and Lockhart both chose to translate the longer version, but neither achieved notable success. There are other translations of this poem, or one of its variants, by Bowring, Frothingham, King, Manchester, Merwin, Turnbull, and Umphrey, with Bowring's coming as close as any to echoing the lyricism of the model.

The final ballad to be considered is possibly the best known of any of the traditional Spanish *romances.* "Conde Arnaldos" has not only been popular in Spain, it also has had the distinction of being translated into English more times than any other poem of its type. At least thirteen authors have attempted it, many of them with great success. Lockhart, John Bowring, and George Borrow were the first, followed by Longfellow and, somewhat later, Gibson. In more recent years there have been translations by James Elroy Flecker, Ida Farnell, W. J. Entwistle, and Nicholson B. Adams. The latest versions are those by George Umphrey, Edwin Honig, John Masefield, and W. S. Merwin. Several of these translations are quite good, and many reveal the typical style and technique of the translator. Gibson's rendition, found below with the original, will be examined first.

¡Quién hubiese tal ventura
Sobre las aguas del mar
Como hubo el Conde Arnaldos
La mañana de San Juan!

Con un falcón en la mano
La caza iba a cazar,
Y venir vió una galera
Que a tierra quiere llegar.

Las velas traía de seda,
La ejarcia de un cendal,
Marinero que la manda
Diciendo viene un cantar

Que la mar ponía en calma,
Los vientos hace amainar,
Los peces que andan al hondo
Arriba los hace andar,

Las aves que andan volando
Las hace a el mastil posar:
. . . .

Allí habló el Conde Arnaldos,
Bien oiréis lo que dirá:
—Por Dios te ruego, marinero,
Digáisme ora ese cantar.—
Respondióle el marinero,
Tal respuesta le fué a dar:
—Yo no digo esta canción
Sino a quien conmigo va.

O never on the ocean wide
Has such a vision shone,
As Count Arnaldos wondering spied,
One morning of St. John.

O'er hill and dale he tracked the game
With falcon on his hand;
When lo! a noble galley came
Right steering for the land.

Its anchors were of beaten gold,
Its sails of satin strong,
And at the helm a sailor bold,
Who sang a wondrous song.

The sea was hushed into a sleep,
The winds they ceased to blow,
The fishes in the ocean deep
Swam upward from below;

The birds that winged their flight along,
Were charmed as they passed;
They felt the glamour of the song,
And lighted on the mast.

Arnaldos cried: "Thou sailor bold,
O teach to me that song!"
The sailor's words were very cold,
Nor was his answer long:
"I cannot teach that song to thee
Unless thou go with me."

The translation is conventional in all respects and follows the original closely. The eight- and six-syllable, iambic lines do not attempt to imitate the external form of the model, but its simple, poetic spirit is preserved and is the most distinguishing feature of the translation. The fourth stanza, particularly, is a beautiful and remarkably accurate rendition of the corresponding four lines of the model.

The version of this *romance* quoted above is that given in the *Cancionero de romances sin año,*[11] and is the one most often reproduced today. In some of the later *cancioneros,* however, the following additional lines spoken by the mariner were inserted between the description of the birds lighting on the mast and the words spoken by Conde Arnaldos.

— Galera, la mi galera
Dios te me guarde de mal,
De los peligros del mundo
Sobre aguas de la mar,
De los llanos de Almería,
Del estrecho de Gibraltar,
Y del golfo de Venecia,
Y de los bancos de Flandes,
Y del golfo de León,
Donde suelen peligrar. —

Lockhart used a version containing the extra lines, as is evident from examination of his translation below.

Who had ever such adventure,
Holy priest, or virgin nun,
As befel the Count Arnaldos
At the rising of the sun?

On his wrist the hawk was hooded,
Forth with horn and hound went he,
When he saw a stately galley
Sailing on the silent sea.

Sail of satin, mast of cedar,
Burnished poop of beaten gold, —
Many a morn you'll hood your falcon
Ere you such a bark behold.

Sails of satin, masts of cedar,
Golden poops may come again,
But mortal ear no more shall listen
To yon gray-haired sailor's strain.

Heart may beat, and eye may glisten,
Faith is strong, and Hope is free,
But mortal ear no more shall listen
To the song that rules the sea.

When the gray-haired sailor chaunted,
Every wind was hushed to sleep, —
Like a virgin's bosom panted
All the wide reposing deep.

Bright in beauty rose the star-fish
From her green cave down below,
Right above the eagle poised him —
Holy music charmed them so.

[11] *Cancionero de romances* (Antwerp: En Casa de Martín Nucio [n.d.]).

"Stately galley! glorious galley!
God hath poured his grace on thee!
Thou alone mayst scorn the perils
Of the dread devouring sea!

False Almeria's reefs and shallows,
Black Gibraltar's giant rocks,
Sound and sand-bank, gulf and whirl-
[pool
All — my glorious galley mocks!"

"For the sake of God, our maker!"
(Count Arnaldos' cry was
[strong) —
"Old man, let me be partaker
In the secret of thy song!"

"Count Arnaldos! Count Arnaldos!
Hearts I read, and thoughts I
[know; —
Wouldst thou learn the ocean secret,
In our galley thou must go!"

The trochaic beat and the syllable count of this translation are more nearly like the original than are those of Gibson's poem, but this is the only respect in which it shows greater fidelity. The simplicity of the Spanish is lost by the addition of the extra verses and by an excessive elaboration of detail. The inclusion of the extra lines diminishes the artistic merit of even the original, and Lockhart's translation of them does little to make them more acceptable. Some of the other verses are quite good (e.g., the second stanza), but in general, Gibson's version is preferable.

The translation by John Bowring, like the two poems above, bears the distinctive hallmarks of the author. It reads as follows:

Who was ever sped by fortune
O'er the ocean's waters, say,
As the happy Count Arnaldos,
On the morn of San Juan's day?
In his hand he held a falcon,
And he went to chase the game,
When a gay and splendid galley
To the shore advancing came.
All its fluttering sails were silken,
All its shrouds of flounces clear,
And the gay and clear-voiced helms-
[man
Sang a song so sweet to hear
That the waves were calm and silent,
And the noisy storm-wind hushed,
And the fish that live the deepest
To the water's surface rushed;
While the restless birds were gathered
Listening on the masts, and still.
"O, my galley! — O, my galley!
God preserve us now from ill."
Thus he spake, the Count Arnaldos,
Thus he spake, and thou shalt
[hear:
"Sing that song, by Heaven I charge
[thee!
Sing that song, good mariner."
But the mariner was silent
And he only answered — "No!
They alone must hear my music,
They alone who with me go."

The model used by Bowring was one containing the first two lines of the extra verses noted in Lockhart's translation. The trochaic meter and the continuous arrangement of verses imitate the Spanish to a reasonable degree, and Bowring's skill as a poet enabled him to produce a literal translation without sacrifice of the lyrical qualities which are so much a part of the charm of the original. It is a very satisfactory translation in every respect.

Only one other translation of this ballad will be examined, although there are several other interesting and different renditions. The version which follows is one of those made by George Umphrey to illustrate the technique of assonance.

> Would that I might have the fortune
> On the shore there by the sea,
> That befell the Count Arnaldos
> Saint John's day of yester-year!
> Hawk on wrist, from chase returning,
> He beheld as in a dream,
> Coming toward him on the seashore,
> A light galley, sailing free.
> Bright its silken sails were gleaming,
> Shrouds that shone with satin sheen;
> And he heard the helmsmen singing
> Words of magic, tones so sweet,
> That the wind forgot its raging
> And the waves their fretting ceased.
> From the depths where they were hiding,
> Fishes came that they might hear,
> And the flying birds enraptured
> Lighted on the ship's lateen.
> Listening to the song, Arnaldos
> Cried aloud with fervent plea:
> "In God's name I ask you, sailor,
> Me that song I beg you, teach."
> But the sailor merely answered,
> Thus his answer, firm and brief:
> "If my song you would be learning,
> You must sail away with me."

Umphrey has an excellent discussion preceding this translation in which he presents the case both for and against the use of assonance in the translation of ballads. The chief arguments opposing it are the difficulties in achieving it successfully and the fact that it is apt to be less pleasing to English ears than is rhyme. On the other hand, the reader or listener who is familiar with the *romances* is vaguely dissatisfied with the substitution of rhyme. Umphrey notes some of the other pertinent considerations when he asserts:

> The few translators who have attempted assonance did not fully understand its technique, underestimated its possibilities, or lacked the courage of their convictions. If the attempt is made, it should be made frankly and resolutely. The two kinds of rime cannot be combined. If assonance is used, the vowel sound or sounds must be repeated often enough to break through the natural insensibility of the English ear to the regular repetition of vocalic sounds only. Consonantal rimes should be avoided, since they would obscure the assonance or give to the assonantal rimes the effect of poor workmanship. Double assonance is more pleasing than single and is more likely to attract attention. If the translator is using single assonance and is troubled by the thought that his carefully constructed rime scheme might pass unnoticed, he would call attention to it by using, from time to time, words ending in the assonating vowel. A strong rhythmic stress on the words in assonance should prove helpful.[12]

Umphrey's translation illustrates well the points he makes above. A trochaic meter is employed, with the final stress falling on the seventh syllable of the alternating eight- and seven-syllable lines. There is an assonating "e" in every other line. He uses only single assonance, but has several words ending with this sound. The translation retains the spirit and thought of the original, and with the additional close imitation of the poetic style and form it is probably as faithful a reproduction of the Spanish as it is possible to achieve. There are many other good translations, however, in addition to those noted above, and here, as in other instances involving a choice between equally competent, but differing, English versions of *romances,* the decision as to which is best must be based ultimately on individual taste and personal preference.

[12] George W. Umphrey, "Spanish Ballads in English. Part II — Verse Technique," *Modern Language Quarterly* 7 (1946): 31.

CONCLUSION

THE TRANSLATIONS PRESENTED IN THE PRECEDING CHAPTERS constitute a relatively small percentage of those *romances* which have found their way into English, although I have made an effort to single out some of the best and most representative. Practically all the major categories are included and most of the better translators, at least those who have been most active in this field. There are, of course, many other outstanding compositions among the hundreds of Spanish ballads in English translation, and it is my hope the reader may be inspired to seek these out for himself. The appendixes, which indicate those *romances* known to exist in English, the names of their translators, and the location of translations, are designed for this purpose.

In many of the poems in this volume, attention has been directed in passing to the type of verse used by the translator. Several different meters and verse forms may be noted, and, in general, these conform to those normally found in the old English ballads. In an excellent article published in 1946, George W. Umphrey analyzed the verse techniques employed by the major translators and identified the most common patterns.[1] A short summary of these, with appropriate reference to the ballads in the present work, is offered for those interested in pursuing the subject further. Briefly stated, there are seven basic types, although numerous variations may be observed.

One of the most popular meters of the old English ballad-makers, and the one used by Lockhart for most of his translations, is the rhyming couplet of fourteen-syllable, seven-stress iambic lines. It is found in his ballad on Bernardo del Carpio (p. 128), in Gibson's

[1] George W. Umphrey, "Spanish Ballads in English. Part II — Verse Technique," *Modern Language Quarterly* 7 (1946): 21-23.

translations on Gayferos (p. 188), and in "The Enchanted Lady" (p. 204). "Lady Alda's Dream" (p. 197), which is Sir Edmund Head's version of "En París está Doña Alda," is another good example of this form.

A second meter often found in the English translations, and chosen for its similarity to the long *romance* lines, is the eight-stress trochaic line of fifteen syllables. A typical example is Gibson's translation of "Paseábase el rey moro — por la ciudad de Granada" (p. 181). It may also be studied in his ballad on "Rosaflorida" (p. 192) and the one on the escape of Don Guarinos (p. 198).

Twelve- or thirteen-syllable lines of six iambics or four anapests were selected at times by the translators in order to give a more rapid, spirited movement to the narrative. This is illustrated by Lockhart's version of Ximena Gómez's plea for justice (p. 50), his ballad on "The Enchanted Lady" (p. 205), and his rendition of one of the ballads on the Infantes de Lara, "The Vengeance of Mudarra." Gibson's use of this pattern may be noted in his ballads on King Rodrigo's loss of Spain to the Moors (e.g., "Los vientos eran contrarios," p. 118).

Perhaps the most popular meter in the English ballads, however, and the one usually preferred by Gibson, is the quatrain of four- and three-stress lines of eight- or six-syllable iambics. Although somewhat akin to the rhyming couplet of fourteen-syllable, seven-stress lines, the quatrain achieves a faster, lighter pace as compared to the slower, more dignified movement of the couplet. Numerous examples will be observed among Gibson's translations of ballads of the Cid (e.g., pp. 42 and 48). Interesting variations of this meter appear in the ballads on pages 74 and 166.

Three-stress iambic lines of six syllables have been used less frequently, but show up in the work of some of the translators. Gibson's use of them is evident in the translations on pages 76 and 216. Several authors, however, notably Frere, Gibson, and Lord Holland, have employed eight-syllable, four-stress iambics in quatrains and in other stanzas of varying length with considerable success. Frere's translation of "Miraba de Campoviejo — el rey de Aragón un día" (p. 150) gives an idea of its style, and it is also found in a ballad by Gibson on p. 139.

Four-stress trochaic lines of eight and seven syllables were first used by Percy in his translation of "Río Verde — Río Verde" (p. 163), and this poem, as has been noted, was frequently used as a model by many of the later translators. Rodd, Gibson, Oxenford, Lockhart, and Longfellow are some of those who were attracted to this meter, and Lord Byron, Monk Lewis, Southey, Borrow, and Scott all used variations of it. Gibson's translations on pages 172, 176, and 202 offer other examples of its use.

The comparison of several versions of the same ballad leads one naturally to form value judgments concerning the respective merits of the translators and translations examined, and this tendency has been evident in many of the discussions accompanying the poems in this volume. In general, the criteria used are those expressed in one of the classic treatises on the art of translation—Alexander Fraser Tytler's *Essay on the Principles of Translation* (London, 1791). Although many books and articles have been written on the subject since that time, the requirements set down by Tytler are excellent statements of what a good translation should be and would still be accepted as valid by most critics. Tytler's first rule was that a translation "should give a complete transcript of the idea of the original work." Next in importance, "the style and manner of writing should be of the same character with that of the original." Third, the translation "should have all the ease of original composition." [2] The first two rules stress faithfulness to the original work, and this criterion would undoubtedly be placed high on any modern translator's list of requirements. One of the twentieth-century writers on the theory of translation, for example, remarks that "by general consent, though not by universal practice, the prime merit of a translation proper is Faithfulness, and he is the best translator whose work is nearest to the original." [3] The desire to be faithful to the model, however, often brings the translator special difficulties since every language has words that have no exact equivalents in other languages and idioms which at best can only be approximated. In such instances, just as in those passages in which more than one meaning is possible, it is the familiarity of the translator with the language and the literary

[2] Alexander Fraser Tytler, Lord Woodhouselee, *Essay on the Principles of Translation* (London: J. M. Dent and Co.; New York: E. P. Dutton and Co., 1907), p. 9.

[3] J. P. Postgate, *Translation and Translations: Theory and Practice* (London: G. Bell and Sons, Ltd., 1922), p. 3.

judgment he possesses which determine the difference between an excellent or poor translation.

Although all the authors whose work is reproduced here satisfy in varying degrees the criteria established by Tytler as the basis for a good translation, the attention given to James Young Gibson is disproportionate to that received by the others. The reasons for this were suggested earlier, and attention has been directed to the excellence of many of his renditions, but a brief general assessment of his contributions is appropriate. In certain respects, this will almost amount to a summary of the characteristics found in most of the best translators and translations.

The comparison of Gibson's translations with the originals and with the work of other generally acknowledged experts in ballad translation confirms the opinion that he is a craftsman of the highest rank. His work is uniformly accurate and pleasing and nearly always consistent with the most important criteria of a good translation. The outstanding characteristic is faithfulness to the spirit and ideas of his models. Almost without exception, his translations are a careful reflection of the best qualities of the originals. A high degree of literary judgment is evident also in the selection of models, even among the Cid ballads where good illustrations of certain aspects of the Cid's history are sometimes difficult to find.

A second noticeable feature of Gibson's work is the excellent quality of the verse. He uses a variety of poetic devices skillfully and artistically, and most of his translations are so smooth and graceful that they might easily pass for original ballads. The difficulty of achieving this effect in translation is usually in direct proportion to the concern the translator shows for preserving the spirit and thought of his model. Lockhart, for example, rates extremely high with regard to the ease of composition of his translations and frequently writes very good poetry. In many of his poems, however, this excellence is achieved at the expense of the ideas and meaning, and many times even the spirit, of the ballads being translated. No such inversion of values is found in Gibson's work. On the contrary, he illustrates a superior ability by producing good poetry in spite of the limitation imposed by a strict adherence to the sense and spirit of the originals.

A further indication of Gibson's extraordinary skill is found in the variety of meters employed in his ballads. The majority of his translations are in the same verse pattern — the quatrain of alternating four- and three-stress iambics. However, this choice resulted not from the inability to use others — all the common ballad patterns and several variations of his own are found in his work — but from a feeling that this meter was best suited for translation of the *romances*. Regardless of the meter used, however, Gibson's translations are characterized by good taste, appropriate, natural expression, and skillful use and control of the poetic medium employed.

As far as imitation of the poetic style of the originals is concerned, Gibson recognized, along with most other translators, that there is no exact and completely suitable parallel in English versification to the assonantal pattern of the *romance*. Consequently, he made no effort to duplicate this phenomenon, but chose instead, for the most part, standard and familiar English ballad meters. Several of those noted above, with minor variations, may be identified in his work.

At least nine out of ten of his Cid ballads are in the popular eight- and six-syllable, iambic lines of the typical English ballad. These are not excessively regular, but are varied by dropping or adding one or more syllables or by substituting other metrical feet. The most frequent change is the omission of the fourth stress in the first line of the typical *a b c b* quatrain. Probably half of the ballads using this meter have one or more stanzas, usually the first one or two, which illustrate this variations.

In several of Gibson's translations, the three-stress lines predominate, and the line length is shortened to from five to seven syllables. Other variations among the Cid ballads include unusual stanza arrangements ("Al arma, al arma"), different line lengths ("La noble Ximena Gómez"), and complicated rhyme, rhythm, and stanza arrangements ("Don Sancho reina en Castilla").

The other historical ballads and the Moorish ballads show a greater variety of verse arrangements. In addition to the meters above, he shows excellent mastery of the eight-syllable, four-stress, iambic pattern and the eight- and seven-syllable trochaic. In both the historical and the Moorish ballads, there are fine examples of the longer ballad meters also; for example, the fourteen-syllable, seven-stress iambics, and Gibson's favorite variation of the twelve-syllable line, the thirteen-syllable, six-stress iambic.

The still longer line of fifteen syllables and eight trochaic stresses is found in some of Gibson's Moorish ballads and in several of the translations in the group of artistic ballads and ballads of chivalry. This last category contains samples of all the verse patterns mentioned above, some fairly regular, others which are combinations or variations of the basic types. Many of the translations of the shorter, artistic ballads and the *romancillos con estribillos* are in short lines of four to nine syllables, with considerable mixing of trochaic and iambic stresses. The greater flexibility and more extensive choice of meter found in this group of translations is consistent with the wider range found in the originals. The historical ballads show a considerable sameness of technique, and Gibson, along with other translators, was more uniform in his treatment.

There are several other individual characteristics peculiar to Gibson's style and methods which appear often enough to merit comment. While the majority of his lines are arranged in quatrains, a great many translations include longer stanzas. Frequently, these parallel logical divisions of the original, but just as often, they represent a shift of some sort in the narrative and seem to be employed as signals to call attention to a change in the story about to take place. This characteristic is akin to another minor stylistic peculiarity: beginning a translation with a line length (and sometimes a meter) different from that used in the main body of the poem. A similar device is noted in his tendency to end a translation with a line using interior rhyme.

Gibson's faithfulness to his models has been much emphasized. While in many of his ballads this amounts to an almost literal line-for-line translation, he was governed always by good taste and a feeling for the dramatic and the artistic. This is most evident in his combination of two or more variants of the same ballad and in the substitution of dialogue for indirect quotation or narrative. The latter is the most common alteration found in his translations, since he almost never omits or adds any significant ideas. Gibson was extremely skillful in recording dialogue, and the use he makes of this technique adds immeasurably to the success and effectiveness of his work.

The importance of Gibson among the translators of Spanish ballads seems firmly established. He translated more ballads and more different kinds of ballads than any other author. Furthermore, comparison of his work with the originals and with other notable translators indicates that from an overall viewpoint his translations are unexcelled. A few of his poems, of course, are surpassed in some respects by those of other writers. Some translators exhibit a wider range of poetic powers and, perhaps, greater virtuosity in the exercise of those powers. With due regard for the accepted criteria of a good translation, however, and considering the ballads of the various translators in their entirety, there is no group of translations of Spanish *romances* which is superior to Gibson's. This should be emphasized especially with respect to the ballads of Lockhart, whose justifiable eminence among translators has long been recognized. By appearing at the right time, and in an agreeable combination of English ballad meter and Spanish *romance* themes, Lockhart's ballads caught the popular fancy and quickly became the accepted versions among non-Spanish readers. The deficiencies of Lockhart's translations — as good as many of them are — quickly appear, however, when they are put next to those of Gibson. Some of his translations are as good as Gibson's, a few surpass the latter's, but many are far inferior. One of the objectives of the present study has been to place the two men in more proper perspective and to raise Gibson to the position he rightfully deserves — a level at least equal to that of Lockhart.

It is my hope, however, that I have not slighted other good translators of ballads and that the reader has been given an adequate introduction to their work and to the pleasure to be found in the Spanish *Romancero*. A significantly large number of authors have dedicated themselves to ballad translation, and many among this group have left compositions which merit further recognition and study. No translation will ever completely satisfy the person familiar with a work of literature in the original, but translations continue to have great value for the student of comparative literature and for the individual interested in furthering his knowledge of the literature or culture of a foreign country. In the case of Spain, familiarity with the ballads contributes enormously to the understanding of both, and scholars and general readers alike remain indebted to many gifted poet-translators who have opened the way to the intriguing and immensely rewarding world of the *romance*.

Appendix A

A LIST OF *ROMANCES* THAT HAVE BEEN TRANSLATED INTO ENGLISH, WITH NAMES OF TRANSLATORS

Note: Each of the following ballads, or a variant thereof, has been translated by the author or authors indicated in parentheses. The list is intended to be used in conjunction with Appendix B to facilitate the locating of an English translation of any particular *romance*. In those instances in which only slightly differing versions of the same ballad were translated, normally only one version, the more popular one, is cited, with the accompanying list of translators embracing those who may have rendered one of the variants. A few of the poems included do not have the true ballad form.

A caza iban, a caza — los cazadores del rey (Jewett)
A cazar va don Rodrigo — y aún don Rodrigo de Lara (Entwistle, Gibson, Lockhart, Oxenford)
A cazar va el caballero — a cazar como solía (Bowring, Lockhart, Merwin)
A coger el trébol, damas — la mañana de San Juan (Gibson)
A concilio dentro en Roma — el padre santo ha llamado (*Foreign Review*, Gibson, Lockhart)
A coronarse de flores — despertaba el alba bella (Bowring)
A Jimena y a Rodrigo — prendió el rey palabra y mano (Gibson, Gerrard Lewis)
A la sombra de mis cabellos — mi querido se adurmió (Bowring)
A la verde, verde — a la verde oliva (Merwin)
A la vista de Tarifa — poco más de media legua (Lockhart)
A los pies de Don Enrique — yace muerto el rey don Pedro (Lockhart)
A media legua de Gelves — hincó en el suelo la lanza (Wilson)
A pie está el fuerte don Diego — fuera de la empalizada (Gerrard Lewis)
A solas le reprehende — a Martín Peláez el Cid (Gibson)
A su palacio de Burgos — como buen padrino honrado (Gibson, Lockhart)
A tal anda don García — por un adarve adelante (Gibson, Merwin)
A tan alta va la luna — como el sol a mediodía (Bowring, Lockhart)
A Toledo había llegado — Ruy Díaz que el Cid decían (Gibson)
A una dama he de servir — la noche y día (Bowring)
Abenámar, Abenámar — moro de la morería (Gibson, King, Rodd, Southey, Wilson)
Abridme, cara de flor — abridme la puerta [Jewish ballad] (Merwin)
Acabadas son las bodas — que allá en Burgos se hacían (Cushing)
Acabado de yantar — la faz en somo la mano (Gibson, Gerrard Lewis)
Afuera, afuera, aparta, aparta — que entra el valeroso Muza (Rodd)

Afuera, afuera, Rodrigo — el soberbio castellano (Gibson: included in his version of "Apenas era el rey muerto"; Merwin, Ticknor)
Ah mis señores poetas — descúbranse ya esas caras (Gibson)
Al arma, al arma, sonaban — los pífaros y atambores (Gibson)
Al casto rey don Alfonso — está Bernardo pidiendo (Cushing, Maturin)
Al cielo piden justicia — de los condes de Carrión (Gibson)
Al dulce y sabroso canto — de las aves placenteras (Wiffen)
Al pie de un túmulo negro — está Bernardo del Carpio (Cushing, Lockhart, Oxenford)
Al rey chico de Granada — mensajeros le han entrado (Rodd)
Al tiempo que el sol esconde — debajo del mar su lumbre (Wilson)
Albornoces y turbantes — no traen los moros de Gelves (Wilson)
Alora la bien cercada — tú que estás en par del río (Honig, Merwin)
Alzé los ojos y vi — a quien amo más que a mí (Bowring)
Allá en Granada la rica — instrumentos oí tocar (Rodd)
Amara yo una señora — y améla por más valor (Bowring)
Amarrado al duro banco — de una galera turquesca (Lord Holland)
Amores trata Rodrigo — descubierto ha su cuidado (Rodd)
Anda cristiano cautivo — tu fortuna no te asombre (Bowring, Rodd)
Andando por estos mares — navegando con la fortuna [Jewish ballad] (Merwin)
Ante el rey Alfonso — estaba ese buen Cid castellano (Gibson, Gerrard Lewis)
Antes que barbas tuviese — rey Alfonso me juraste (Maturin, Oxenford)
Apenas era el rey muerto — Zamora ya está cercada (Gibson)
Apretada está Valencia — puédese mal defensar (Gibson, Gerrard Lewis)
Apriesa pasa el estrecho — porque le van dando caza (Lockhart)
Aquel monte arriba va — un pastorcillo llorando (Merwin)
Aquel rayo de la guerra — alférez mayor del reino (Bowring)
Aquella hermosa aldeana — de los campos de Madrid (Merwin)
Aquese famoso Cid — con gran razón es loado (Gibson, Gerrard Lewis)
Aquese infante don Sancho — hizo lo que no debía (Oxenford)
Aqueste domingo — no muy de mañana (Bowring)
Arrancando los cabellos — maltratándose la cara (Wilson)
Arriba canes, arriba — que mala rabia os mate (King, Lockhart, Merwin, Wilson)
Asentado está Gayferos — en el palacio reale (Gibson, Rodd)
Así no marchite el tiempo — el abril de tu esperanza (Wilson)
¡Ay de mí! dice el buen padre — a cinco hijos que tenía (Merwin)
Ay Dios de mi tierra — saquéisme de aquí (Bowring)
Ay Dios, que buen caballero — el maestre de Calatrava (King, Rodd)
Ay Dios, que buen caballero — fué don Rodrigo de Lara (Oxenford)
Ay luna que reluces — blanca y plateada (Bowring)
Ay ojuelos verdes — ay los mis ojuelos (Bowring)
Bajaba el gallardo Hamete — a las ancas de una yegua (Wilson)
Bañando está las prisiones — con lágrimas que derrama (Cushing, Lockhart, Merwin)
Batiéndole las ijadas — con los duros acicates (Wilson)
Bella Zaida de mis ojos — y del alma bella Zaida (Rodd, Wilson)
Blanca sois, señora mía — más que el rayo del sol (Bowring, Head, Masefield, Merwin)
Bodas hacían en Francia — allá dentro de París (Head)

Bullicioso era el arroyuelo — y salpicóme (Bowring)
Cabalga Diego Laínez — al buen rey besar la mano (Gibson, Lockhart)
Caballero de lejas tierras — llegaos acá y paréis (Bowring, Head)
Caballeros granadinos — aunque moros, hijosdalgo (Rodd)
Cansadas ya las paredes — de guardar en tanto tiempo (Ticknor)
Cansados ya de pelear — los seis hermanos yacían (Merwin)
Castellanos y Leoneses — tienen grandes divisiones (Ford)
Castillo, dáteme, date — sino dártehe yo combate (Bowring)
Castillo de San Cervantes — tú que estás par de Toledo (*Blackwood's Magazine*)
Cata Francia, Montesinos — cata París la ciudad (Rodd)
Católicos caballeros — los que estáis sobre Granada (Wilson)
Celebradas ya las bodas — a do la corte yacía (Gibson, Gerrard Lewis, Lockhart)
Cercado está Santa Fe — con mucho lienzo encerado (Gibson, Rodd, Wiffen)
Cercado tiene a Baeza — ese arráez Andalla Mir (Merwin)
Cercado tiene a Coimbra — aquese buen rey Fernando (Gibson)
Cercado tiene a Sevilla — el santo rey don Fernando (Lockhart)
Cercado tiene a Valencia — ese buen Cid castellano (Gibson)
Compañero, compañero — casóse mi linda amiga (Bowring)
Con cartas sus mensajeros — el rey al Carpio envió (Ford)
Con dos mil jinetes moros — Reduán corre la tierra (Trapier, Wilson)
Con el rostro entristecido — y el semblante demudado (Gerrard Lewis)
Con los mejores de Asturias — sale de León Bernardo (Borrow, Cushing, Maturin, Oxenford)
Con más de treinta en cuadrilla — hidalgos Abencerrajes (Rodd)
Con nuevo ejército pone — en nuevo estrecho a Numancia (Maturin)
Con rabia está el rey David — rasgando su corazón (Bowring)
Con solos diez de los suyos — ante el rey Bernardo llega (Cushing, Lockhart)
Con tres mil y más Leoneses — deja la ciudad Bernardo (Cushing, Gibson, Lockhart, Longfellow)
Conde Niños por amores — es niño y pasó la mar (Trapier)
Considerando los condes — lo que el de Vivar vale (Gibson, Gerrard Lewis)
Contándole estaba un día — al valeroso Bernardo (Cushing)
Contaros he en que me vi — cuando era enamorado (Merwin)
Coronado de vitorias — aquellas dichosas sienes (Gibson)
Corrido Martín Peláez — de lo que el Cid ha fablado (Gibson)
Cual bravo toro vencido — que escaba la roja arena (Wilson)
Cuando aquel claro lucero — sus rayos quiere enviar (Rodd)
Cuando de los enemigos — en roja sangre bañando (Wilson)
Cuando las pintadas aves — mudas están y la tierra (Maturin, Moir, Oxenford, Wiffen)
Cuando yo triste, nací — luego nací desdichada (Frere)
Cuidando Diego Laínez — por las menguas de su casa (Gibson, Lord Holland, Gerrard Lewis, Ticknor)
De Antequera partió el moro — tres horas ante el día (Entwistle)
De Castilla van marchando — a Navarra con su gente (Gibson)
De concierto están los condes — hermanos Diego y Fernando (Gibson, Gerrard Lewis)
De Francia partió la niña — de Francia la bien guarnida (Borrow)
De Granada sale el moro — que Aliatar era llamado (Matthew Lewis, Rodd)
De honor y trofeos lleno — más que el gran marte ha sido (Rodd, Wilson)

De la gran Constantinopla — su emperatriz se partía (Oxenford)
De lejos mira a Jaén — con vista alegre y turbada (Lockhart, Wilson)
De los trofeos de amor — ya coronado sus sienes (Wilson)
De Mantua salen apriesa — sin tardanza ni vagare (Rodd)
De Mantua salió el marqués — Danés Urgel el leale (Lockhart, Rodd)
De Mérida sale el palmero — de Mérida esa ciudad (*Foreign Quarterly Review*, Rodd)
De Rodrigo de Vivar — muy grande fama corría (Gibson, Lord Holland, Lockhart)
De su fortuna agraviado — y sujeto a quien le agravia (Wilson)
De tres heridas mortales — de que mucha sangre vierte (Rodd, Wilson)
De una torre de palacio — se salió por un postigo (Merwin)
De velar viene la niña — de velar venía (Bowring)
De verde y color rosado — en señal que vive alegre (Wilson)
De Zamora sale el Dolfos — corriendo y apresurado (Gibson, Maturin)
Decidme vos, Pensamiento — dónde mis malos están (Bowring)
Deja el alma que es libre — señor Alcaide (Bowring)
Del perezoso Morfeo — los roncos pífaros suenan (Wilson)
Del rey Alfonso se queja — ese buen Cid castellano (Gerrard Lewis)
Descolorida zagala — a quien tristezas hicieron (Merwin)
Desde un alto mirador — estaba Arselia mirando (Wilson)
Desesperado camina — ese moro de Villalba (Wilson)
Despedísteme Señora, vida mía — ¿Dó me ire? (Bowring)
Después que Bellido Dolfos — ese traidor afamado (Gibson)
Después que el rey don Rodrigo — a España perdido había (Gibson, Lockhart, Merwin, Rodd)
Después que Gonzalo Bustos — dejó el cordobés palacio (Cushing, Maturin, Oxenford)
Después que reptó a Zamora — don Diego de Ordóñez (Gibson, Gerrard Lewis)
Dí Juan, de qué murió Blas — tan mozo y tan mal logrado (Bowring)
Día era de los reyes — día era señalado (*Foreign Review*, Gibson)
Diamante falso fingido — engastado en pedernal (Bryant)
Dicen que me case yo — no quiero marido, no (Bowring)
Dime Bencerraje amigo — ¿qué te parece de Zaida (Wilson)
Discurriendo en la batalla — el rey Sebastiano bravo (Maturin)
Doliente estaba, doliente — ese buen rey don Fernando (Gibson, Gerrard Lewis)
Don Rodrigo de Bivar — está con doña Jimena (Gibson, Gerrard Lewis)
Don Rodrigo, rey de España — por la su corona honrar (*Foreign Quarterly Review*, Oxenford)
Don Sancho reina en Castilla — Alfonso en León, su hermano (Gibson)
¿Dónde estás señora mía — que no te duele mi mal (Bowring, Merwin)
¿Dónde os vais, caballero — dónde os vais y me dejáis [Jewish ballad] (Merwin)
Donde se acaba la tierra — y comienza el mar de España (Wilson)
Doña María Padilla — no's mostréis tan triste vos (Gibson, Lockhart)
Dueña si habedes honor — mirad bien por mi facienda (Wiffen)
Dulces árboles sombrosos — humillaos cuando veáis (Bowring)
Durandarte, Durandarte — buen caballero probado (Bowring, *Fraser's Magazine*)
Durmiendo está el rey Almanzor — a un sabor a tan grande (Wilson)

Durmióse Cupido al son — de una fuente de cristal (Bowring)
Ebro caudaloso — fértil ribera (Moir)
El alcaide de Molina — manso en paz y bravo en guerra (Bryant)
El animoso Celín — hijo de Celín Audalla (Wilson)
El año de cuatrocientos — que noventa y dos corría (Masefield)
El cabello negro — y la niña blanca (Bowring)
El Cid fué para su tierra — con sus vasallos partía (Gibson)
El conde Fernán González — que tiene en Burgos su campo (Maturin)
El cuerpo preso en Sansueña — y en París cautiva el alma (Lockhart)
El escudo de fortuna — en quien sus golpes descargan (Wilson)
El gallardo Abenumeya — hijo del rey de Granada (Wilson)
El hijo de Arias Gonzalo — el mancebito Pedro Arias (Gibson, Gerrard Lewis)
El más gallardo ginete — que jamás tuvo Granada (Wilson)
El rey don Sancho reinaba — en Castilla su reinado (Gibson)
El rey moro tenía un hijo — que Tarquino le yamaban (Merwin)
El vasallo desleale — el desterrado, el traidor (*Foreign Review*)
En Burgos está el buen rey — asentado a su yantar (Lord Holland)
En campaña, madre — tocan a leva (Bowring)
En Castilla está un castillo — que se llama Rocafrida (Gibson, Merwin)
En Ceuta está Don Julián — en Ceuta la bien nombrada (Lockhart)
En consulta estaba un día — con sus grandes y consejo (Gibson, Lockhart)
En dos yeguas muy ligeras — de blanco color de cisne (Wilson)
En el cuarto de Comares — la hermosa Galiana (Rodd)
En el más soberbio monte — que en los cristales del Tajo (Wilson)
En el mes era de abril — de mayo antes un día (Maturin)
En el nombre de Jesús — que todo el mundo ha formado (Rodd)
En el regazo de abril — duerme el sol entre las flores (Bowring)
En el tiempo que Celinda — cerró airada la ventana (Wilson)
En el valle de Pisuerga — vive entre peñas un angel (Bowring)
En esa ciudad de Burgos — en Cortes se habían juntado (Longfellow)
En Francia estaba Belerma — alegre y regocijada (Rodd)
En Francia la noblecida — en ese tiempo pesado (Rodd)
En la corte del Casto Alfonso — Bernardo a placer vivía (Merwin)
En la ciudad de Granada — grandes alaridos dan (Gibson, Lockhart)
En la villa de Antequera — cautiva está Vindaraja (Wilson)
En las almenas de Toro — allí estaba una doncella (Gibson)
En las huertas de Almería — estaba el moro Abenámar (Rodd)
En las salas de París — en el palacio sagrado (Rodd)
En las sierras de Altamira — que dicen del Arabiana (Merwin)
En las torres de Alhambra — sonaba gran vocería (Lord Byron, Rodd)
En los campos de Alventosa — mataron a don Beltrán (Rodd)
En los reinos de León — el quinto Alfonso reinaba (Lockhart, Merwin)
En los solares de Burgos — a su Rodrigo aguardando (Gibson, Gerrard Lewis)
En los tiempos que me vi — más alegre y placentero (Bowring, Gibson, Lockhart)
En Palma estaba cautiva — la bella y hermosa Zara (Wilson)
En París está Doña Alda — la esposa de don Roldán (Gibson, Head, Lockhart, Masefield)
En Sant Pedro de Cardeña — está el Cid embalsamado (*Foreign Quarterly Review*, Gibson)

En Santa Gadea de Burgos — do juran los fijosdalgo (Gibson, Maturin)
En Sevilla está una hermita — cual dicen de San Simón (Jewett)
En Toledo estaba Alfonso — que a Cortes llamado había (*Foreign Review*)
En Toledo estaba Alfonso — que non cuidaba reinar (Gibson)
En un balcón de su casa — estaba Azarque de pechos (Wilson)
En un dorado balcón — cuya fuerte y alta casa (Wilson)
En un pastoral albergue — que la guerra entre unos robles (Wiffen)
En Valencia estaba el Cid — doliente del mal postrero (Gerrard Lewis)
En Zamora está Rodrigo — en cortes del rey Fernando (Gibson)
Encontrándose dos arroyuelos — al pasar de un verde valle (Bowring)
Ensíllenme el potro rucio — del alcaide de los Vélez (*Fraser's Magazine*, Percy, Rodd, Wilson)
Entrado ha el Cid en Zamora — en Zamora aquesa villa (Gibson)
Entre muchos moros sabios — que hubo en Andalucía (Wilson)
Es el trofeo pendiente — del ramo de aqueste pino (Merwin)
Esa guirnalda de rosas — hija, ¿quién te la endonara (Merwin)
Escuchó el rey don Alfonso — las palabras halagüeñas (Gibson)
Ese buen Cid Campeador — que Dios en salud mantenga (Gibson, Gerrard Lewis, Maturin, Scott)
Ese conde don Manuel — que de León es nombrado (Gibson)
Esperanza me despide — el galardón no paresce (Merwin)
Esta zagaleja, madre — de los azules ojuelos (Merwin)
Estaba la linda infanta — a sombra de una oliva (McVan, Merwin, Wilson)
Estábase el conde Dirlos — sobrino de don Beltrane (Rodd)
Estábase la condesa — en el su estrado asentada (Gibson, Lockhart)
Estando el rey don Fernando — en conquista de Granada (Lockhart, Masefield, Pinkerton, Rodd)
Estando toda la corte — de Abdilí, rey de Granada (Percy, Rodd, Wilson)
Estando toda la corte — de Almanzor, rey de Granada (Lockhart)
Estando yo en mi choza — pintando la mi cayada (Merwin)
Estén atentos los hombres — sin haberse de admirar (Merwin)
Estraño humor tiene Juana — que cuando más triste estoy (Gibson)
Fertiliza tu vega — dichoso Tormes (Bowring, Gibson)
Fijó, pues, Zaide los ojos — tan alegres cual conviene (Wilson)
Fontefrida, Fontefrida — Fontefrida y con amor (Anderson, Bowring, Entwistle, Gibson, King, Merwin, Ticknor, Umphrey, Winter)
Fuerte, galán, y brioso — que a toda Granada espanta (Wilson)
Galeritas de España — parad los remos (Bowring, Gibson, Lockhart)
Grande estruendo de campanas — por toda París había (Rodd)
Grande rumor se levanta — de gritos, armas, y voces (Gibson, Lord Holland, Lockhart)
Grandes guerras se publican — entre España y Portugal (Jewett)
Gritando va el caballero — publicando su gran mal (Bowring)
Guarte, guarte, rey don Sancho — no digas que no te aviso (Lockhart)
Hablando estaba en celada — el Cid con la su Jimena (Gibson)
Hablando estaba en el claustro — de San Pedro de Cardeña (Gibson)
Helo, helo, por do viene — el infante vengador (Entwistle, Gibson, Lockhart)
Helo, helo, por do viene — el moro por la calzada (Gibson, Rodd)
Hermano Perico — que estás a la puerta (Southey)
Jerez, aquesa nombrada — cercada era de cristianos (Lockhart)
La bella malmaridada — de las lindas que yo vi (Gibson: in *Journey to Parnassus*; Lockhart)

La bella Zaida Cegrí — a quien hizo suerte avara (Wilson)
La era de mil y ciento — y treinta y dos que corría (Gibson)
La hermosa Zara Cegrí — bella en todo y agraciada (Wilson)
La mañana de San Juan — a punto que alboreaba (Pinkerton, Rodd, Southey, Wilson)
La más bella niña — de nuestro lugar (Bowring)
La niña morena — que yendo a la fuente (Gibson, Lockhart)
La noble Jimena Gómez — hija del conde Lozano (Gibson)
La silla del buen Sant Pedro — Victor Papa la tenía (Gibson)
Las huestes del rey Rodrigo — desmayaban y huían (Gibson, Lockhart, Merwin, Moir)
Las soberbías torres mira — y de lejos las almenas (Wilson)
Límpiame la jacerina — vé presto; no tardes, paje (Wilson)
Lisaro que fué en Granada — cabeza de los Cegríes (Lockhart)
Los fieros cuerpos revueltos — entre los robustos brazos (Scott)
Los tiempos de mi prisión — tan aborrecida y larga (Ticknor)
Los vientos eran contrarios — la luna era crecida (Gibson, Matthew Lewis, Merwin, Rodd)
Llegado es el rey don Sancho — sobre Zamora esa villa (Gibson)
Llegó Alvar Fáñez a Burgos — a llevar al rey la empresa (Gibson)
Llegó la fama del Cid — a los confines de Persia (Gibson)
Llevadme, niño, a Belén — que os deseo ver, mi Dios (Bowring)
Llorando Diego Laínez — yace sentado a la mesa (Gibson, Lord Holland)
Madre, la mi madre — el amor esquivo (Gibson)
Madre mía, amores tengo — ay de mí, que no los veo (Bowring)
Madre mía, aquel pajarillo — que canta en el ramo verde (Bowring)
Mal mis servicios pagaste — ingrato rey Alfonso (Oxenford)
Mala la visteis, franceses — la caza de Roncesvalles (Gibson, Matthew Lewis, Lockhart, Rodd)
Mañanita de San Juan — mañanita de primor (Pursche)
Marinero soy de amor — y en su piélago profundo (Gibson, Percy)
Más envidia he de vos, conde — que mancilla ni pesar (Bowring)
Me casó mi madre — chiquitita y bonita (Merwin)
Media noche era por filo — los gallos querían cantar (Rodd)
Mentirosos Adalides — que de las vidas ajenas (Gibson)
Mi padre era de Ronda — y mi madre de Antequera (Bowring, Gibson, Merwin)
Mientras duerme la niña — flores y rosas (Bowring)
Mientras duerme mi niña — céfiro alegre (Bowring)
Mira Zaide, que te aviso — que no pases por mi calle (Rodd, Wiffen, Wilson)
Miraba de Campoviejo — el rey de Aragón un día (Frere, Lockhart, Merwin, Rodd)
Miro a mi morena — como en el jardín (Bowring)
Mis arreos son las armas — mi descanso es pelear (Bowring, Entwistle, Lockhart, Merwin)
Moriana en un castillo — juega con el moro Galvane (*Foreign Quarterly Review*, Gibson, Wilson)
Moriscos, los mis moriscos — los que ganáis mi soldada (Bowring, Merwin)
Morir vos queredes, padre — San Miguel vos haya el alma (Gibson, Gerrard Lewis)
Moro alcaide, moro alcaide — el de la vellida barba (Bowring, Lord Byron, Merwin, Percy, Rodd, Southey)

Muchas veces oí decir — y a los antiguos cantar (Rodd)
Mucho ha que el alma duerme — bien será que recuerde (Bowring)
Muerto yace Durandarte — debajo una verde haya (Rodd)
Muerto yace el rey don Sancho — Bellido muerto le había (Gibson)
Muerto yace ese buen Cid — que de Vivar se llamaba (Gibson, Gerrard Lewis, Maturin, Merwin)
Muy doliente estaba el Cid — de trabajos muy cansado (Gerrard Lewis)
Muy revuelta anda Jaén — rebata tocan apriesa (Rodd)
Muy revuelta está Granada — en armas y fuego ardiendo (Rodd)
Niña de quince años — que cautiva y prende (Bowring)
No con azules tahalíes — corvos alfanjes dorados (Bryant, Lord Holland, Southey, Wilson)
No con poco sentimiento — mira a los condes infames (Gibson)
No con tal braveza lleno — Rodamonte el africano (Pinkerton, Rodd, Wilson)
No lloréis mi madre — que me dais gran pena (Bowring)
No quiero ser casada — sino libre enamorada (Bowring)
No se puede llamar rey, — quien usa tal villanía (Cushing, Lockhart)
No tiene heredero alguno — Alfonso el Casto llamado (Cushing)
Non es de sesudos homes — ni de infanzones de pro (Gibson, Lord Holland)
Non quisiera, yermos míos — haber visto tal guisado (Gibson)
Nunca fuera caballero — de damas tan bien servido (Gibson, Lockhart)
Obedezco la sentencia — maguer que no soy culpado (Gibson)
Ocho a ocho y diez a diez — Sarracinos y Aliatares (Carter, Pinkerton, Rodd, Southey, Wilson)
¡Oh Belerma!, ¡Oh Belerma! — por mi mal fuiste engendrada (Gibson, Matthew Lewis, Lockhart)
¡Oh canas ignominiosas — dice el señor de Tarifa (Oxenford)
¡Oh Valencia, oh Valencia! — ¡Oh Valencia valenciana (Gibson)
Oíd, señor don Gayferos — lo que como amiyo os hablo (Lockhart)
Opreso está el rey Alfonso — oprimido y acuitado (Oxenford)
Partíos dende, los moros — vuestros muertos soterrad (Gibson)
Paseábase el buen conde — todo lleno de pesar (Bowring)
Paseábase el rey moro — por la ciudad de Granada (Bowring, Lord Byron, Entwistle, Gibson, Matthew Lewis, Masefield, Maturin, Merwin, Rodd, Southey)
Pensativo estaba el Cid — viéndose de pocos años (Gibson, Lord Holland)
Pésame de vos, el conde — porque así os quieren matar (Bowring, *Fraser's Magazine,* Ticknor)
Pidiendo a las diez del día — papel a su secretario (Gibson, Gerrard Lewis)
Ponte a las rejas azules — deja la manga que labras (Lockhart)
Por aquel postigo viejo — que nunca fuera cerrado (Gibson)
Por arrimo su albornoz — y por alfombra su adarga (Wilson)
Por divertirse Celín — fiestas ordena en Granada (Wilson)
Por el jardín de las damas — se pasea el rey Rodrigo (Maturin)
Por el mes era de mayo — cuando hace la calor (Bowring, Entwistle, Frothingham, Gibson, King, Lockhart, Manchester, Merwin, Turnbull, Umphrey)
Por el rastro de la sangre — que Durandarte dejaba (Rodd)
Por el val de las estacas — pasó el Cid a mediodía (Gibson)
Por Guadalquivir arriba — cabalgan caminadores (Gibson)
Por la calle de su dama — paseando se halla Zaide (Matthew Lewis, Percy, Rodd, Wilson)

Por la matanza va el viejo — por la matanza adelante (Little, Rodd)
Por la muerte que le dieron — en Zamora al rey don Sancho (Gerrard Lewis)
Por la parte donde vido — más sangrienta la batalla (Rodd)
Por la plaza de Sanlúcar — galán paseando viene (Pinkerton, Rodd, Wilson)
Por la puerta de la Vega — salen moros a caballo (Gibson, Lockhart)
Por las sierras de Moncayo — vi venir un renegado (Wilson)
Por los caños de Carmona — por do va el agua a Sevilla (Merwin)
Por los palacios del rey — duques, condes van entrando (Merwin)
Por mando del rey Alfonso — el buen Cid es desterrado (Gibson, Gerrard Lewis, Maturin)
Por una triste espesura — en un monte muy subido (*Fraser's Magazine*)
Preguntado está Florida — a su esposo placentero (Wilson)
Preso en la torre del oro — el fuerte Arbolán estaba (Wilson)
Preso está Fernán González — el gran conde de Castilla (Gibson, Lockhart)
Pues por besarte Minguillo — me riñó mi madre a mí (Bowring)
Pues que no me sabéis dar — sino tormento y pasión (Bowring)
¿Qué de vos y de mí, Señora — qué de vos y de mí dirán (Bowring)
Que no cogeré yo verbena — la mañana de San Juan (Bowring)
Que por mayo era, por mayo — cuando hace la calor (*See* "Por el mes era de mayo.")
¿Qué producirá mi Dios — tierra que regáis así (Bowring)
¿Quién es aquel caballero — que tan gran traición hacía (Cushing, Ticknor)
Quien gentil señora pierde — por falta de conocer (Bowring)
¡Quién hubiese tal ventura — sobre las aguas del mar (Adams, Borrow, Bowring, Entwistle, Farnell, Flecker, Gibson, Honig, Lockhart, Longfellow, Masefield, Merwin, Umphrey)
Recibiendo el alborada — que viene a alegrar la tierra (Gibson)
Recoge la rienda un poco — para el caballo que aguija (Wilson)
Reduán, bien se te acuerda — que me diste la palabra (Borrow, Lockhart, Merwin, Rodd)
Regalando el tierno vello — de la boca de Medoro (*Fraser's Magazine*)
Renegaron de su ley — los romancistas de España (Ticknor)
Resuelto ya Reduán — de hacer su palabra buena (Lockhart, Wilson)
Retirado en su palacio — está con sus ricos homes (Cushing, Oxenford)
Retraída está la infanta — bién así como solía (Bowring, Lockhart)
Rey don Sancho, rey don Sancho — cuando en Castilla reinó (Gibson)
Rey don Sancho, rey don Sancho — no digas que no te aviso (Adams, Burnham, Entwistle)
Rey don Sancho, rey don Sancho — ya que te apuntan las barbas (Gibson, Gerrard Lewis)
Reyes moros en Castilla — entran con gran alarido (Gibson, Lockhart)
Riberas de Duero arriba — cabalgan dos Zamoranos (Gibson)
Riñó con Juanilla — su hermana Mingüela (Lockhart, Ticknor)
Río Verde, Río Verde — tinto vas en sangre viva (Gibson, Longfellow, Percy, Rodd)
Romerico, tú que vienes — de do mi señora está (Bowring)
Rompiendo el mar de España — en una justa turquesca (Wilson)
Rosa fresca, rosa fresca — tan garrida y con amor (Anderson, Bowring, Gibson, Masefield, Merwin, Ticknor)
Ruy Velásquez, el de Lara — gran maldad obrado había (Cushing, Oxenford)
Sale la estrella de Venus — al tiempo que el sol se pone (Bowring, Moir, Percy, Pinkerton, Rodd)

Saliendo de Canicosa — por el val de Arabiana (Oxenford)
Sembradas de medias lunas — capellar, marlota, y manga (Wilson)
Sentado está el señor rey — en su silla de respaldo (Gibson, Lord Holland)
Servía en Orán al rey — un español con dos lanzas (Wilson)
Sevilla está en una torre — la más alta de Toledo (Wilson)
Si a do quieren reyes — allá leyes van (Bowring)
Si atendéis que de los brazos — vos alce, atended primero (Gibson)
Si d'amor pena sentís — por mesura y por bondat (Merwin)
Si de mortales feridas — fincare muerto en la guerra (Gibson, Gerrard Lewis, Maturin)
Si el caballo vos han muerto — subid, rey, a mi caballo (Lockhart)
Si mil almas tuviera — con que amaros (Bowring)
Si muero en tierras agenas — lejos de donde nací (Bowring)
Si tan bien arrojas lanzas — como las cañas arrojas (Wilson)
Si te durmieres, morena — ten aviso que el sueño (Merwin)
Si tienes el corazón, Zaide — como la arrogancia (Wilson)
Siempre Fray Carrillo estás — cansándonos acá fuera (Bowring)
Siete años que lo tinch muerto — y tancat dins de ma cambra [Catalan ballad] (Merwin)
Sobre Baza estaba el rey — lunes, después de yantar (Merwin)
Sobre el corazón difunto — Belerma estaba llorando (Rodd)
Sobre el muro de Zamora — vide un caballero erguido (Gerrard Lewis)
Sola me estoy en mi cama — namorando mi cojín (Merwin)
Soplan ventecillos — temblarán las sauces (Bowring)
Suspira por Antequera — el rey moro de Granada (Gibson)
Tan celosa está Adalifa — de su querido Abenámar (Wilson)
Tan claro hace la luna — como el sol a mediodía (Merwin)
Ten, amor, el arco quedo — que soy niña y tengo miedo (Bowring)
Tiempo es el caballero — tiempo es de andar de aquí (Bowring, Merwin)
Tirad, hidalgos, tirad — a vuestro trotón el freno (Maturin)
Todas las gentes dormían — en las que Dios había parte (Merwin)
Topáronse en una venta — la muerte y amor un día (Gibson)
Tres cortes armara el rey — todas tres a una sazón (Gibson, Gerrard Lewis)
Tres hijuelos había el rey — tres hijuelos que no más (*Foreign Quarterly Review*, *Fraser's Magazine*, Gibson, Merwin)
Triste estaba el caballero — triste está sin alegría (Bowring)
Triste yo que vivo en Burgos — ciego de llorar desdichas (Merwin)
Un castillo, dos castillos — una princesa hi havía [Catalan ballad] (Merwin)
Un sueño soñaba anoche — soñito del alma mía (Honig, Merwin)
Una bella lusitana — dama ilustre y de valía (Lockhart)
Una dama muy hermosa — que otra mejor no hay [Jewish ballad] (Merwin)
Vámonos, dijo, mi tío — a París esa ciudade (Gibson)
Vanse mis amores — madre mía y déjanme (Bowring)
Vanse mis amores — quiérenme dejar (Bowring)
Vengo brindado Mariana — para una boda el domingo (Merwin)
Verde primavera — llena de flores (Bowring)
Víspera de los reyes — la primer fiesta del año (Merwin)
Volved los ojos, Rodrigo — volvedlos a vuestra España (*Blackwood's Magazine*)
Ya cabalga Calaínos — a las sombras de una oliva (Lockhart, Rodd)
Ya cabalga Diego Ordóñez — del real se había salido (Gibson, Gerrard Lewis)

Ya de Escipión las banderas — llegan a ver las murallas (Maturin)
Ya Diego Ordóñez se parte — ya de real se ha salido (Lockhart)
Ya llegaba Abindarráez — a vista de la muralla (Lockhart)
Ya no tocaba la vela — la campana de Alhambra (Wilson)
Ya que acabó la vigilia — aquel noble Cid honrado (Maturin)
Ya que la aurora — dejaba de Titón el lecho (Wilson)
Ya repican en Andújar — y en la guardia dan rebato (Rodd)
Ya se asentaron los dos reyes — y el moro blanco tres (Merwin)
Ya se asienta el rey Ramiro — ya se asienta a sus yantares (Merwin)
Ya se parte de Toledo — ese buen Cid afamado (Gibson, Lockhart, Maturin)
Ya se parte el rey Alfonso — de Toledo se partía (Gerrard Lewis)
Ya se salen de Castilla — castellanos con gran saña (Merwin)
Ya se salen de Valencia — con el buen Cid castellano (Gibson)
Ya se salen por la puerta — por la que salía al campo (Gibson, Gerrard Lewis)
Ya se salía el rey moro — de Granada, en Almería (Gibson)
Ya tan alta va la luna — como el sol a mediodía (Merwin)
Yo me adamé una amiga — de dentro en mi corazón (Bowring, Merwin)
Yo me era mora Moraima — morilla de un bel catar (Bowring, Merwin, Ticknor, Umphrey)
Yo me estaba allá en Coimbra — que yo me la hube ganado (King, Lockhart)
Yo me iba, mi madre — a Villa Reale (Merwin)
Yo me levantara, madre — mañanica de Sant Joan (Borrow, Bowring, *Fraser's Magazine*)
Zagala, dí que harás — cuando veas que soy partido (Bowring)
Zagaleja de lo verde — gradiosita en el mirar (Bowring)
Zaida ha prometido fiestas — a las damas de Granada (Wilson)

Appendix B

ALPHABETICAL LIST OF TRANSLATORS AND LOCATION OF TRANSLATIONS

Note: The following list is a guide to the location of English translations of the *romances* included in Appendix A. The several references noted after the names of certain translators indicate the minimum sources essential to a complete survey of that author's ballad renditions. Some translations have been widely reproduced, and no effort has been made to include after each translator's name every reference in which his work has appeared.

Adams, Nicholson B. *The Heritage of Spain*. New York: Henry Holt and Co., 1943, pp. 79, 80.

Anderson, Ruth Matilde. *Translations from Hispanic Poets*. New York: Hispanic Society of America, 1938, pp. 29-31.

Blackwood's Magazine (Anonymous). Vol. 8 (1821), 359-60.

Borrow, George Henry. *Ballads of All Nations*. London: A. Rivers, Ltd., 1927.

———. *Targum* or *Metrical Translations from Thirty Languages and Dialects*. London: Jarrold & Sons, 1892.

———. *The Works of George Henry Borrow*. Edited by Clement Shorter. New York: G. Wells, 1923-1924, 9: 47, 51, 54; 16: 97, 99.

Bowring, Sir John. *Ancient Poetry and Romances of Spain*. London: Taylor and Hessey, 1824.

———. "Poetical Literature of Spain." *Retrospective Review* 4 (1821): 358.

Bryant, William Cullen. *The Prose Writings of William Cullen Bryant*. New York: D. Appleton, 1884, 1: 93-102.

———. *Poems by William Cullen Bryant*. New York: D. Appleton, 1854, 2: 52, 62, 66.

Buceta, Erasmo. "Two Spanish Ballads Translated by Southey." *Modern Language Notes* 34 (1919): 329-36.

Burnham, Jean Willard. *Translations from Hispanic Poets*. New York: The Hispanic Society of America, 1938, p. 33.

Byron, Lord. "Childe Harold," Canto IV.

Carter, Francis. *A Journey from Gibraltar to Malaga*. London, 1777.

Cone, S. Wallace. *United States Magazine and Democratic Review* 16 (1845): 13-16.

Cushing, Caleb. *Reminiscences of Spain*. 2 vols. Boston: Carter, Hendee and Co., 1833.

Entwistle, W. J. *European Balladry*. Oxford: The Clarendon Press, 1939, pp. 152-92.

Farnell, Ida. *Spanish Prose and Poetry.* New York and Oxford: University Press, 1920, p. 84.

Flecker, James Elroy. *The Collected Poems of James Elroy Flecker.* New York: Doubleday, Page and Co., 1916, p. 108.

Ford, J. D. M. *Main Currents of Spanish Literature.* New York: Henry Holt and Co., 1919, pp. 33-67.

Foreign Quarterly Review (Anonymous). Vol. 4 (1829): 89-100.

Foreign Review and Continental Miscellany (Anonymous). "The Romancero del Cid of Escobar," 4 (1829): 438-54.

Fraser's Magazine (Anonymous). "Romantic Poetry of Spain," 6 (1832): 44-49.

Frere, John Hookham. *Works of the Right Honorable John Hookham Frere.* 2d ed. London: B. M. Pickering, 1874, 2: 399 ff.

Frothingham, Alice W. *Translations from Hispanic Poets.* New York: The Hispanic Society of America, 1938, p. 23.

Gibson, James Young. *The Cid Ballads and Other Poems and Translations from Spanish and German.* Edited by Margaret Dunlop Gibson. London: Kegan Paul, Trench, and Trubner, 1887; 2d ed., 1898.

Head, Sir Edmund. *Ballads and Other Poems.* London: Smith Elder and Co., 1868, pp. 8, 24, 27.

Holland, Lord (Henry Richard Fox). *Some Account of the Life and Writings of Lope de Vega.* 2d ed. London: Longman, Hurst, Rees, Orme, and Brown, 1817.

Honig, Edwin. *García Lorca.* Norfolk, Conn.: New Directions Books, 1944, pp. 24-30.

Jewett, Sophie. *Folk Ballads of Southern Europe.* New York and London: G. P. Putnam's Sons, 1913, pp. 55, 97, 139.

King, Georgiana G. *A Brief Account of the Military Orders in Spain.* New York: The Hispanic Society of America, 1921, pp. 92-208.

———. *Heart of Spain.* Cambridge, Mass.: Harvard University Press, 1941, pp. 76-78.

Lewis, Gerrard. *Ballads of the Cid.* London: Sampson, Low, Marston, Searle, and Rivington, 1883.

Lewis, Matthew Gregory. *The Monk: A Romance.* London: Brentano's, Ltd., 1924. (1st ed. 1796.)

———. *Romantic Tales.* London: Chapman and Hall, 1848. (1st ed. 1808.)

———. *Life and Correspondence.* London: H. Colburn, 1839, 2: 338 ff.

Little, Luella Thurston. "English Translation of Spanish Ballads." Master's thesis, University of Washington, 1937.

Lockhart, John Gibson. *The Spanish Ballads.* London: Warne, 1823. (2d ed. 1841.)

———. *Ancient Spanish Ballads.* London: J. Murray, 1842. (This book has also appeared in the following editions: New York, 1842; London, 1854; London, Boston, and New York, 1856; London, 1859; Boston, 1861; London, 1870; New York, 1887; London, 1890; New York and London, 1912.)

———. *Don Quixote.* Motteux translation. 5 vols. Edinburgh: Printed for Hurst, Robinson and Co., London, 1822. (Translations of Lockhart located in notes throughout the five volumes.)

Longfellow, Henry Wadsworth. *Outre-Mer.* Rev. ed. Boston and New York: Houghton Mifflin Co., 1866. (1st ed. 1833.)

Longfellow, Henry Wadsworth. *The Seaside and the Fireside.* Boston: Ticknor, Reed and Fields, 1850, p. 3.

———. *The New England Magazine* 4 (1833): 406.

Manchester, Paul T., ed. *Joyas Poéticas.* New York: Frederick Ungar Publishing Co., 1951, p. 106.

Masefield, John. *On the Hill.* Melbourne, London, Toronto: Wm. Heinemann, 1949, pp. 89-108.

Maturin, Edward. *United States Magazine and Democratic Review* 17 (1845): 290-96, 353-66, 433-38.

McVan, Alice J. *Translations from Hispanic Poets.* New York: The Hispanic Society of America, 1938, p. 22.

Merwin, W. S. *Spanish Ballads.* New York: Doubleday and Company, Inc., 1961.

Moir, George. "Early Narrative and Lyric Poetry of Spain." *Edinburgh Review* 39 (1824): 393-432.

Oxenford, John. *The New Monthly Magazine* 76 (1846): 84-89, 379-84; 77 (1846): 106-9, 269-72.

Percy, Thomas. *Reliques of Ancient English Poetry.* London: J. Dodsley, 1765.

———. *Ancient Songs.* Edited by David Nichol Smith. Oxford: Oxford University Press, 1932.

Pinkerton, John. *Select Scottish Ballads.* 2d ed. 2 vols. London: J. Nichols, 1783. (1st ed. 1781.)

Pursche, Anna. *Translations from Hispanic Poets.* New York: The Hispanic Society of America, 1938, p. 27.

Rodd, Thomas. *Ancient Ballads from the Civil Wars of Granada and the Twelve Peers of France.* 2d ed. London: T. Ostell, 1803. (1st ed. 1801.)

———. *History of Charles the Great and Orlando.* 2 vols. London: T. Rodd and T. Boosey, 1812.

———. *The Civil Wars of Granada and the History of the Zegries and Abencerrages.* Pt. I. London, 1803.

Scott, Sir Walter. "The Chronicles of the Cid." *Quarterly Review* 1 (1809): 134-53.

Southey, Robert. *Chronicles of the Cid.* London: Longman, Hurst, Rees, and Orme, 1808.

———. *Southey's Common-Place Book.* London: Longman, Brown, Green, and Longmans, 1849-1851, vol. 4.

———. *Letters Written During a Short Residence in Spain and Portugal.* Bristol: Printed by Bulgin and Rosser for J. Cottle, 1797, pp. 378-87.

Spence, Lewis. *Legends and Romances of Spain.* London: G. G. Harrop and Co., 1920.

Thornbury, George Walter. *Life in Spain.* New York: Harper and Bros., 1860.

Ticknor, George. *History of Spanish Literature.* 3 vols. London: Trubner and Co., 1863, 1: 95-141.

Trapier, Elizabeth du Gue. *Translations from Hispanic Poets.* New York: The Hispanic Society of America, 1938, pp. 20, 24.

Turnbull, Eleanor L. *Ten Centuries of Spanish Poetry.* Edited by Eleanor L. Turnbull. Baltimore: The Johns Hopkins Press, 1955, p. 103.

Umphrey, George W. "Spanish Ballads in English. Part II — Verse Technique." *Modern Language Quarterly* 7 (1946): 31-33.

Wiffen, Jeremiah Holmes. *The Works of Garcilaso de la Vega.* London: Hurst, Robinson and Co., 1823, preface and appendix.

———. *Foreign Review and Continental Miscellany* 1 (1828): 72 ff.

Wilson, Epiphanius. *Moorish Literature.* Vol. 18 of *The World's Great Classics.* Edited by Justin McCarthy et al. New York and London: The Colonial Press, 1901, pp. 3-142.

Winter, Yvor. *Poetry* 29, no. 27 (1926): 307.

INDEXES

INDEX OF BALLAD TEXTS REPRODUCED IN THIS SURVEY

(The asterisk indicates that the *romance*, or one of its variants, existed prior to 1550.)

GENERAL INDEX